"This extremely lucid, practical, and authoritative method for inventing and performing divisions on the lute fills a gap that has been waiting to be filled since the sixteenth century. Rich in historical sources and musical examples, it also gives the reader insight into the musical mind of one of the world's finest living lutenists."

> —**Kate Clark**, Founder of the Attaignant Consort, Professor of Historical
> Flutes at the Royal Conservatorium, Den Haag, and
> co-author of *The Renaissance Flute*

"*Playing with Patterns on the Lute* is a brilliant and inspiring contribution to the lute world. Its clear, step-by-step approach makes it an invaluable resource for students and seasoned professionals alike."

> —**Peter Croton**, Lute teacher, Schola Cantorum Basiliensis
> and Bern University of the Arts

"As an experienced lute player and teacher of renown, Nigel North has generously poured his profound knowledge of the relevant material, acquired through decades of study and performance, into this clearly structured, practice-oriented work. It will undoubtedly prove beneficial to lutenists seeking to develop evidence-informed improvisational skills and subsequently apply them to the variety of sixteenth-century musical repertoires."

> —**Michał Gondko**, lutenist and co-director of the ensemble La Morra

"This is a book for every lutenist. Accessible and logical, the reader is led with discerning clarity through the ornamentation practices of Renaissance lutenists. Codifying their customs with disarming simplicity, this is the book that today's lute players have been awaiting, authored by one of the most experienced teachers and remarkable players of our time."

> —**Professor John Griffiths**, University of Melbourne,
> Editor, *Journal of the Lute Society of America*

"This is a great book, finally addressing a lute player's perspective on the theme of diminutions. After a thorough yet compact analytic overview of diminutions in the repertoire of the sixteenth century, we are led through a method leaning on original sources with many patterns. While the author remains as systematic as ever, he also pays attention to musical creativity and guides us to the subtle combination of consistency and variety. Of all the practical texts I've worked with, it's the only one based in the somewhat complex lute idiom, mixing its combination of melodic and chordal aspects. An absolute standard work for lute players working with sixteenth-century music."

> —**Simon Linné**, Professor of Lute, Leipzig University of Music and Theatre

"This is a book that should be in the library of every lutenist, and indeed everyone interested in the performance of Renaissance music! Nigel has done a masterful job of distilling a complex, and often confusing practice into well-organized, easy-to-follow concepts reinforced by exercises designed to guide players to fluency. His system mirrors the way lutenists were taught in the sixteenth century. A magnificent achievement!"

> —**Paul O'Dette**, Professor of Lute, Eastman School of Music,
> University of Rochester

PLAYING WITH PATTERNS ON THE LUTE

A Study and Method for Playing Sixteenth-Century Divisions

Nigel North

OXFORD
UNIVERSITY PRESS

Oxford University Press is a department of the University of Oxford.
It furthers the University's objective of excellence in research, scholarship,
and education by publishing worldwide. Oxford is a registered trade mark of
Oxford University Press in the UK and in certain other countries.

Published in the United States of America by Oxford University Press
198 Madison Avenue, New York, NY 10016, United States of America.

Library of Congress Cataloging-in-Publication Data
Names: North, Nigel author
Title: Playing with patterns on the lute : a study and method for playing
    sixteenth-century divisions / Nigel North.
Description: [1.]. | New York : Oxford University Press, 2025. | Includes
    bibliographical references and index.
Identifiers: LCCN 2025028549 (print) | LCCN 2025028550 (ebook) |
    ISBN 9780197808733 paperback | ISBN 9780197808726 hardback |
    ISBN 9780197808764 | ISBN 9780197808740 epub
Subjects: LCSH: Embellishment (Music)—16th century | Lute music—
    16th century—Analysis, appreciation | Lute—Methods | LCGFT: Methods (Music) |
    Scores
Classification: LCC MT80.N67 2026 (print) | LCC MT80 (ebook) |
    DDC 787.8/3143—dc23/eng/20250729
LC record available at https://lccn.loc.gov/2025028549
LC ebook record available at https://lccn.loc.gov/2025028550

DOI: 10.1093/9780197808764.001.0001

Paperback printed by Sheridan Books, Inc., United States of America
Hardback printed by Lightning Source, Inc., United States of America

The manufacturer's authorized representative in the EU for product safety is
Oxford University Press España S.A. of Parque Empresarial San Fernando de Henares,
Avenida de Castilla, 2 – 28830 Madrid (www.oup.es/en or product.safety@oup.com).
OUP España S.A. also acts as importer into Spain of products made by the manufacturer.

CONTENTS

ACKNOWLEDGEMENTS

After many years spent in the company of baroque music, basso continuo, and the baroque lute, my attention was drawn to the beauty of Renaissance music. The wonderful musician and friend who helped show me this world was Kate Clark, traverso player, founder of the Attaignant Consort, and dear friend. I have learned so much from making music with Kate and am forever grateful. When we taught a workshop together on diminutions, I caught up with all the things I had missed thus far. After this, I continued learning from our concerts and recordings together. Thank you, Kate.

This initial inspiration was soon followed by more music-making: lute duets with my friend and colleague Michał Gondko. His playing of Renaissance music was the first lute playing that really captured my heart and showed me how understandable, expressive, and attractive this music can be, in the right hands. As with Kate Clark, I learned so much from just playing music together. Thank you, Michał.

My lack of knowledge and experience became more evident to me as the years passed, and many students in Bloomington, Indiana (USA), and at various workshops around the world were my next catalyst. When exploring sixteenth-century intabulations of vocal music, the inevitable questions from students were always present: How do we learn to add divisions to our intabulations? Which book, original or modern, should we study for this? Thank you, to all students, for prompting me to answer fully these very basic questions, without which I may not have started my own education. I do hope that this present book will provide some answers and offer a way to learn more.

During the progress of creating this book, several people have generously helped by reading and offering feedback, proofreading with lute players' eyes, and generally keeping me focused. For this I must thank Erik Ryding, John Griffiths, Simon Linné, Peter Croton, and Paul O'Dette. I am in debt and grateful to my wife, Sigrid T'Hooft, for her patient support and technical help. Through her love and patience in our first year together, I was able to disappear into my room to prepare the manuscript and then rejoice together when all was finished.

Having studied this subject of division-making as a personal quest, I came to realize I needed to share it with others. I wish that the result will be of use and interest to lutenists of all levels. While the inspiration for the work has certainly been a team effort, any remaining mistakes or omissions are all completely my own.

Nigel North, Gent, 2025

All tablature and music examples were made with FRONIMO (3.0)

PART 1
FUNDAMENTALS OF DIVISIONS

CHAPTER 1

INTRODUCTION

1.1. Ornamentation Types: Divisions and Graces

There were two distinctly different ways to embellish lute music in the sixteenth century: *divisions* and *graces*.

- *Divisions* (also known as diminutions, *passaggi*, *coloraturen*, *glossas*, etc.)

On the lute in the sixteenth century, divisions were always plucked by right-hand fingers and were not slurred by the left hand. They were created by taking a long note and dividing it into smaller notes. These smaller notes (divisions) were usually played by alternating the thumb and index of the right hand, producing *good* and *bad* notes.

Thumb = good/strong. Index = bad/weak.

Plucking and not slurring produced a stronger tone and rhythmic clarity. Notated left-hand slurs are not found until the seventeenth century. The first publication of Kapsberger for Chitarrone is the earliest example of notated slurs (G. G. Kapsberger, *Libro primo d'intavolatura di chitarrone*, Venice, 1604). Before 1604, lutenists may have slurred fast notes, but we have no evidence of the practice. Many tablature sources take the trouble to notate the right-hand dot, indicating the index finger, and these dots would not be needed if slurs were expected. Unnotated use of left-hand slurs would therefore seem unlikely.

- *Graces*—small ornaments applied to individual notes (often referred to in the sixteenth century as mordents, or *mordenten*), played by plucking the written note and then slurring the added notes with left-hand fingers only (trills, shakes, mordents, *appoggiaturas*, falls, fore-falls, *trilli*, etc.).

One of the earliest Italian manuscript sources (the *Capirola Lute Book*, Venice, ca. 1517) includes two grace ornament signs in the Italian tablature (see Chapter 2). In the *Varietie of Lute-lessons* (Robert Dowland, London, 1610), Jean Baptiste Besard wrote in his *Necessary Observations* that when playing divisions we should avoid adding graces (which he calls sweet relishes and shakes):

> You should have some rules for the sweet relishes and shakes if they could be expressed here, as they are on the Lute: but seeing they cannot by speech or writing be expressed, thou wert best to imitate some cunning player, or get them by thine own practice, only take heed, least in making too many shakes thou hinder the perfection of the Notes. In somme, if you affect biting sounds, as some men call them '(Mordenten)' which may well be used, yet use them not in your running, and use them not at all but when you judge them decent.
>
> (*Necessarie Observations belonging to the Lute*, John Baptisto Besardo, f. C3v)

Playing with Patterns on the Lute. Nigel North, Oxford University Press. © Oxford University Press 2025.
DOI: 10.1093/9780197808764.003.0002

This present book is devoted to the first type of ornament, hereafter called divisions.

For graces you will find a short summary in Chapter 2, Graces.

1.2. In Search of a Method for Lutenists

Throughout the sixteenth century, lutenists ornamented their music. This is easily seen from a quick glance through extant printed and manuscript sources. We also know that professional lutenists could and would improvise ornaments when playing, and this was an important part of their musical art. We have a wealth of examples woven into the lute repertoire from this period but, as far as I am aware, we have no actual method which shows how lutenists learned this art 400–500 years ago.

During the sixteenth century (especially towards the end of the century), singers and players of wind instruments and bowed strings were treated to several printed embellishment methods. (Details of these may be found in Appendix 1.) As a lutenist, if one attempts learning divisions from these vocal and instrumental treatises, a clear didactic method can be seen, but the types of divisions found there do not always transfer well onto the lute. They are from the same musical world, but do not fit the lute like a glove. In fact, if we take the existing lute repertoire to represent the living, breathing example of what lute players did, then lute-style divisions seem to have been much simpler than those used by other instrumentalists and singers.

In these existing generic sixteenth-century methods, we can see that they present patterns and formulas to be practised, memorized, and used in performance. Four basic sets of material are used in most of the methods:

- Cadential patterns
- Intervallic patterns
- Standard melodic phrases (which were not specifically cadential or intervallic)
- Ornamented versions of composed vocal works, usually applied to the soprano voice, but sometimes to the bass, or to a bass instrument which could play in all registers (such as the *viola bastarda*).

In these methods, with examples of divisions in the preceding four categories, we can see a great variety of style, virtuosity, and artistic achievement. In the sixteenth-century lute repertoire, we also see such a rich treasure of musical ideas. We can imagine that this art of ornamenting sixteenth-century lute music with improvised divisions was mostly passed down and taught from master to student or apprentice. The vocabulary and style were probably plucked from the air and from the music which surrounded the players at that time. As in many improvised arts of the present day, this may have been done by ear and not by notation, rather like basso continuo for plucked instruments in the seventeenth and eighteenth centuries. For the modern-day lutenist, lacking an ornamentation manual of the Renaissance, we need to extract a method from our solo, duo, and ensemble repertoire. This vast repertoire contains idiomatic material which can be learned, memorized, and reproduced in performance. The purpose of this book is to supply a basic study and method for lutenists wishing to learn to improvise divisions on the lute, based on the patterns found in our repertoire of the time. While we can observe changes in style from composer to composer, and country to country, the method offered here would be applicable to all styles and periods of the sixteenth century.

1.3. The Function of Divisions

WHY WERE DIVISIONS USED AND WHAT WAS THEIR FUNCTION AND PURPOSE?

On the lute, when plucked and not slurred, divisions give variety, sustain of a long note, and the possibility to contribute dynamics, direction, and shape to a phrase. The principal reason for divisions on the lute must be that the lute has a naturally short sustain, and long notes were represented by several shorter notes. We can see this technique in sixteenth-century intabulations of vocal pieces in which divisions often replace the sustain of a long sustained vocal note.

WHERE CAN WE FIND EXAMPLES OF SIXTEENTH-CENTURY DIVISIONS?

* Solo works—Original compositions

Fantasias, dances, variations on grounds or popular songs, found in most European sources (e.g., Passamezzo Antico and Moderno, Romanesca, La Gamba, Une jeune fillette, etc.), ballad tunes in England (Go from my Window, Walsingham, Greensleeves, etc.).

* Solo works—Intabulations

These were arrangements of original vocal works, intabulated into a score or *partitura*, written in tablature, and made playable on the lute. Ornamenting these intabulations was one of the most important aspects of the art of intabulation. In his publication, *A briefe and plaine Instruction to set all Musicke of eight divers tunes in Tablature for the Lute* (London, 1574), Adrian Le Roy describes adding divisions to a piece to make it more *finely handled*. Intabulations account for at least 50 percent of the surviving solo lute repertoire of the sixteenth century.

* Ensemble

Lute duets are an important source for the study of divisions; the treble and ground duet texture (one lute plays the ground and the other plays a single line of divisions) makes the ornamentation examples very clear. Examples of trebles and grounds can be found in Part 2: Tablature Case Studies of this volume. See John Johnson (*The Queen's Treble*), Francesco da Milano (*Fantasia a dui liuti*), and the *Contrapunto Primo* from Galilei's *Fronimo*. In this category we must include the *contrapunto*: an independent ornamented, melodic line, played over an harmonic accompaniment. The two *Contrapunti* (by B.M.) included in Vincenzo Galilei's 1584 edition of *Fronimo* are two of the very finest. A uniquely English practice was the Mixed Consort (also known as the Broken Consort or Consort of Six) consisting of violin, flute, bass viol, lute, cittern, and bandora. In the surviving lute parts from Thomas Morley's and Philip Rosseter's *Consort Lessons*, and various manuscript sources which contain similar material (e.g., Cambridge University Library, Dd.3.18), we find a style of division writing very similar to the English lute duet.

WHEN DOES A LUTENIST NEED TO BE ABLE TO IMPROVISE OR PREPARE DIVISIONS?

There are four different types of composition to which we can add divisions:

* A composed, pre-existing single line of a composition (often the cantus or treble voice).

- A composed, pre-existing multi-voiced composition (often in four voices: cantus, alto, tenor, and bass), such as an intabulation of a motet or madrigal.
- Divisions on a ground, chord progression, or even a popular tune, from which the lutenist invents divisions and makes a new piece of music, without the restraints of the melodic lines of any one voice.
- A new single line (such as a *contrapunto*) which can be added to a pre-existing composition.

The first two types of composition have as an *anchor* the original musical lines. We do not compose, but merely ornament or decorate. The third and fourth both require invention of new melodic, ornamented lines, not necessarily found in the original.

Types of composition might include:

- An improvised treble on a ground or chord progression (e.g., Romanesca, Passamezzo Antico) in lute solo or lute duet form.
- Solo dances for lute which have no written ornamented repeat.
- When we make a new intabulation in the style of the sixteenth century.
- A *contrapunto* or a *bastarda* type of ornamented lute part, perhaps based on a vocal model.
- Improvising a decorated part in an ensemble.

In his book *Del sonare sopra'l basso,* Siena (1607, f. C3v), Agostino Agazzari lists all the techniques a good skilled lutenist must have when improvising an ornamented part in an ensemble. This is where the lute is an ornamental instrument, not a basso continuo instrument. Agazzari considered the lute a *stromento nobilissimo* ('most noble instrument') and the ornamental techniques a good lutenist should have were many and varied:

> *Devesi dunque, hora con botte, e ripercosse dolci; hor con passaggio largo, et hora stretto, e raddoppiate, poi con qualche sbordonata, con belle gare e perfidie, repetendo, e cavando le medesime fuge in diverse corde, e luoghi; in somma con lunghi gruppi e trilli, et accenti à suo tempo, intrecciare le voci.*
>
> One should therefore now strike percussively, now with a gentle touch, sometimes with a slow *passaggio*, and now with a fast one, with doublings [? two voices, or notes twice as fast, or an echo?] and then some deep basses, with imitative and dissonant passages, repeating and moving the imitations on different strings and registers; to sum up, with long gruppi, trills and accents (in their proper place) weave the voices together. (Agazzari, *del sonare*, Siena, 1607, p. 8)

In 1555, Bermudo gives us a more sober view of embellishment in lute (or vihuela) music:

> *Tenga por auiso principal el que deste libro se quisiere aprouechar: que en la musica no heche glosas. La mayor corrupcion y perdida de musica que entre tañedores hallo; es las importunas glosas.* (Bermudo, *Declaración*, Osuna, 1555, fol. xxix)
>
> For anyone wishing to benefit from this book, here is a piece of general advice: don't smother the music in glossas. The worst corruption and spoiling of music that I find among instrumentalists comes from inappropriate diminution. (Translation, John Griffiths)

1.4. Guidelines, Terms, and Abbreviations Used

This book is written for a Renaissance lute in G. Notation is standard throughout: French tablature (which is the tablature with letters). G lute tuning is the most common tuning used for the 6, 7, 8, 9, and 10 course lute in standard Renaissance tuning, and French tablature notation is currently in use by professionals and amateurs alike. I do not dismiss other tablatures (Italian, German, Neopolitan, Spanish—Luis Milan), but rather wish to make the method easily accessible to everyone. Even if you love playing from German tablature, it is almost guaranteed that French tablature would have come first in your studies. Most players will have begun on a Renaissance lute in G and have developed their first reading skills based on the G lute pitches. It is not only very good but essential to read notation on the lute and know what the notes are. Even if practice, repetition, and a good ear are all important skills for improvising divisions, it is also helpful and important to know what you are doing. All examples for the lute in this book, however, will be presented in tablature only. Space does not allow for parallel transcription into staff notation. This can be done by the student at their own pace, if need be.

While there are several words for this type of ornamentation (divisions, diminutions, *passaggi*, *glossas*, etc.), in general we will use *divisions*. I have found that most lutenists today use and understand this term. The following is a list of terms and abbreviations used throughout the book.

Anchor notes	These are the main, principal notes of the composition, or vocal line; *anchor* notes are usually consonant with the harmony and are placed on the beat as *good* notes.
Bar	Bar or measure
Divisions	A series of ornamental notes which embellish a longer note. Alternative names of the time include *passaggi, diminutions, coloraturen, glossas*.
LH	Left hand
Ms.	Manuscript
RH	Right hand
Tab	Tablature
1583/2 (example)	This is used to identify the printed source in relation to the standard reference method of RISM, such as we find in the bibliography of Howard Mayer Brown, *Instrumental Music Printed Before 1600* (1967).
1, 3, 5, etc.	In notes and instructions, these numbers will refer to the notes of the *triad* in question (1st, 3rd, or 5th) or the note at an interval above the bass of the chord.

CHAPTER 2

GRACES

2.1. Sixteenth-Century Graces for the Lute

In Chapter 1 we mentioned the two basic types of ornamentation used by lutenists and established that this book is only concerned with developing the skill to improvise the first type, divisions. The second type of ornament, which we can distinguish by the term *graces*, has been much written about in the twentieth and twenty-first centuries. In the sixteenth century we have examples of divisions in almost every lute piece, but few actual instructions for how to play graces: *trilli, tremoli, mordenten, accenti,* and so on. By the seventeenth century we start to find sources which have tables of ornaments, names for the graces, and explanations of how to play them (e.g., Alessandro Piccinini, 1623; Nicolas Vallet, 1614; Thomas Robinson, 1603; Marin Mersenne, 1636).

Besard's comments (see Chapter 1) are typical of the frustrating lack of real evidence of how to perform graces in the sixteenth century. Sixteenth-century tablature notation of graces is very scant. When it exists, the notation varies from source to source, composer to composer, scribe to scribe, and so on. For example, the printed books of German tablature and the Spanish vihuela books do not notate them. There are, however, two Italian sources from the sixteenth century which are worthy of our attention. From these we can see that the notation and use of graces was very much alive even from the early part of the century.

2.2. The *Capirola Lutebook*, ca. 1517

Compositione di meser Vincenzo Capirola, US- Cn Case MS VM.C25, Newberry Library, Chicago.

Capirola gives us two signs for *tremoli*. The first, which appears more often than the second, is a red number, made of dots written to the right of the principal note. In Italian tablature (without the colour) it would look like this:

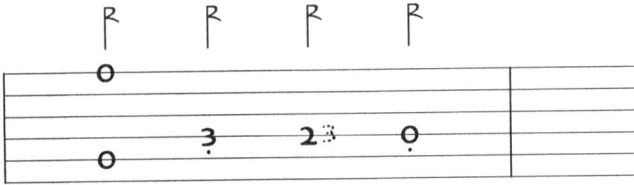

Following Capirola's instructions, the player must hold the black note (here a tab *2* on the 3rd course) and shake that note with the red *3* to the right. No number of repercussions is indicated, but it does seem as though it begins with the real, black note. It is a main-note trill. Translating this into French tablature, it would sound like this:

Playing with Patterns on the Lute. Nigel North, Oxford University Press. © Oxford University Press 2025.
DOI: 10.1093/9780197808764.003.0003

The second of the *tremoli* is indicated by two red dots above a black tablature note and is a mordent or trill with a lower auxiliary. In Italian tablature (without the colour) it would look like this:

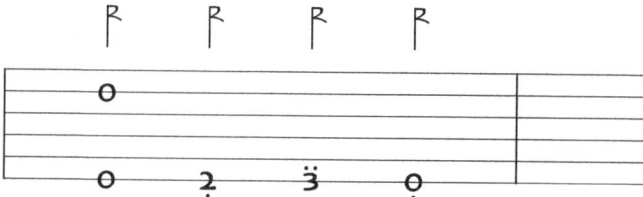

Translating this into French tablature, it would sound like this:

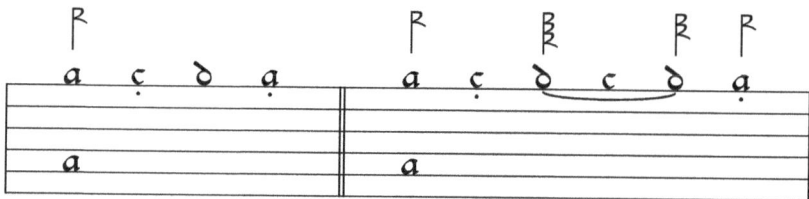

2.3. Pietro Paulo Borrono (1548)

Intavolatura di lauto del divino Francesco da Milano et dell' Eccellente Pietro Paulo Borrono. Libro secondo, Venice, 1548 (1548/3).

This printed book was a collaboration of two masters from Milan, Francesco and Borrono. A unique and unexpected grace sign appears only in the works of Borrono. Perhaps it was part of his style of playing and new to lute playing. Reading Borrono's instructions, it could be thought of as an appoggiatura from above. The execution of it may, however, be very different from the more common comma (e.g., *b,*) found in seventeenth- and eighteenth-century lute sources. Perhaps it is a very quick grace which gives more of an accent to that note, rather than a dissonance to be enjoyed and dwelt upon, similar to quick-accented grace notes on many folk instruments around the world.

Here is an example from Borrono:

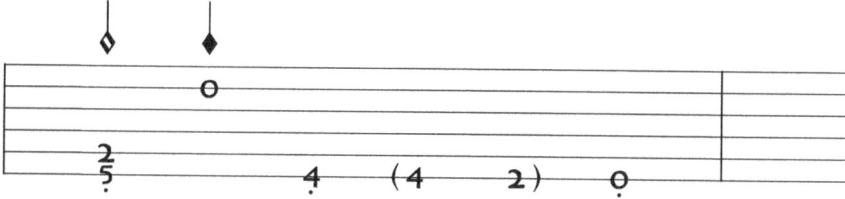

Translating this into French tablature, it would sound like this:

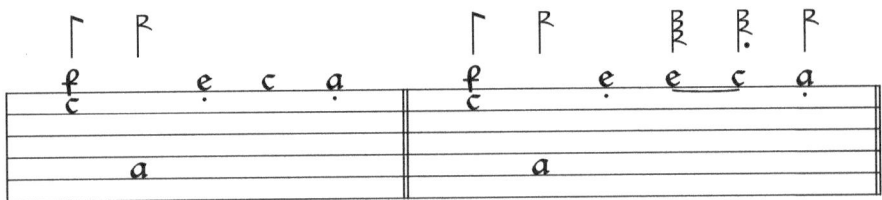

2.4. The Most Common Sixteenth-Century Graces Explained

When reading the sources and treatises for other instruments, we can identify the following types of graces in use in the sixteenth century. There are more notated signs and some consistency when we arrive in the seventeenth century.

Main note trill with upper auxiliary (as in the first of Capirola's *tremoli*):

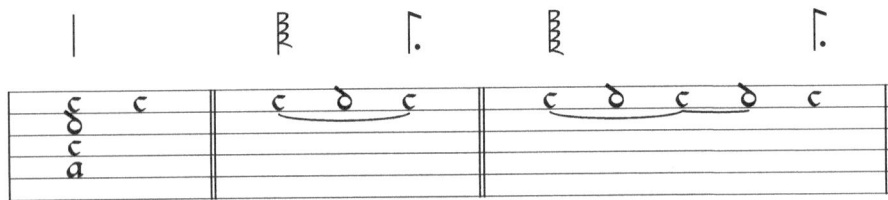

Main note trill with lower auxiliary (as in the second of Capirola's *tremoli*):

Double fall forward (slide, Schleifer, *intonazione*):

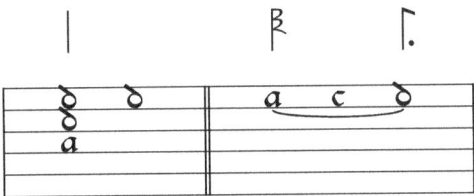

Fall forward (found mostly from ca. 1600 onwards):

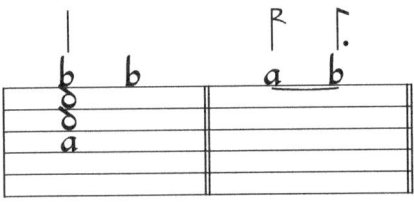

Except for the unique instructions by Borrono described earlier, an *appoggiatura* from above is found mostly from ca. 1600 onwards. The instructions of Nicholas Vallet (*Le Secret des Muses*, Amsterdam, 1615) show what became standard for this grace: a comma (,) to the right of the tablature letter. He gave no rhythm signs to his examples and did not specify a rhythm.

Examples from Vallet:

Vibrato was considered a grace/ornament in the seventeenth century, and lutenists used various signs to indicate *vibrato*. In the sixteenth century there were no signs, but Mersenne (*Harmonie universelle*, Paris 1636–1637) mentions that it had been greatly used in earlier times.

CHAPTER 3

GENERAL RULES

The general concept of *dividing*, or playing *divisions/passaggi/diminutions*, is that we break down the long notes of an original vocal line (or notes of a chord) and play quicker ones to fill up the same amount of time.

3.1. Two Modes

There are two distinct modes for division playing, melodic and harmonic:

- The first, of which it may be easier to conceive, is when we have a melodic line already composed (often the *cantus* voice) and use this line for our *anchor notes* and divide that into faster notes, within certain limits. The **lute rules for divisions** in the following section apply to this mode of dividing. It is a simple form of *improvising*. If we can't create anything new, at any moment, we can always resort to playing the original, unornamented.
- The second mode is when we divide over a harmonic foundation, such as divisions over a ground (a repetitive series of chords). (See Part 2: Tablature Case Studies, The *Greensleeves Treble and Ground Duet*, or *The Queen's Treble*, John Johnson.) In this mode, we are free to create by improvising or composing a new melodic line of divisions which is concordant with the harmony. A subsidiary mode of this would be a *contrapunto*; a newly created line (composed or improvised) which can be combined with a previously composed piece, such as a madrigal, a motet, or an instrumental work. (For examples of these see Part 2: Tablature Case Studies, Francesco da Milano, *Fantasia a dui liuti*, or the *Contrapunto* from *Fronimo*.)

Studying the composed divisions of our repertoire is both practical and tangible. I assume that the sixteenth-century professionals who left pieces with composed divisions also improvised in a similar style when they played. We only have the written examples to emulate in our own playing. One goal in studying division playing on the lute is to be able to improvise and create in the moment. We may well find that this skill will develop if we first create by composing, and by practising and memorizing the *patterns* needed for this creation.

First, we need to follow a few basic rules. These rules can be seen modelled throughout our sixteenth-century repertoire. A similar list (*Regole della diminutione*) can be found in the manuscript *Il dolcimelo*, ca. 1600 (see Appendix 1). This manuscript was compiled by Aurelio Virgiliano as a method for teaching diminutions to all bowed string and wind instrumentalists (see Part 2: Tablature Case Studies and the *Recercata per viola da bastarda, e lauto* from this manuscript).

Playing with Patterns on the Lute. Nigel North, Oxford University Press. © Oxford University Press 2025.
DOI: 10.1093/9780197808764.003.0004

3.2. Lute Rules for Divisions

RULE 1: MOVE BY STEP

In general, move by step so that a division figure can be basically melodic:

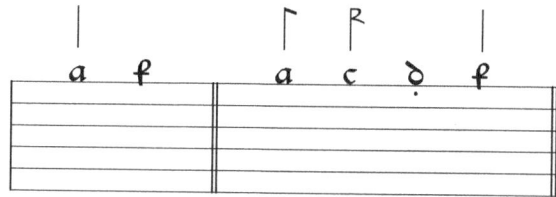

This seems less elegant because it is not by step:

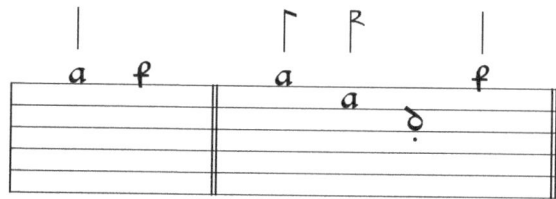

RULE 2: ALTERNATE 'GOOD' AND 'BAD' NOTES

Alternate 'good' and 'bad' notes when moving by step. Use right-hand (RH) thumb and index as a default technique, especially if you are only playing a single line:

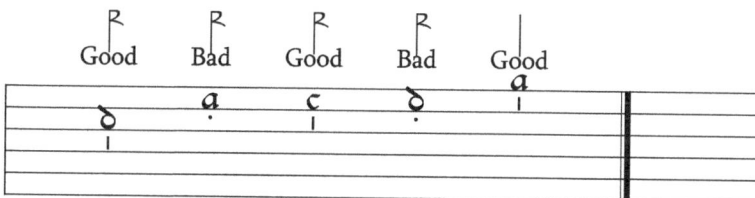

RULE 3: ANCHOR NOTES

The good notes on the beat, which are consonant with the harmony, may be thought of as *anchor notes*, or stepping stones on which to land. The term *anchor notes* will be used throughout this book. An *anchor note* is often the original note of the melody we are dividing. Bar 1 in the following example shows *anchor notes*. These are then divided into a simple division, moving by step, using good and bad notes played with alternating RH thumb and index (bar 2):

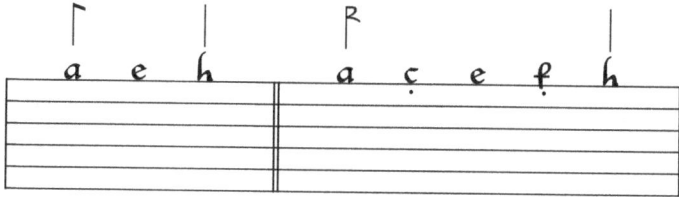

Here we see a longer division on one harmony, ascending and descending, with the notes of the chord or triad providing the *anchor notes*:

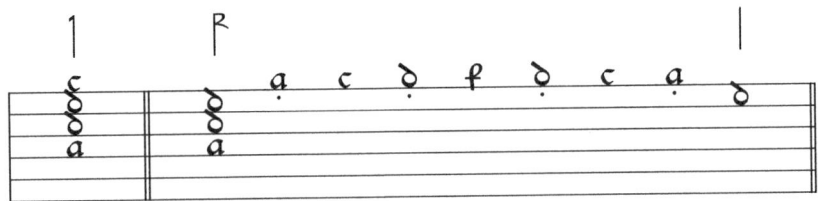

RULE 4: MOVING BY LARGER INTERVALS

Moving by a third can often feel and sound as though it is only by step, as in this example:

For intervals greater than a third, the new note should be consonant with the harmony. (This rule was occasionally abandoned by famous sixteenth-century lutenists with good taste. See later discussion.) Remember: notes consonant with the harmony are *good* notes and should be plucked with the RH thumb (or middle finger). Off-beat, *bad* notes, notes that are not consonant with the harmony, should usually be plucked with the RH index finger. In this example, the *cantus* moves correctly by ascending a fourth to a note consonant with the harmony:

This example, however, would be in bad taste. The *cantus* moves from a G to a D, above a C major chord:

In this example we see John Dowland breaking the rule. *The Frog Galliard*, bar 24, shows a typical division which jumps to a dissonant note but does sound good to the ears! This is probably because there is a harmonic hint of a high D (tablature *h* on the 1st course) which then proceeds in the normal pattern of a descending octave. Bar 1 shows the original, and bar 2 with the imagined missing high D.

The Frog Galliard, John Dowland, bar 24

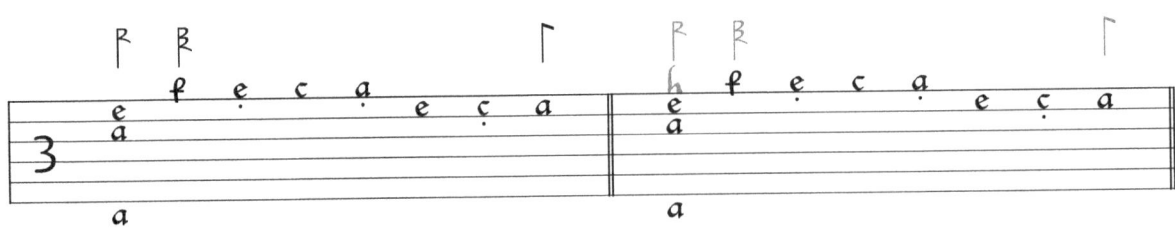

RULE 5: CADENCES

The first place to consider ornamenting is a *cadence*, and we can use one of many standard cadential formulas. (*Cadential* patterns are explained and documented in Chapter 4: Twelve Types of Divisions, and Part 3: Method with Exercises.)

This example shows a standard *cadential* formula, plain and then with divisions:

RULE 6: STATIC NOTES

The second place to consider ornamenting is when you decorate the written note and return to it. This may be termed a *static* figure or pattern. (*Static* patterns are explained and documented in Chapter 4: Twelve Types of Divisions, and Part 3: Method with Exercises.)

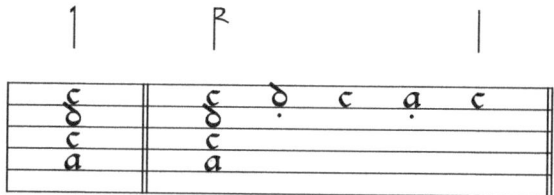

RULE 7: CONNECTING NOTES BY THE INTERVAL BETWEEN THEM

The third place for consideration is when we connect two notes which are an interval of a third or more apart. This can be for two notes from the same melodic voice (an *interval* division) or a way to connect two chords, going from one voice in the first chord to a different voice in the second chord (a *connector* division). (Both will be explained and documented in Chapter 4: Twelve Types of Divisions, and Part 3: Method with Exercises.)

This example shows *anchor* notes with intervals of ascending thirds, followed by simple divisions by step, using good and bad notes:

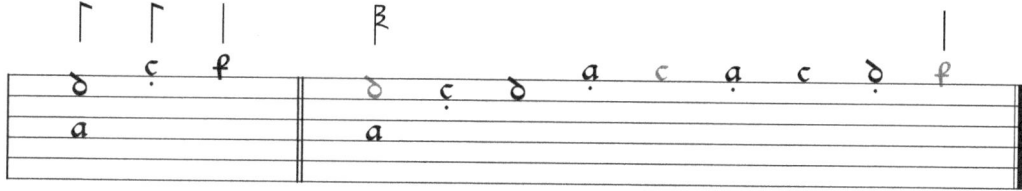

This example is similar, but shows a *connector* division, joining the middle voice of the chord to the final note in the upper voice, using an ascending octave scale. The anchor notes are shown in grey:

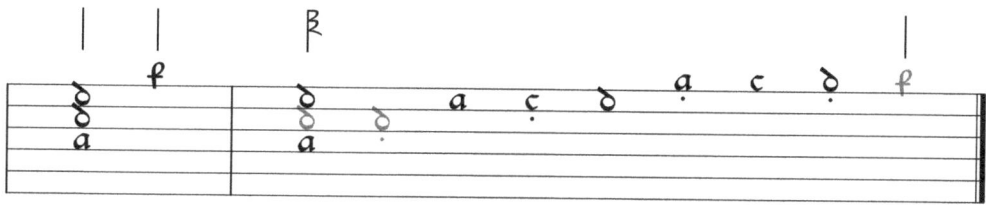

RULE 8: DISSONANCES

The dissonances which were generally allowed in the sixteenth century were *cadential* suspensions. Similar suspensions which are not at a cadence are also found. Expressed in intervals above the bass the accepted *cadential* and *non-cadential* dissonances were: 4–3, 7–6, and 9–8.

Examples of these three types of dissonances, in tablature:

Outside of those dissonances, 'blue notes' (non-harmonic notes, on the beat) were rare, and when used could be highly expressive, sometimes sounding like an *appoggiatura* from the baroque period. Their use may also have been for a special effect or a way to connect a phrase melodically.

From John Dowland's Galliard, *Mignarda*, we have a good example of a blue note dissonance. An interval of a ninth above the bass doesn't just resolve to the eighth next to it but continues to descend in a division. In this example we can see bars 1–4 followed, by their divisions, bars 9–12. The dissonances are shown in grey and occur on the first beats of bars 3 and 11.

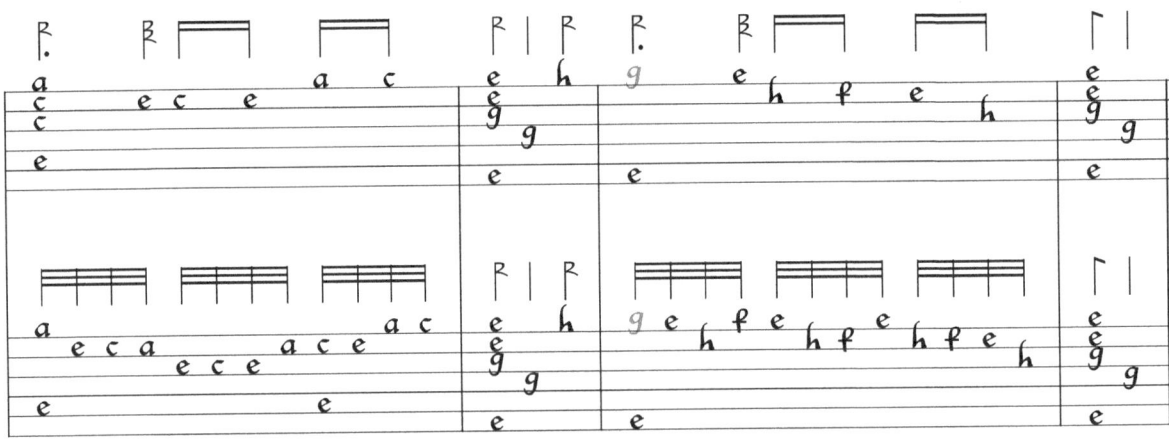

One of my favourite examples of a blue note can be found in Dowland's *Lachrimae* in the consort version by Thomas Morley (*Consort Lessons*, 1599 and 1611). The original lute part is lost, and the lute part in the following is taken from the Cambridge Consort Lute part book (GB:Cul Ms. Dd 3.18). In bar 7 of the repeat of the A section, on the fourth beat, the lute has a written long appoggiatura: B♭ against an F major chord. (Grey tablature letter *d* on the 1st course.) This type of dissonance was not commonplace in 1599! The surviving parts are represented here:

Stave 1: Lute
Stave 2: Treble viol
Stave 3: Flute
Stave 4: Bass viol

EXAMPLE *Lachrimae Pavan* (extract), Thomas Morley, *Consort Lessons* (1599 and 1611), bar 7.

Lute

Treble viol

Flute

Bass viol

RULE 9: RHYTHM

Many of the diminution manuals (see Appendix 1) describe three rhythmic levels of divisions. This is also what we find in the lute repertoire, although many pieces have only the first two levels. Two examples in the Tablature Case Studies (see Part 2) use only two levels of division rhythm. *Mille regretz* (intabulated by Narvaez) uses only quarter notes and eighth notes for embellishment:

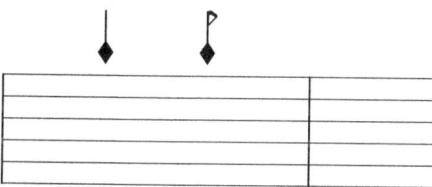

In French tablature, this would be notated:

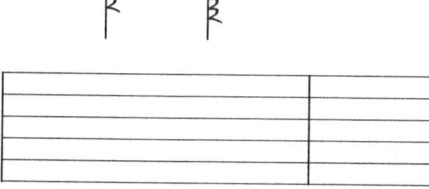

The Queen's Treble (treble and ground duet) by John Johnson, also uses the same two levels of rhythm for the divisions.

For an easy example of the use of three levels, we can look to the first piece in the Tablature Case Studies: *Nach Willen Dein* (Paul Hofhaimer), in three intabulations by Hans Newsidler. The first version (1536) is the simplest and has only one level:

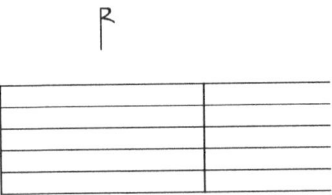

The second version (1549) has two levels of speed for the divisions:

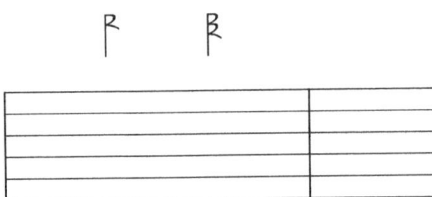

The third version (1536) is the most advanced level, with three division speeds:

In Chapter 12, Tablature Case Study #7, *Contrapunto primo* from Galilei's *Fronimo* (1584), we find all three levels used throughout.

When we imagine a division figure before playing it, the most useful thing for our ears and fingers is the rhythm. When we can hear internally a rhythm to connect two notes, then we can find the right melodic pattern to fit the rhythm. Here are some rhythmic examples from John Johnson:

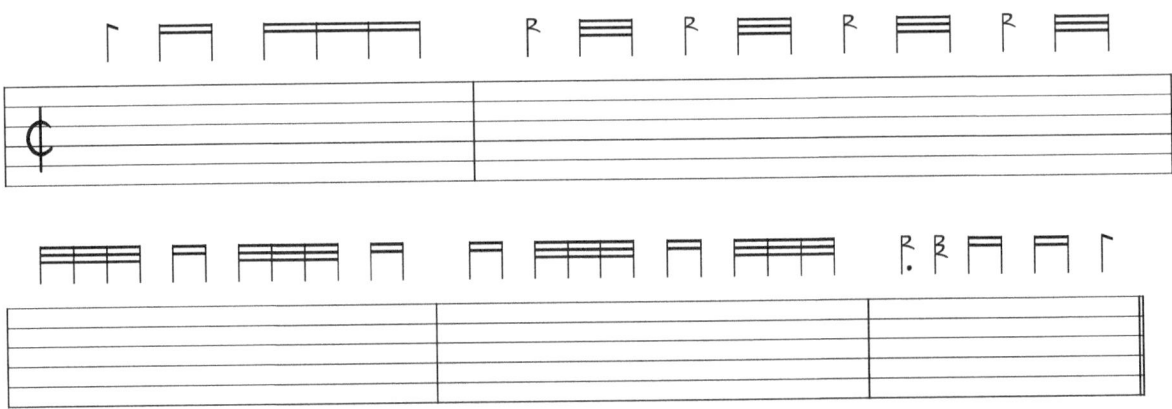

In triple time, the patterns will vary, often by extending the length of one of the anchor notes. Here are more examples from John Johnson, this time in triple meter:

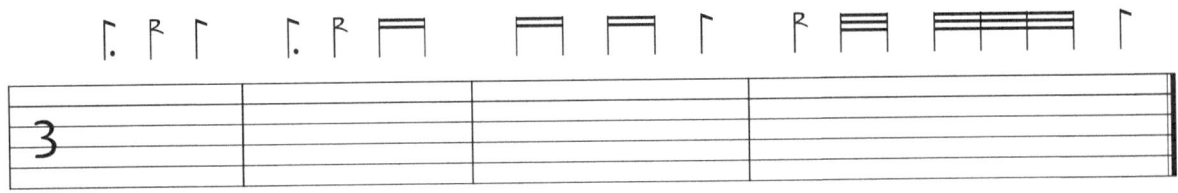

Observing the written divisions of the sixteenth century, we can see that imitation is often heard and felt when the rhythmic figures are imitated, even if the melodic figures are not identical. Short division figures, repeated and imitated (such as in the trebles of John Johnson), will be rhythmically imitative. The melodic or harmonic content will not always be completely identical, but if the rhythm is the same, we hear it as imitative. See Part 2: Tablature Case Studies, and Chapter 13: The Queen's Treble, John Johnson.

CHAPTER 4

TWELVE TYPES OF DIVISIONS

When analysing or describing a particular division pattern in this book, I will use the following definitions in the list of 12 types of divisions. Defining lute divisions in this way has come from studying the repertoire for solo lute, lute duet, and ensemble. When reading and playing, I have found it particularly helpful to identify each figure and store it in my memory so I can retrieve it when needed in an improvised performance. This process of practising and memorizing for later use is a common protocol in many improvised traditions.

Every division pattern has two anchor notes, the first and last main notes, which are being connected with a division. The two notes that begin and end a division help to define it. For example, an ascending division on an interval of a fifth will define the pattern connecting two notes, such as C–G (tab *d* on the 3rd course to tab *a* on the 1st course).

I have identified 12 different species or types of division figures, and it was with this perspective that I created the Tablature Case Studies (Part 2 of this volume). In Part 3: Method, you will find explanations, examples, and exercises for practising the most common types. Here we will just define the 12 types of divisions. Types one through six have proven to be the most common in our repertoire.

Twelve different species of divisions found in original lute repertoire:

1. *Cadential*
2. *Triad*
3. *Static*
4. *Interval*
5. *Doubler*
6. *Filler*
7. *Lead-in*
8. *Connector*
9. *Tirata*
10. *Contrapunto* and *bastarda*
11. *Broken chords*
12. *Recomposed*

4.1. Cadential

The first place to play or find an ornament in almost all music is at cadences. *Cadential* figures were standard, and they exist in a variety of speeds found in all lute works. Cadences had melodic, contrapuntal, and harmonic patterns and provide major punctuation in any composition.

Cadential figures can be found in:

- Solo works (dances, fantasies, preludes, and toccatas)
- Intabulations
- Grounds
- Everywhere!

Playing with Patterns on the Lute. Nigel North, Oxford University Press. © Oxford University Press 2025.
DOI: 10.1093/9780197808764.003.0005

The *groppo* was one of the most common cadential figures, and we find many variant patterns.
A standard *groppo* pattern:

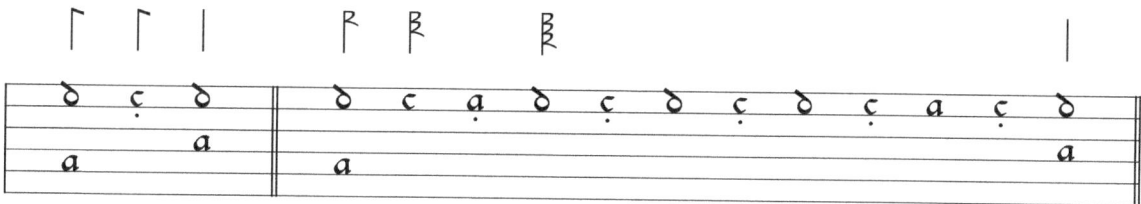

Here are some examples from sixteenth-century lutenists.
Alonso Mudarra, 1546:

Francesco da Milano, Fantasie N#66:

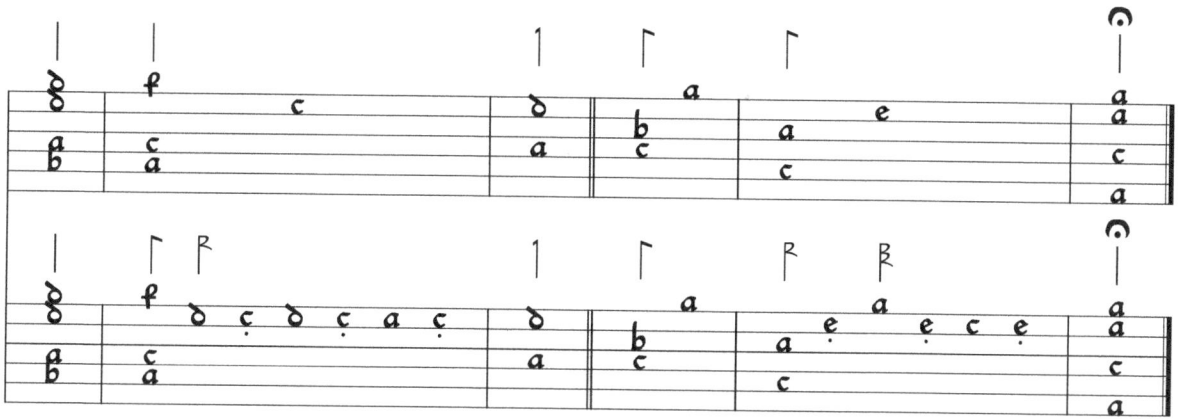

John Dowland, *Lachrimae Pavan*:

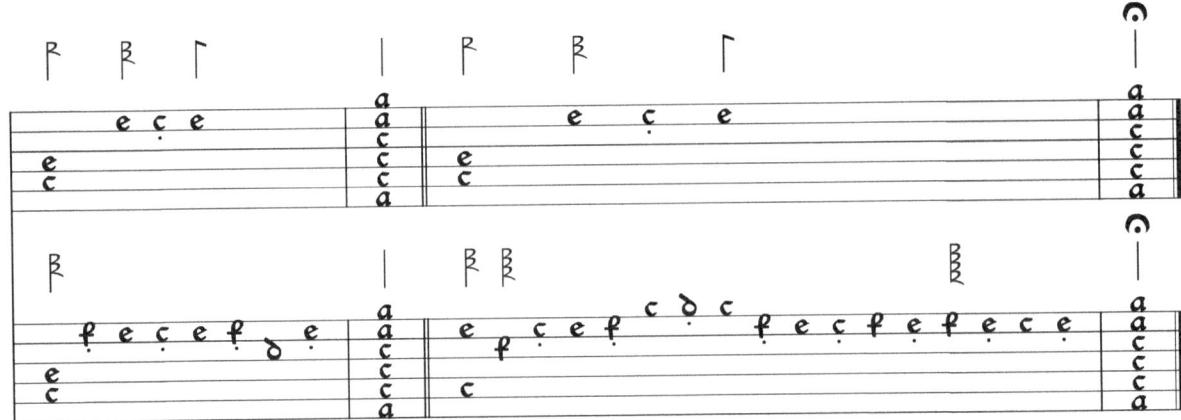

4.2. Triad

When studying *The Queen's Treble* (John Johnson) in Tablature Case Studies (see Part 2 of this volume), we can see how prevalent *triad* figures are, and how inventive Johnson was in his division writing, using the simplest of techniques. One aspect of English division style is the frequent use of *triad* patterns.

    Triad divisions based on 1, 3, and 5 on any note come in four different modes:

- *Simple*

Divisions with the consonances (1, 3, 5) as the good notes and 2 and 4 connecting them as
    bad notes. Range of 5 notes only.

Here are some simple examples:

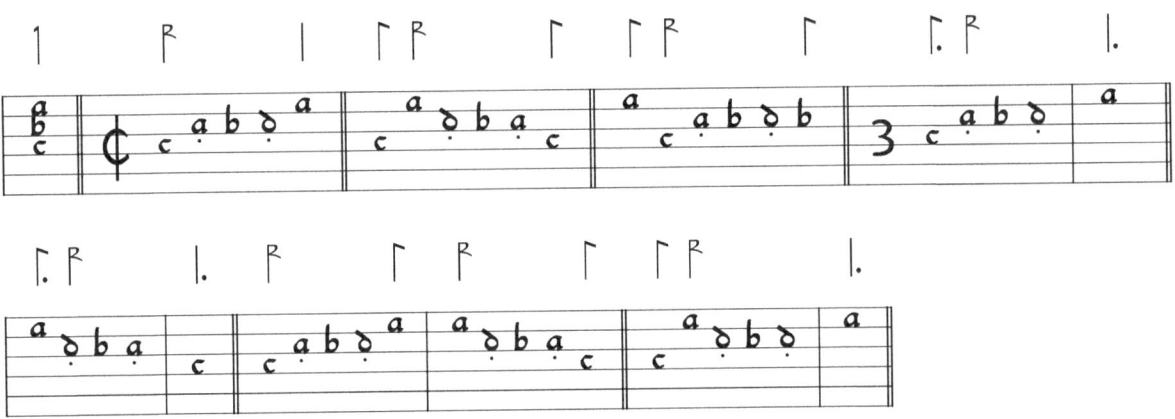

- *Extended*

Simple *triad* divisions can also be extended to include one or two other notes above 5, or
    below 1. All *triad* figures can be made to fall easily under the hand. Extended *triad*
    figures have a range of 6 or 7 notes.

An extended *triad* pattern from Francesco da Milano (Fantasie #34):

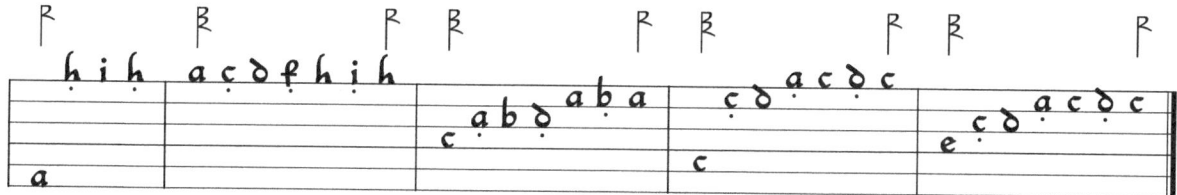

- *Octave extensions*

Divisions which are based on the *triad* can also extend from 5 to 8 and cover the whole octave. The good notes on the beat are still consonant with the *triad*. Range of eight notes, often with a feeling of two phrases combined, a fourth and a fifth, which was how the modes were thought of—a combination of an interval of a fifth and another of a fourth.

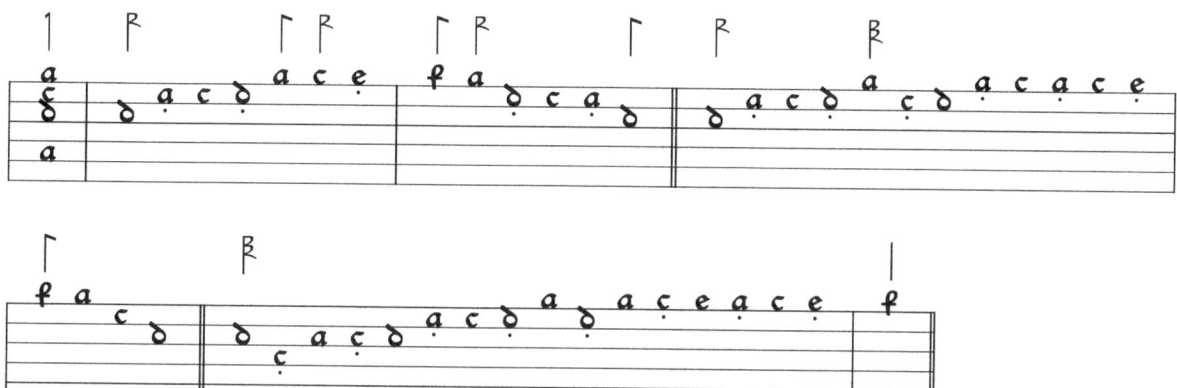

- *Harmonic triads*

There are some figures which do not move by step but principally use 1, 3, and 5, with the occasional passing note of 2, 4, or 6, and which sound more like arpeggiation.

These examples are all taken from *Contrapunto* (B.M.) *Fronimo*, Galilei, 1584 (see Part 2: Tablature Case Studies). Upper stave is the *tenore* lute part; lower stave, the *contrapunto*.

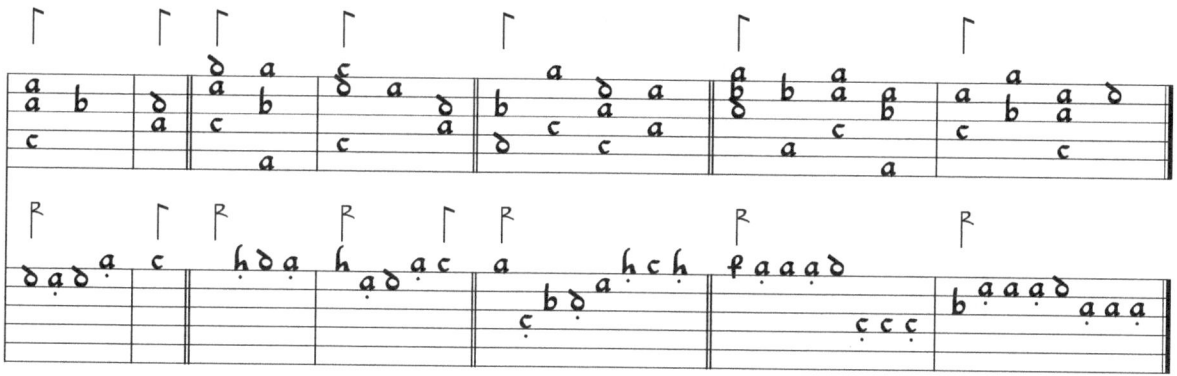

Another example, from John Dowland, *Queen Elizabeth's Galliard* (1610):

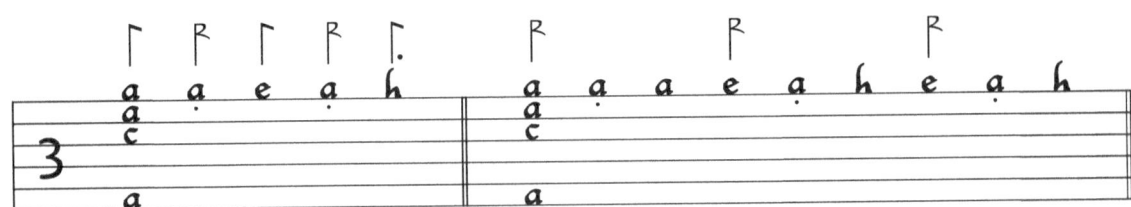

4.3. Static

- Any division which centres around the written, or main note.
- Starting and ending with the same original note.
- It is a very common division type.
- It can even include repetition of the written note.
- A cadential *groppo* is often used as a *static* division on the final tonic.
- A *static* division is one of the best ways to represent a sustained sound on the lute. We find many *static* divisions in intabulations of vocal music, for this very reason.

Some examples from lute repertoire which illustrate *static* divisions:

John Johnson, *The Quadro Pavan*:

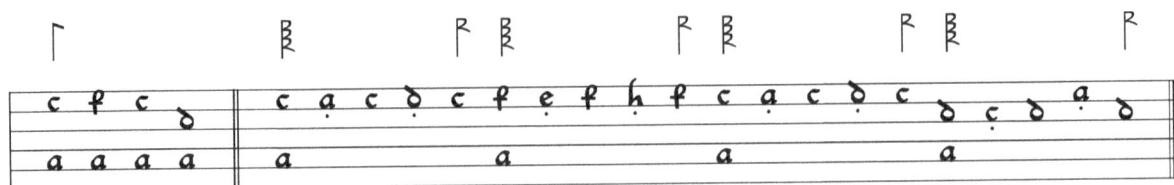

John Johnson, *The Galliard to the Flat Pavan*, lute duet:

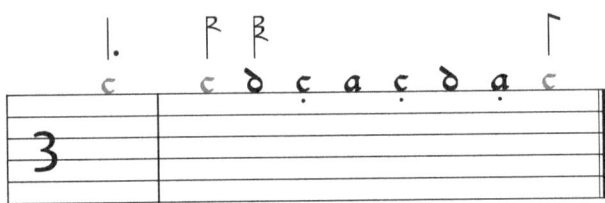

John Dowland, *Sir John Smith, his Almain*:

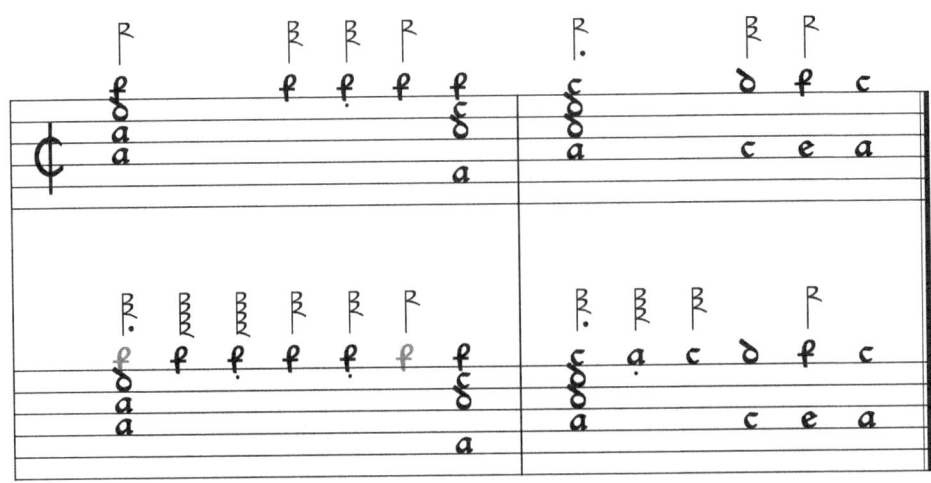

John Dowland, *Galliard on a Galliard of Daniel Batchelar*:
An example of a *static* division on a final chord, as a *filler* (see section 4.6):

4.4. Interval

This type of division is perhaps the one with the most variety and frequency.

Contrary to a *static* figure, *interval* figures are constructed around two notes, the first and last note. These two notes form an *interval* which is connected by a division. We find divisions on any of these *intervals*: 2nd, 3rd, 4th, 5th, 6th, 7th, 8ve, and any of these with an octave extension such as a 9th or 10th. They all have certain standard patterns, ascending and descending, that can be learned and copied. There will be much more to study in Part 3. To illustrate this important division type, here are a few examples for the *intervals* of a second and an octave:

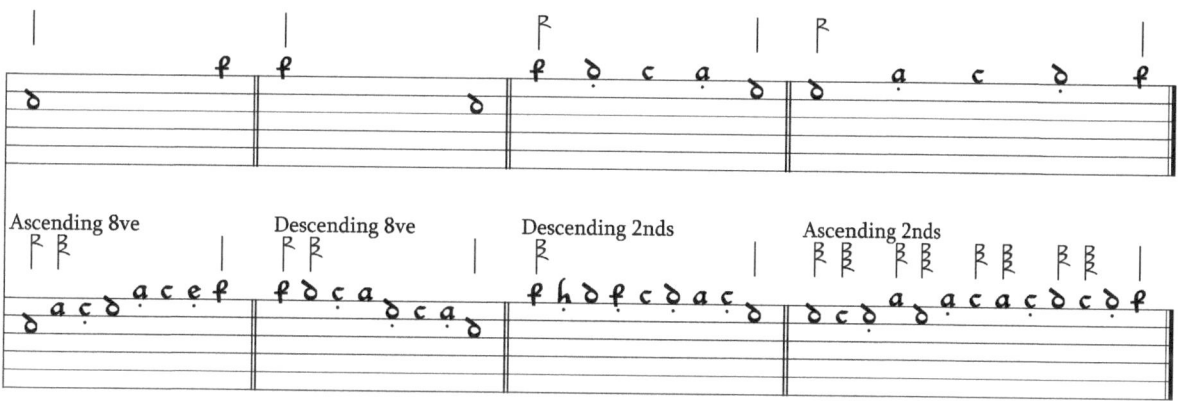

4.5. Doubler

In the list of techniques a lutenist can use when ornamenting in an ensemble, Agazzari used the term *raddoppiate*. From this, I adapted the word *doubler* to describe a simple figure which becomes a division at twice the speed, often at the end of a phrase. The doubling of the speed propels the music forward and may also imply a crescendo. It is a division which exaggerates and highlights a phrase.

Here are some examples.

A cadential *doubler*, with the *doubler* shown in grey tablature letters:

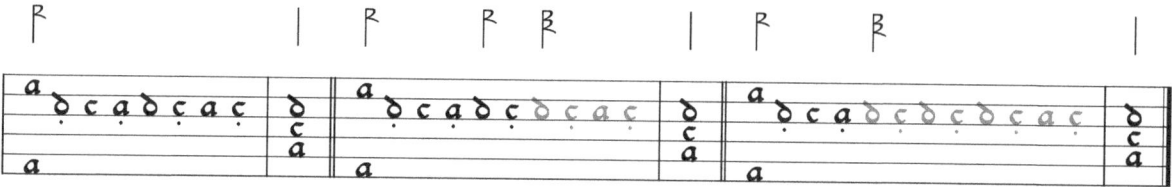

A melodic *doubler*, with the *doubler* shown in grey tablature letters:

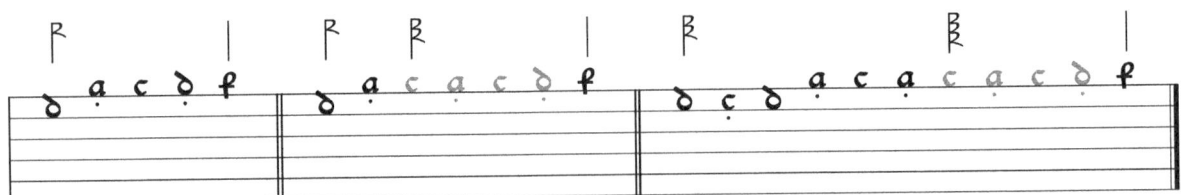

The following are examples from original pieces.
Newsidler: *Nach Willien dein*:

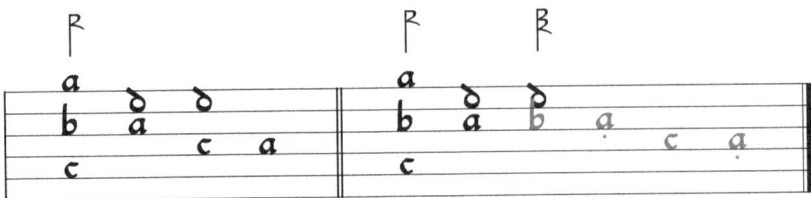

John Dowland, *Lachrimae Pavan*:

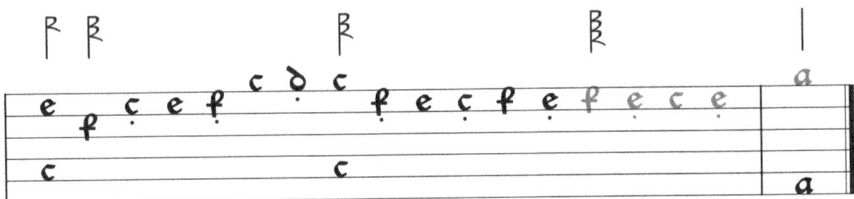

4.6. Filler

A *filler* division is one which, melodically and rhythmically, fills the space of a long note, or bar. The most common occurrence is at the end of dance strains, main sections, or the final bar of any piece. Two common types are:

*   Harmony-based *filler*, using broken 5/3 chords, with ornamentation around 3 or 5.
*   Melodic interval-based *filler*, often using the octave interval as a division.

This is an example of a harmony-based *filler*.
John Dowland, *Galliard Can she excuse*:

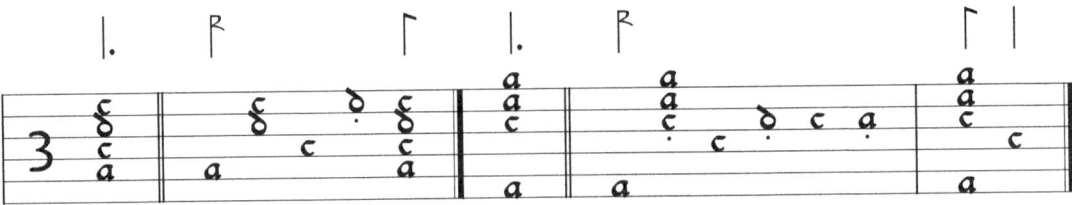

The following is an example of a melodic-based *filler*.

John Dowland, *Mr Langton's Galliard*:

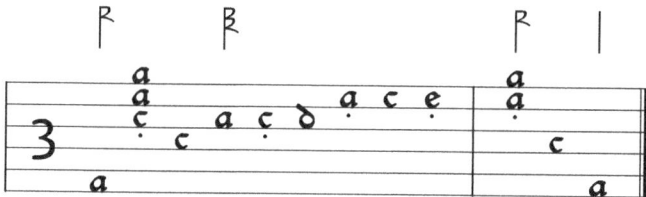

The following are examples of combined harmonic and melodic *fillers*.
Adriansen (1584):

John Dowland, *Lachrimae Pavan*:

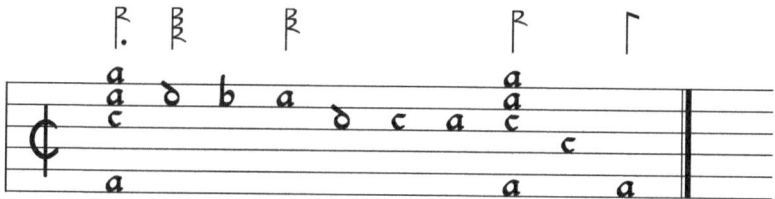

Adrian Le Roy (1568):

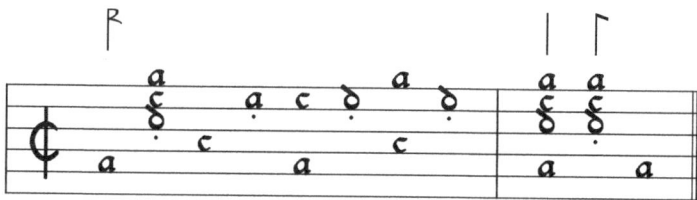

4.7. Lead-in

A *lead-in* is a short division figure which leads into the real beginning of a piece, often an intabulation. More common in the early part of the century, this division type is often found in the form of a *groppo* which leads into the tonic at the very beginning of a movement. The following examples all come from the *Capirola Lute Book*. They show the same rhythm, but only the third is a *groppo* figure.

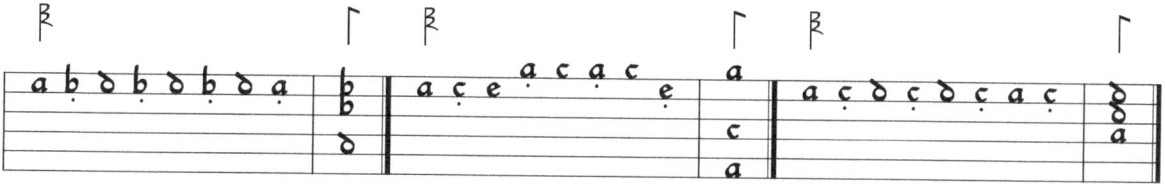

4.8. Connector

This division type is an *interval* division which connects two chords, with anchor notes from each chord not necessarily in the same voice. This is something which a lute can do but which cannot be done by a single voice in a madrigal or motet. The following example shows a *connector* division from the second B strain into the first C strain of the Pavan. The tenor of the first chord (B natural, tab *c* on the 3rd course) connects to the *cantus* high D (tab *h* on the 1st course). The first and last notes of the division can be seen in grey.

John Dowland, *Pipers Pavan* (C.U.L Add. Ms 3056):

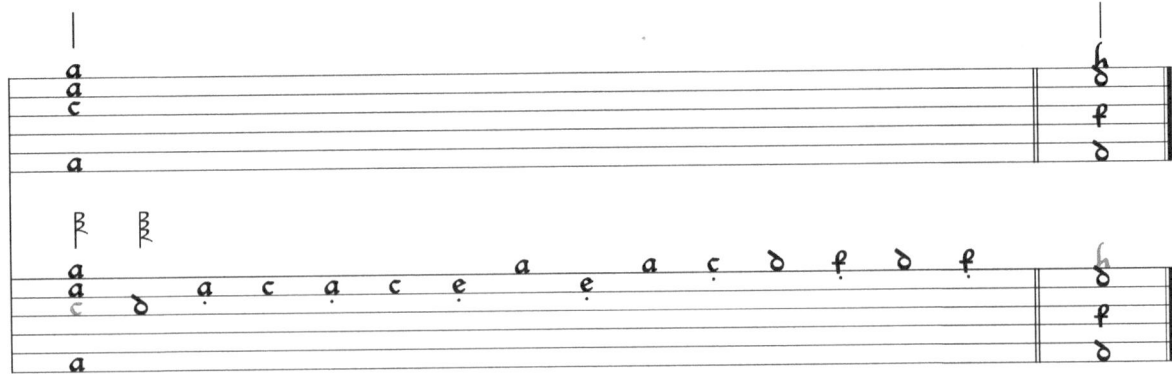

The next example is a very common one. The tenor voice from the first chord links to the *cantus* voice of the second chord. The first and last notes of the division can be seen in grey.

Two different *connectors* from Newsidler's setting of *Nach Willen Dein*; the first and last notes of both divisions can be seen in grey:

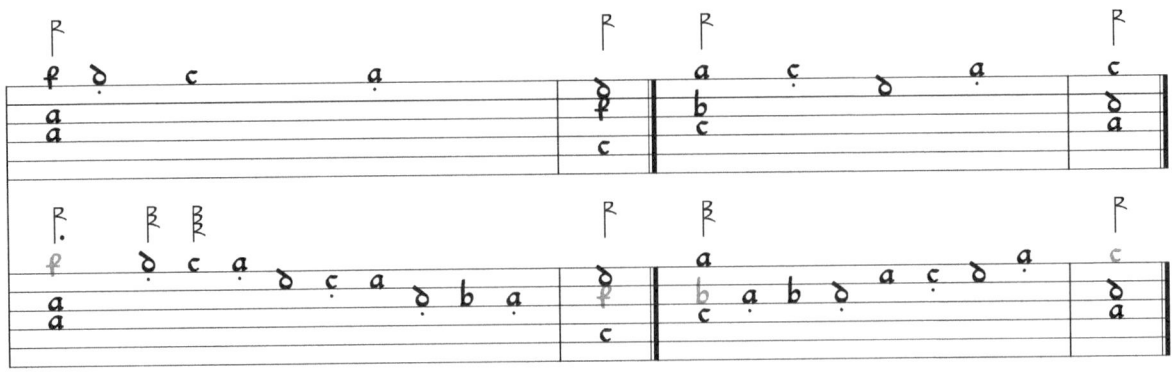

Here is a phrase from Narvaez's famous setting of the chanson, *Mille Regretz* (Josquin?). In this excerpt, bass G (tab *c* on the 4th course) connects to D in the *cantus* (tab *a* on the second course). The first and last notes of the division can be seen in grey.

4.9. Tirata

For our purposes on the lute, a *tirata* may generally be understood as a fast scale, usually moving by step, ascending or descending, covering an interval of more than an octave. A *tirata* might also sometimes fall under the banner of a *filler* or *connector*.

Here are three examples from original lute sources. The first and last notes of each division can be seen in grey.

Francesco da Milano, *Ricercar 33*:

Francesco da Milano, *Ricercar 34*:

Terzi, *Contrapunto* (1593):

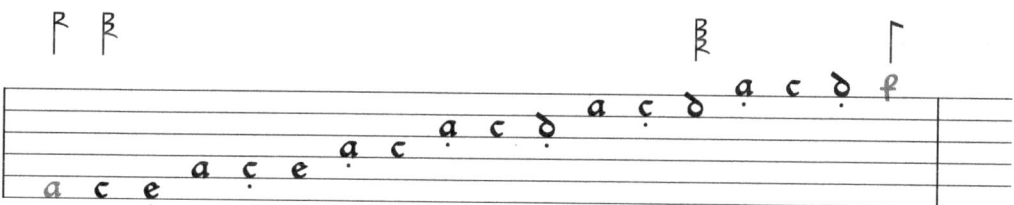

4.10. *Contrapunto* and *Bastarda* Style

A *contrapunto* is a newly composed single line, which adds to an original composition. A well-known example would be *La Spagna* for two lutes, Francesco da Milano. It was often based on a vocal model, a *tenor*, or repeated harmonic pattern or ground bass.

The skill of improvising a *contrapunto* was considered by Agazzarri (1607) as one of the many essential skills a good lutenist needed when playing as an ornamental instrument in an ensemble. Many *contrapunti* are found in intabulations of vocal models, to which is added a new part weaving amongst all voices. An excellent and perhaps the earliest example of this may be found in Diego Ortiz's *Trattado de Glosas*, Rome (1553), in which he composes a 'fifth' voice to two 4-part madrigals, *O Felici Occhi miei* (Arcadelt) and *Doulce Memoire* (Sandrin).

A type of *contrapunto* which became prevalent towards the end of the sixteenth century was the *bastarda*, a type of division, usually virtuosic, which had a large *ambitus* and which travelled through all the voices. Composers often wrote these for the viola da gamba, and the instrument used was then called the *viola bastarda*, representing more a style of playing a bass viol rather than indicating a specialised and different instrument. In Part 2: Tablature Case Studies, the Terzi duet version of *Susanne un jour* (Lassus) represents an example of *bastarda* divisions, even though the duet setting is called a *Contrapunto sopra Susanne un jour*.

4.11. Broken Chords

While most divisions are melodically and rhythmically conceived, there is an element of harmonic divisions, in some lute writing. This could also include the early form of *separée* as found, for example, in the solo lute works of De Rippe and Le Roy. Here are some examples which easily demonstrate this unusual but idiomatic style.

Dumpe (Philip van Wylder, *Marsh Lute Book*):

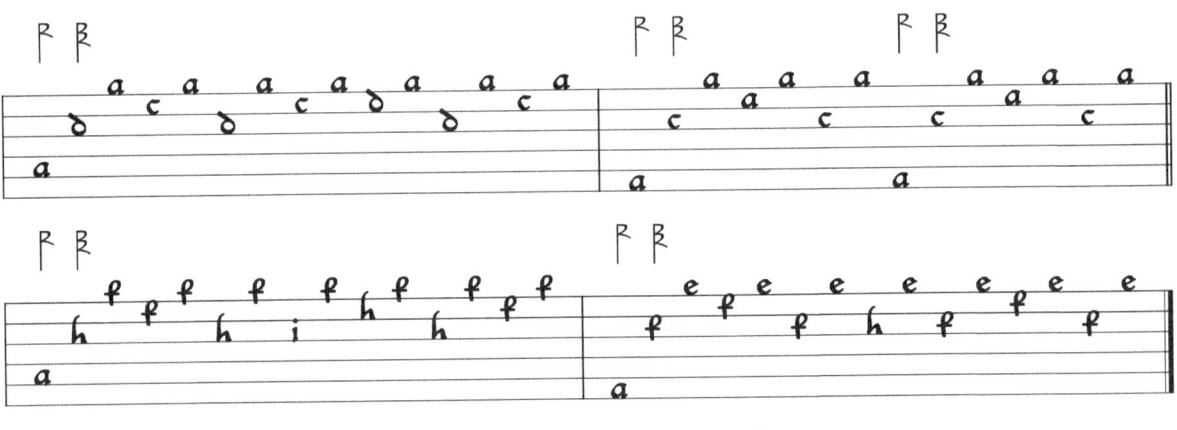

Passingmeasures Pavan (John Johnson), Dd 2.11, f.62v:

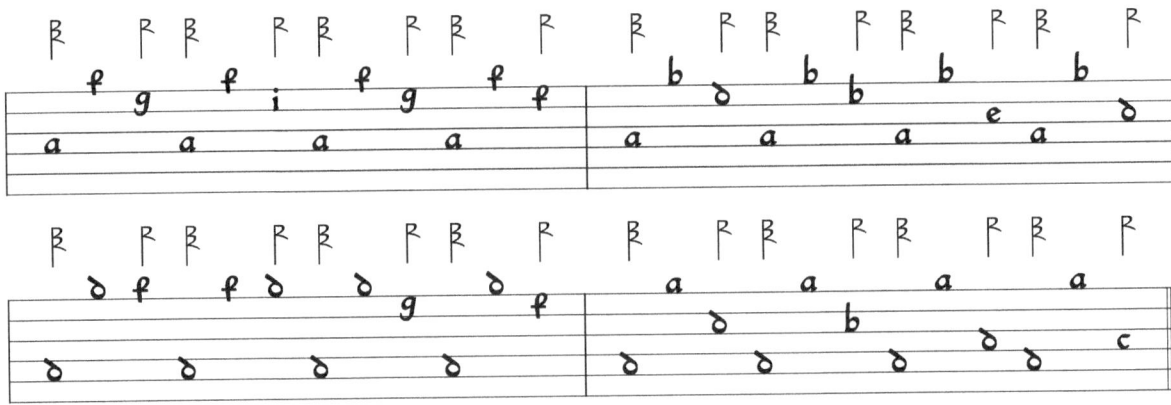

4.12. Recomposed

This type of division is one which extends outside the original melodic range but fits the harmony. Much of the consort lute parts of the English 'Broken Consort' would fit into this category. When we turn to John Dowland, we can find some beautiful and easily understood examples. The following extracts are all from John Dowland.

Earl of Essex, his Galliard (bars 39–42 and 47–50). Bars 39–42, which on repeat become bars 47– 50, show how Dowland abandons the original melodic *anchors*.

The King of Denmark's Galliard (A Varietie of Lute-lessons, 1610). Bars 1–8 represent the first complete strain of three. The complete galliard is in the form of variations. The first variation begins at bar 25, and here the harmony and the rhythm act as anchors.

King of Denmark's Galliard (bars 1–8 and 25–32), notated here for a 7-course lute with 7 = D:

Galliard to Lachrimae. As Dowland's lute style matured, so did his division writing, becoming freer and less restricted to the original *anchor* notes. The *Galliard to Lachrimae* is a late piece, published in *A Pilgrim's Solace* (1612) with many fine examples of division writing. Here are three extracts which illustrate this type of division.

Galliard to Lachrimae (bars 1–3 and their repeat, bars 11–13), notated here for 9-course lute: 7 = F; 8 = E♭; 9 = D:

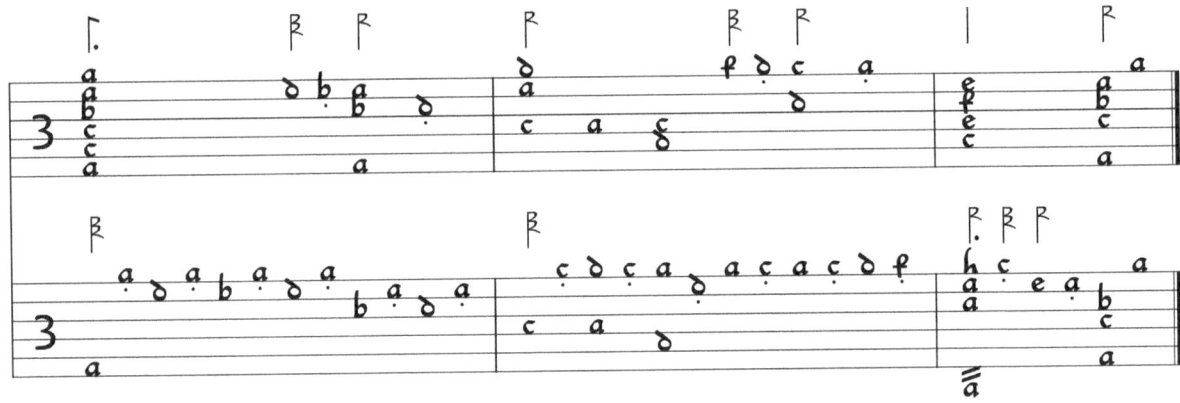

Galliard to Lachrimae (bars 8–10 and their repeat, bars 18–20):

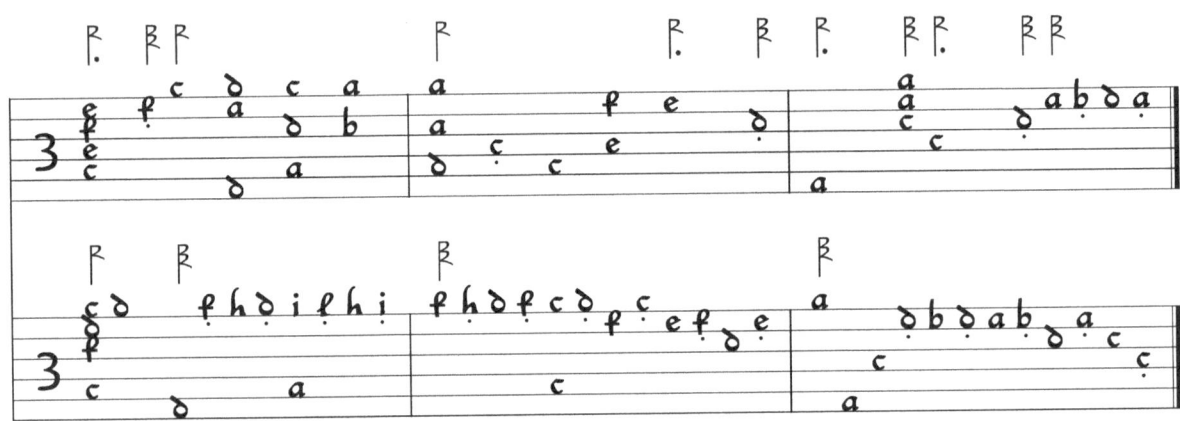

Galliard to Lachrimae (bars 21–22 and their repeat, bars 32–33):

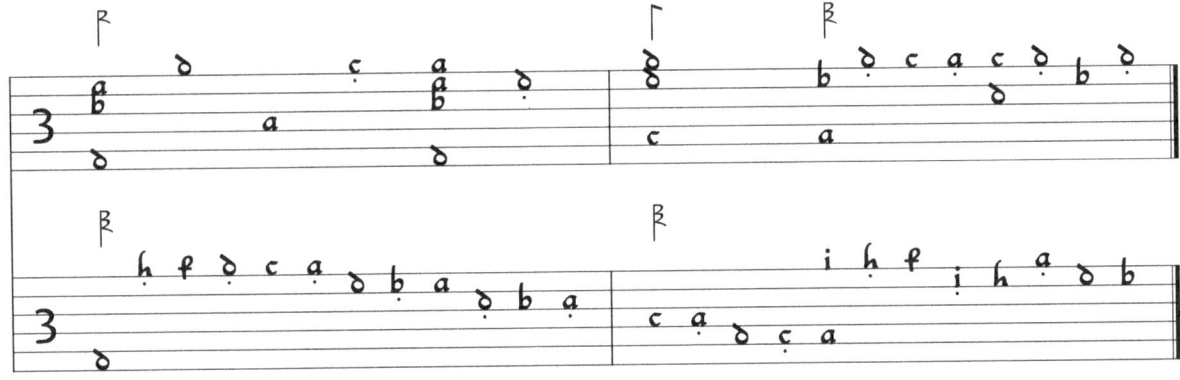

Pavan 'La Mia Barbara' from *Schele ms.* (D: Ha.Ms MB 2768). The divisions in this excerpt sound and play more like a lute part from a consort version!

PART 2
TABLATURE CASE STUDIES

Examples of solo and duo lute pieces, with notated scores showing an analysis of the types of divisions used.

CHAPTER 5

TABLATURE CASE STUDIES: INTRODUCTION

5.1. Introduction

In Part 1 we established that lutenists embellished their music with divisions, but there are no surviving teaching methods or treatises to document this learning process. Our solo and duo repertoire for lute contains all the examples we need, and the music of Part 2 was chosen to represent the whole century and the variety contained therein. The *Twelve Types of Divisions* and *General Rules* described in Part 1 have all been extracted from this lute repertoire. This process is what I have always imagined to be the method used by Johann Joseph Fux in his *Gradus Ad Parnassum* (1725), now a standard textbook for learning sixteenth-century counterpoint. Fux praises the works of Palestrina and may well have extracted his counterpoint method from studying the works and compositional techniques of Palestrina. In the following studies we can see how each lutenist embellished their music, and each score is annotated to show the types of divisions used. The annotations in the tablature should aid your awareness of the divisions you are playing. You will also notice that some divisions can be seen in more than one category (e.g., *interval* and *connector*, or *triad* and *interval*).

5.2. Annotations

Each division has a first and last note, and these anchor notes are coloured *grey*. The whole division is then enveloped in a circle. Above these circles, you will find a description of the division described in abbreviations. These labels refer to the *Twelve Types of Divisions* described in Part 1. Those used are listed in the following table. For example, 'INT 2nd ↑' will mean an ascending interval division between two notes a second apart.

5.3. Abbreviations

Abbreviations used in the annotations which describe the various division types:

INT	Interval
↑	Ascending
INT 5th ↑	An ascending interval of a fifth
↓	Descending
INT 5th ↓	A descending interval of a fifth
CAD	*Cadential*
GR	A *cadential groppo* division

Playing with Patterns on the Lute. Nigel North, Oxford University Press. © Oxford University Press 2025.
DOI: 10.1093/9780197808764.003.0007

ST	*Static* division (as defined in Part 1)
TRIAD	*Triad* division (as defined in Part 1)
TRIAD EX	*Extended triad* division (as defined in Part 1)
TRIAD H	*Harmonic triad* (as defined in Part 1)
TIR	*Tirata* (as defined in Part 1)
DB	*Doubler* (as defined in Part 1)
SEQ	Sequence
IM	Imitation
CON	*Connector*
FIL	*Filler*
DIS	Dissonance
REC	*Recomposed*

CHAPTER 6

NACH WILLEN DEIN, PAUL HOFHAIMER (1459–1537)

Three Versions by Hans Newsidler (1536 and 1544)

Original four-part lied:
George Foster, *Teutsche Liedlein* (Vol. 1), Nürnberg, 1539, Lied #43.
　　Lute intabulations (originally in German tablature) by Hans Newsidler:

- *Ein Newgeordent Küntslich Lautenbuch*, Nürnberg, 1536 (1536/6) f. l iii
- *Das Ander Buch,* Nürnberg, 1549 (1549/6) f. 4v (#16)
- *Der ander theil des Lautenbuchs,* Nürnberg, 1536 (1536/7) ff. Gg–Gg ii

This four-part song was popular with lutenists. Of the six printed by Hans Newsidler, the simplest one intabulates the tenor and bass only. In all other versions, Newsidler intabulates soprano, tenor, and bass, omitting the alto. It was common practice in the early sixteenth century to omit one voice so that the piece would be more naturally and easily played on the lute. While a song like this is usually considered to be a *tenor lied* where the main melody is in the tenor voice, lute intabulations took no regard of this. As we can see, most divisions are in the *cantus* voice. In fact, lute intabulations often transform a vocal piece into a new instrumental work which does not necessarily convey the text or the affect of the original song. The three versions shown here are graded in playing levels, from simple to advanced, mostly in the use of divisions, clearly showing the three different rhythmical levels of divisions discussed in Part 1. As often found, the *musica ficta* varies from one version to another (see, e.g., bar 2, tenor B♮ or B♭).
Division types used: *static, cadential, interval, connector, doubler, triad, recomposed.*
　　Almost all divisions can be easily identified from our list of division types. Compare the variety in the *static* divisions of bar 1, all moving by step, and the *cadential* divisions throughout the piece. Version 3 has some strong dissonances on the beat, something which is not often used, except at *cadential* points. See bars 2, 4, 17, and 26.
　　Some *interval* divisions can also be seen as being *triads,* such as bar 6. For an ascending *interval* division, one common devise is to descend before ascending. This gives more notes to the division and makes a certain rhythm possible (see bars 3, 6, 15, 19, etc., for examples). In bar 8, when we look from version 1 to the other two, we see a classic *doubler* on beats 1 and 2. Similar use of the *doubler* can also be seen in the *cadential groppo* of the third version. Cadential *doublers* may be seen in the third version in bars 4, 8, 11, 13, 14, and 16.

Playing with Patterns on the Lute. Nigel North, Oxford University Press. © Oxford University Press 2025.
DOI: 10.1093/9780197808764.003.0008

The original four-part lied:

Nach Willen dein mich dir allein
in Treuen zu erzeigen,
für all auf Erd bist du mir wert,
und gib mich dir füe eigen.
Ganz in dein Pflicht der Zuversicht
lasst dir mein Dienst gefallen,
dann glaub fürwahr, in Frauenschar
liebst du mir ob ihn allen.

With your consent, to you alone,
I show myself in true faith,
for all that is on the earth
you are the most precious to me,
that would be worth all that is there on earth,
and I give myself to you.
Completely in your duty of trust
Please accept my service,
then, believe me indeed, that among all
womankind
I love you more than all others.

EXAMPLE *Nach willen dein*, Paul Hofhaimer. Nürnberg, 1539. Score of the original four-part lied.

Annotated tablature score of the three versions by Newsidler:

EXAMPLE *Nach willen dein*, Paul Hofhaimer. Intabulated by Hans Newsidler, 1563, 1549.

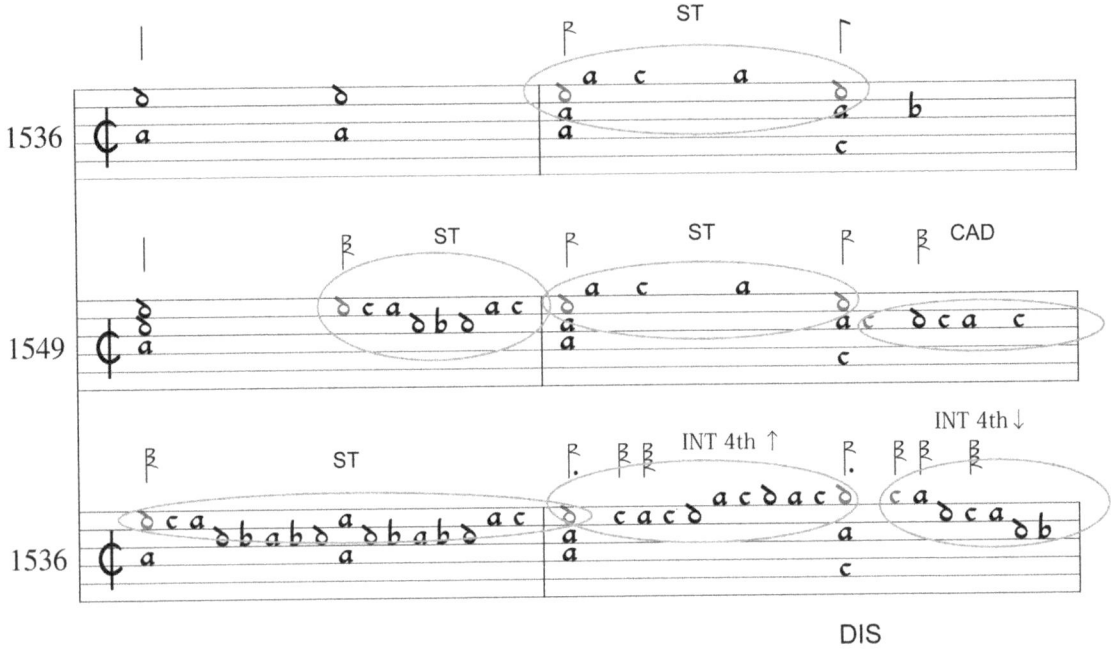

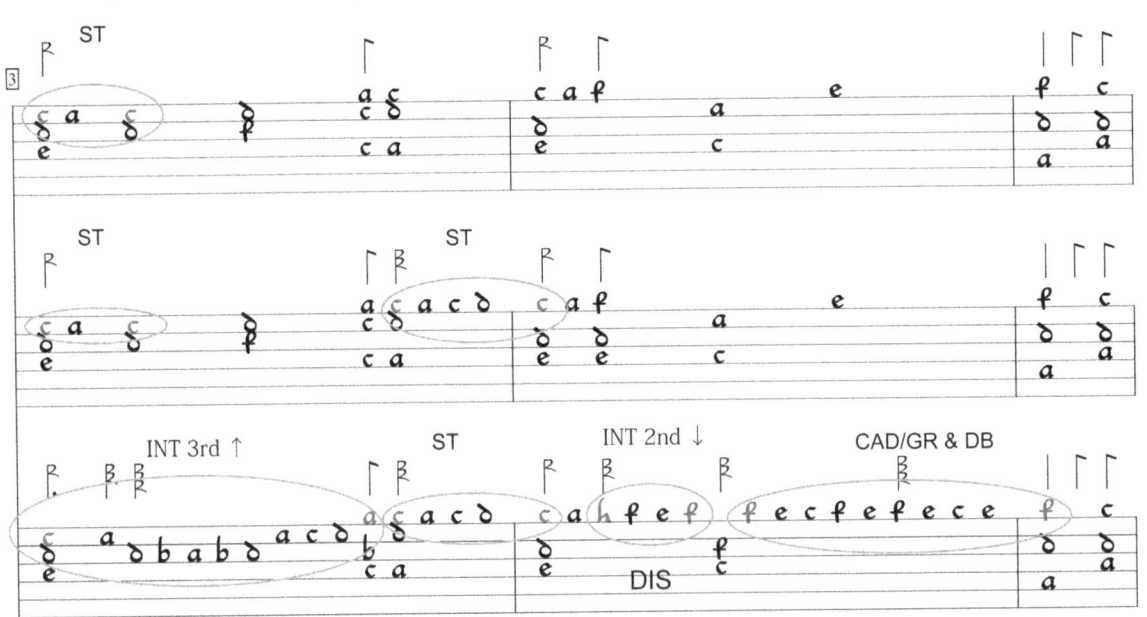

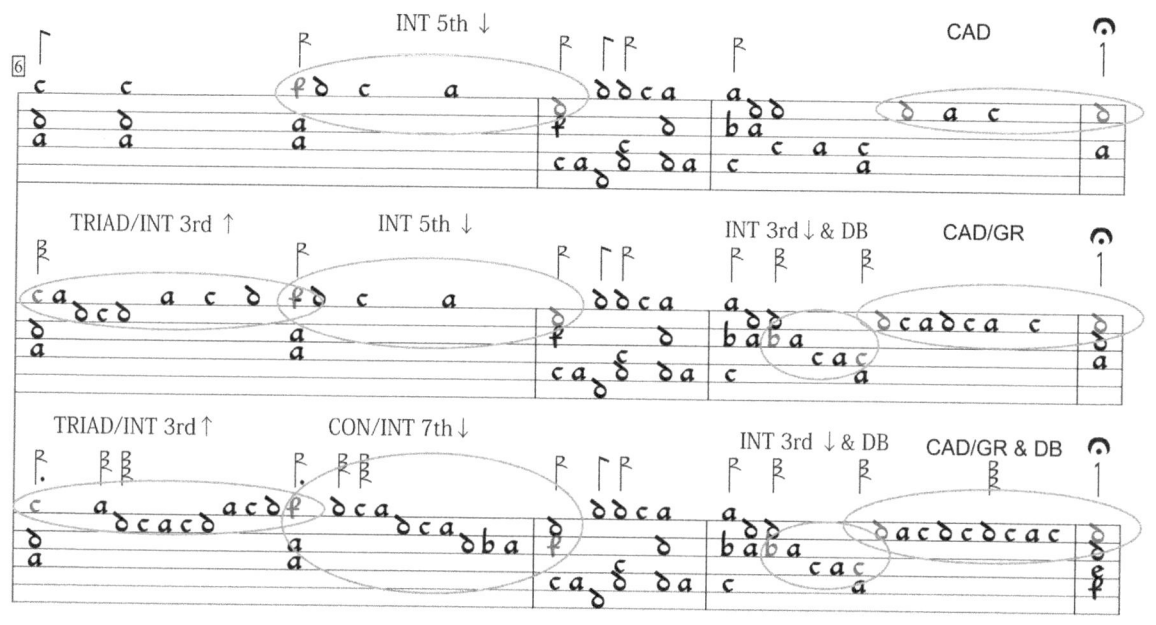

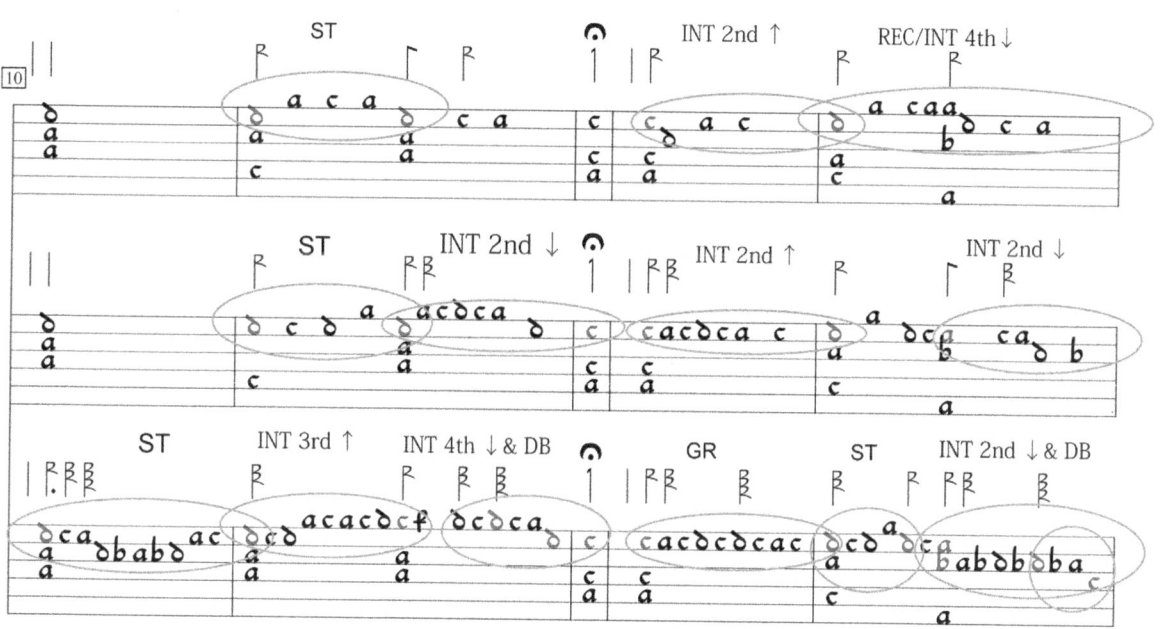

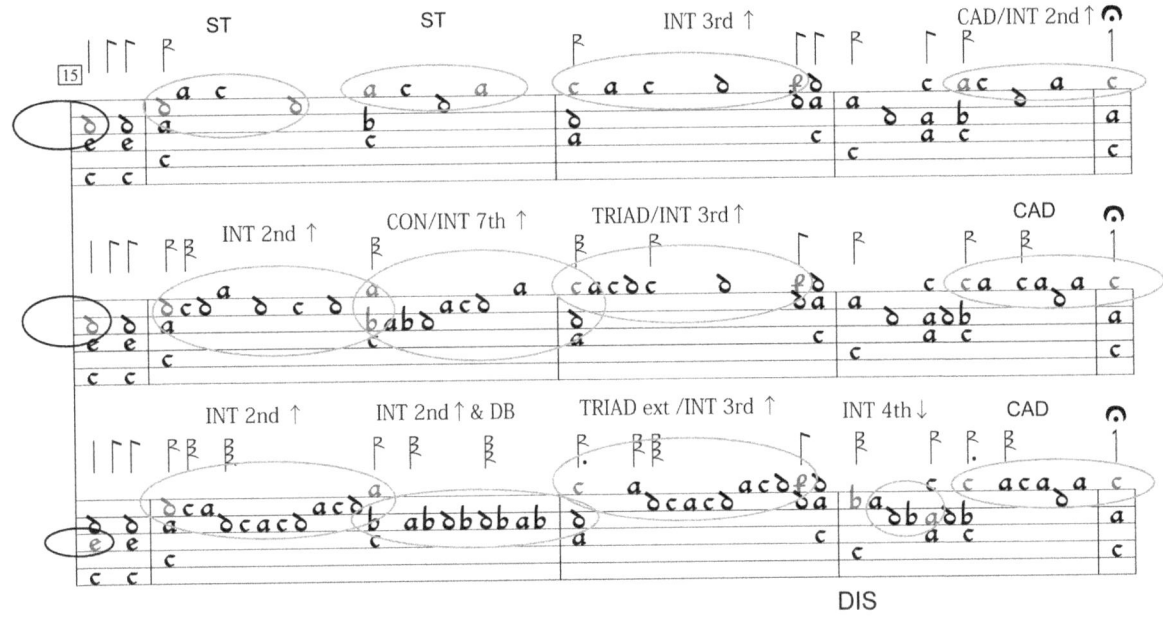

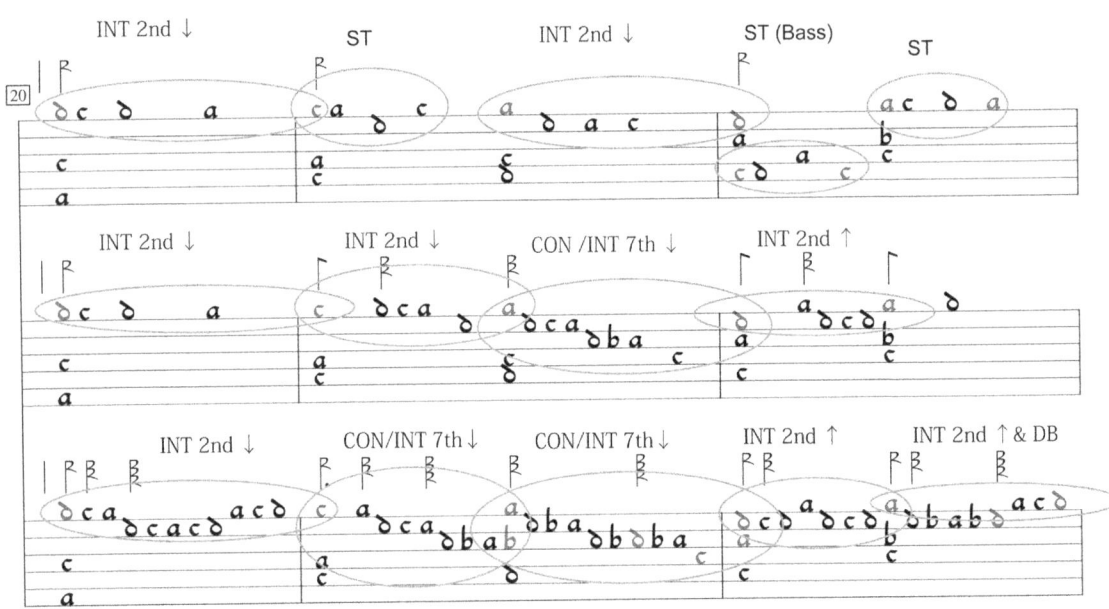

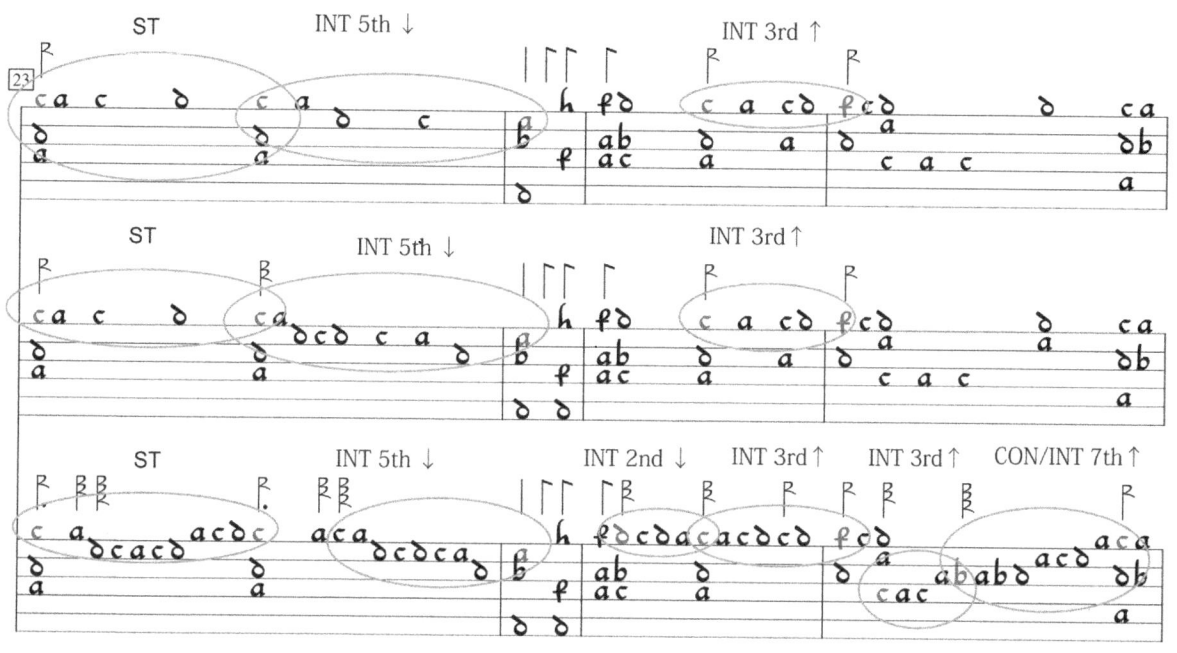

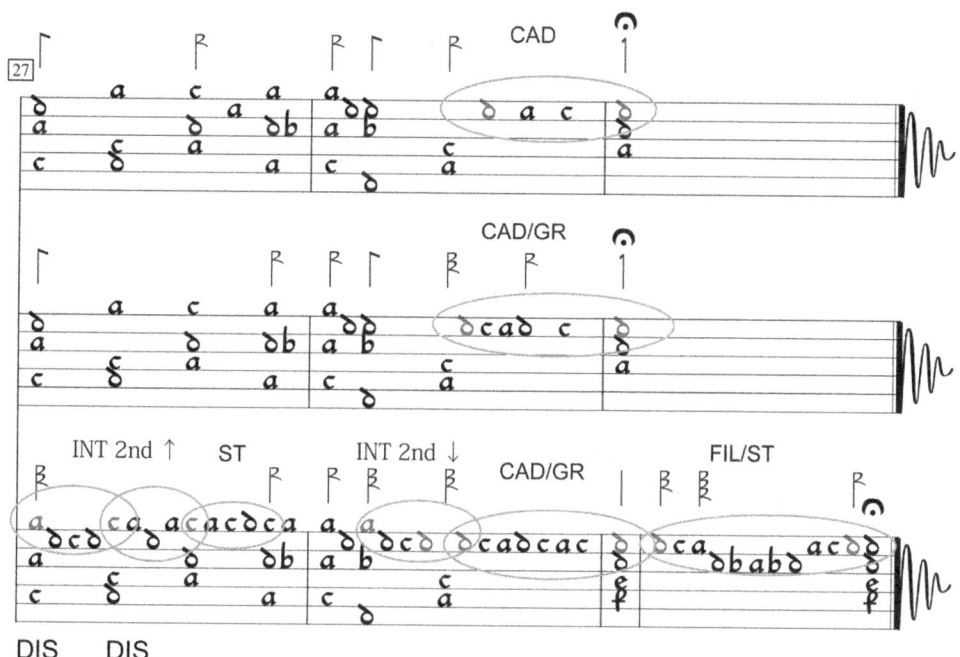

CHAPTER 7

JE PRENS EN GRÈ, CLEMENS NON PAPA (CA. 1510–CA. 1555)

As Set by Mattheus Waisell (1573)

Original four-part chanson:

- Pierre Attaingnant (publisher), *6ème livre contenant xxvii chansons nouvelles*, Paris, 1539
- Tielman Susato (publisher), *1er livre des chanson*, Antwerp, 1543

Lute intabulation by Matthäus Waissel (originally in German tablature):

- *Tabulatura*, Matthäus Waisell, Frankfurt an der oder, 1573 (1573/3) based on an earlier printed intabulation:

Pierre Phalèse, *De chansons & motetz (Livre Troisieme)*, Louvain, 1547 (1547/9)

This well-crafted yet simple intabulation uses standard formulas to good effect as is often found in the books of Phalèse.

7.1. Division Types Used

STATIC

The *static* division is the one most often used, one step up, one step down, sometimes with a *doubler*, and these appear in all voices. For example, *cantus*: bar 2; alto: bar 3; tenor: bar 13; bass: bar 23.

INTERVAL

A descending second is often used in a *compound interval* form; the division goes up first so that there is a longer journey down! Examples may be found in bars 6, 18, 20, and 52.

Descending octave scales are used for *fillers* (bars 12 and 55), the second of which adds a *doubler*. Ascending octave scales are used as *connectors* in bars 40 and 48.

CADENTIAL

We can observe that each lutenist had their preferred, signature *cadential groppo* rhythm. Waissel is consistent with his here in bars 11, 22, 32, 42, 51, and 55. Each one has the same rhythm, showing three rhythmic levels of division completed with a *doubler* which takes the phrase forward to the next chord.

Playing with Patterns on the Lute. Nigel North, Oxford University Press. © Oxford University Press 2025.
DOI: 10.1093/9780197808764.003.0009

Printing the original *cantus* with the divisions was a common practice in some of the wind/string/vocal diminution treatises. Here is the chanson, with the *cantus* part of the vocal original and Waissel's intabulation in annotated French tablature.

Je prens en grè, Clemens non papa, intabulated by Matthäus Waissel:

Je prens en grè la dure mort
Pour vous madame par amours
Navrè m'avez mais a grand tort,
Dont brief je finiray mes jours.
La chose me vient a rebours
Souffrir si tost la mort amere
O dure mort, que faites vous
Mourir me fault c'est chose clair.

Willingly do I accept cruel death,
Because of my love for you, my lady
You have wounded me, but unjustly so,
Thus, my days will soon end.
The matter appears backwards to me,
To suffer so soon the bitterness of dying.
O cruel death, what are you doing?
I must die, that much is clear to me.

EXAMPLE *Je prens en grè* (Clemens non papa). Intabulated by Waissel, 1573. Original *cantus* part with Waisell's intabulation.

CHAPTER 8

MILLE REGRETZ, ATTRIBUTED TO JOSQUIN DES PREZ (CA. 1450–1521)

As Set by Luis Narvaez (1538)

Original four-part chanson:

- Tielman Susato (publisher), *L'unziesme livre des chansons*, Antwerp, 1549

Intabulation (vihuela): *La cancion del emperador (Mille regretz)*

- Luis de Narvaez, *Los seys libros del Delphin de musica*, Valladolid, 1538

Narvaez's well-known intabulation corresponds with Josquin's written pitches if we assume an A-tuned vihuela (or lute). For our purposes here, you will see two scores. The first is a score with original pitches and no text. As this book is designed for G-tuned lutes, the second score shows the *cantus* part transposed down a tone, to correspond with the G-tuned lute/vihuela tablature beneath. The Narvaez barring has been adapted to fit with the chanson. Original Italian/Spanish tablature transcribed into French.

Division types used:

The two principal division types used are *static* and *interval*.

Static:

These are used in all voices, most often in the soprano, but also alto, tenor, and bass.

Interval:

The *interval* of a fifth, ascending and descending, is the most popular interval used, and is perhaps the most significant melodic feature which gives this intabulation its unique quality. Other *intervals* (2nd, 3rd, and 4th) are used less often.

Bar 2: The bass divisions are worthy of comment. The first half of the bar is imitated in the second half, and they are really *static* as they return to the anchor note before moving on. But we hear ascending fifths.

Bars 6–7: The intabulated bass division connects the tenor anchor notes. The bass is tacet at this point!

Bar 8: The descending fifth division connects the soprano A to a D which is non-existent in the original but is consonant with the harmony.

Bar 14: The descending fifth *interval* connects the alto D to a non-existent but consonant G (tablature *c* on the 4th course).

Bars 19–20: We can see an ascending fourth (tablature 1st course, *c* bar 19) connected to tablature 1st course *h* at the end of the same bar) followed by a descending second (tablature 1st course, *h* to *f*).

Bar 27: The soprano division is imitated in the alto with a division in bar 28.

Bars 35 and 37 have a descending fifth which is a *connector*, joining the alto to the tenor.

Playing with Patterns on the Lute. Nigel North, Oxford University Press. © Oxford University Press 2025.
DOI: 10.1093/9780197808764.003.0010

Overall, the melodic divisions are minimal, with much rhythmic imitation from one phrase to another and some unusually constructed divisions, yet it feels balanced and in no way empty or unornamented.

Here are some examples of interval divisions of a fifth and a second.

Examples of interval divisions of a 5th (ascending & descending)

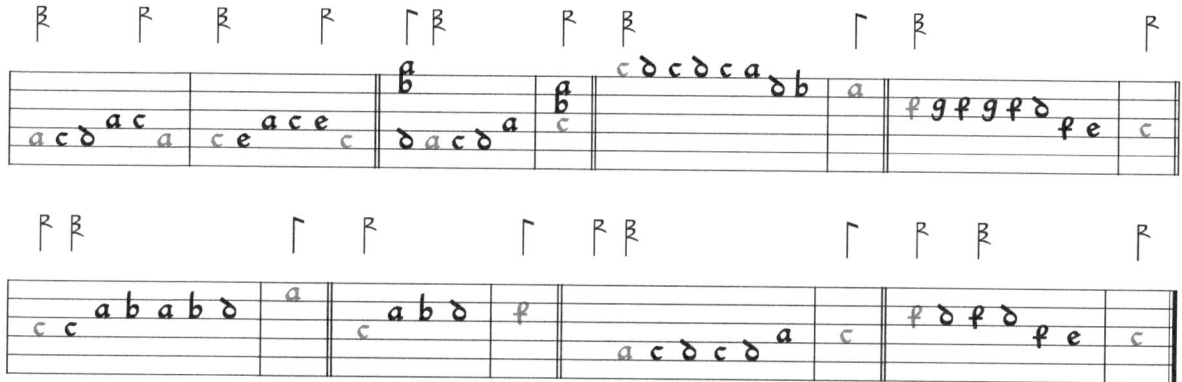

Examples of descending interval divisions of a 2nd

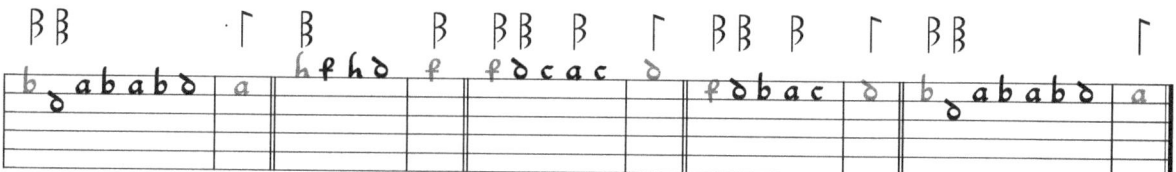

Unlike many intabulations, this one is lacking cadential ornaments and *fillers* and the final plagal cadence has no divisions. Perhaps a good place for us to improvise some? Hans Gerle's intabulation (*Tabulatur auff die Laudten*, Nürnberg, 1533, 1533/1, ff. 40v–41) has a division which can serve for the final cadence. Here it is, with a *doubler* added at the end of the division:

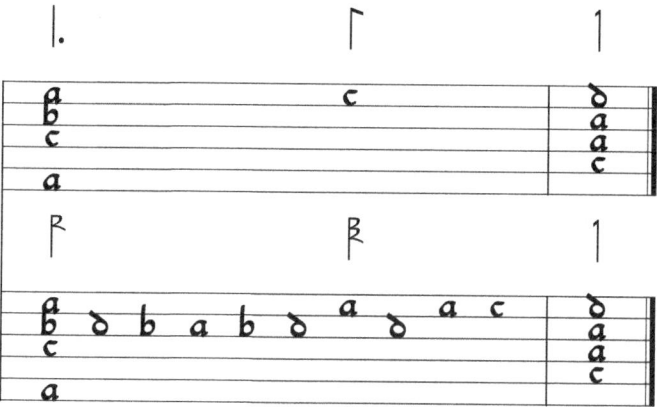

A score of the original four voices:

EXAMPLE *Mille regretz*, attributed to Josquin des Prez. Score of the original four-part chanson, without text

? Josquin des Prez
pub. Antwerp, 1549

Mille regretz

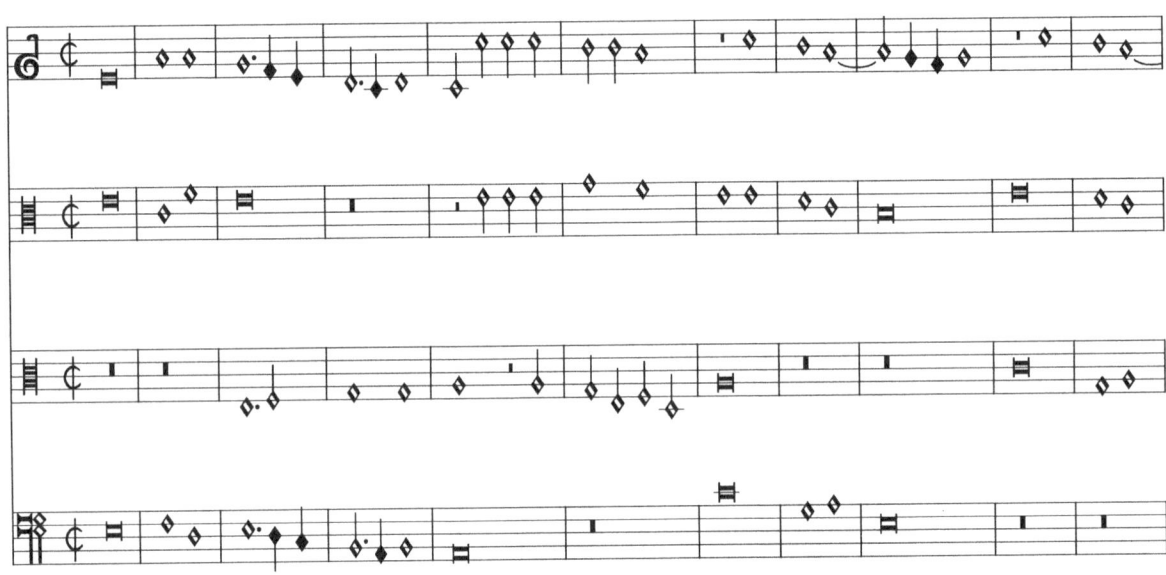

A score with the *cantus* transposed, and an annotated G-lute tablature:

Mille regretz de vous abandonner
Et d'eslonger vostre fache amoureuse,
Jay si grand dueil et paine douloureuse,
Qu'on me verra brief mes jours desfiner.

A thousand regrets for abandoning you
and for turning away your loving face,
I am in such deep mourning and painful sorrow,
that I will soon see my days come to an end.

EXAMPLE *Mille regretz*, attributed to Josquin des Prez. Original *cantus* part, transposed down a tone, with intabulation for vihuela/lute by Narvaez.

? Josquin des Prez
pub. Antwerp, 1549

Mille regretz

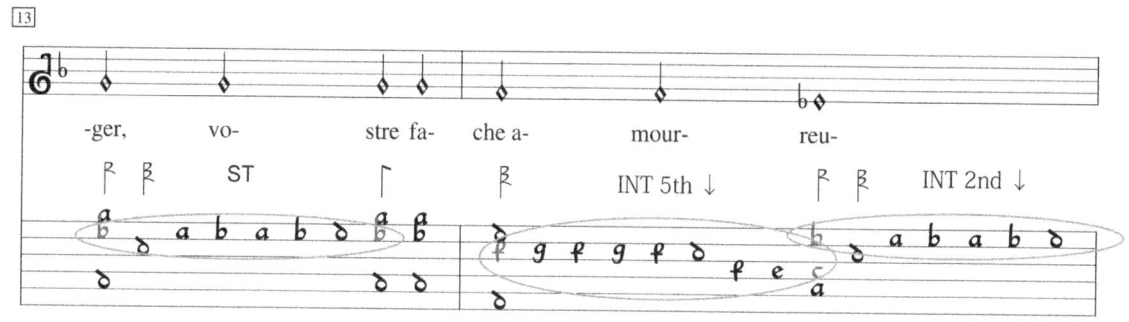

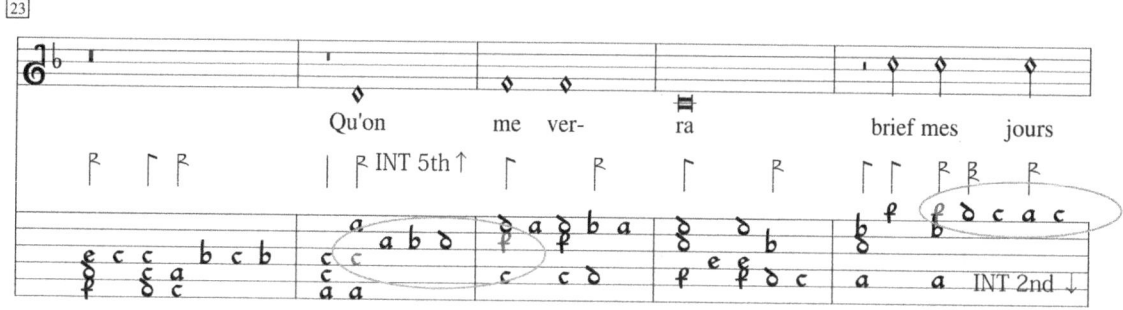

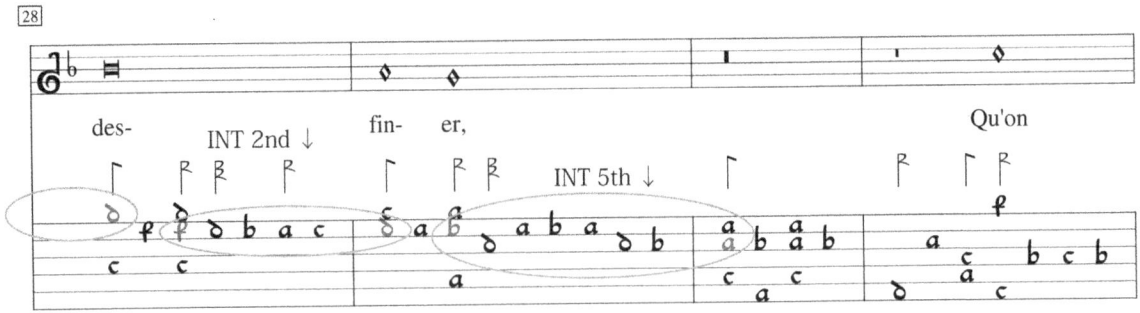

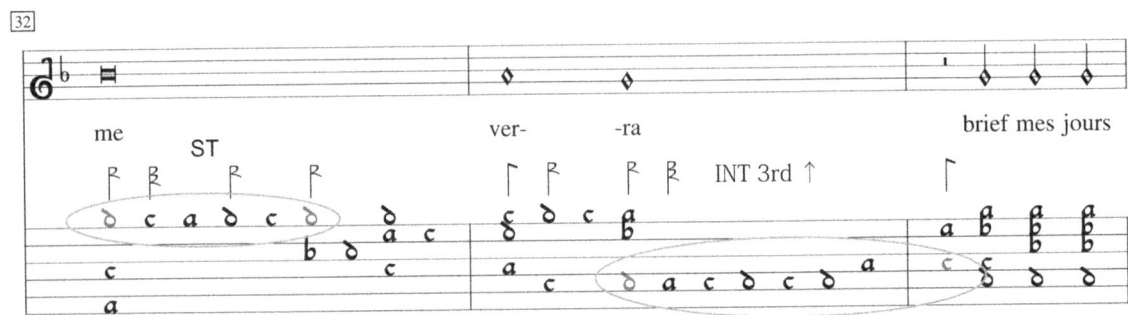

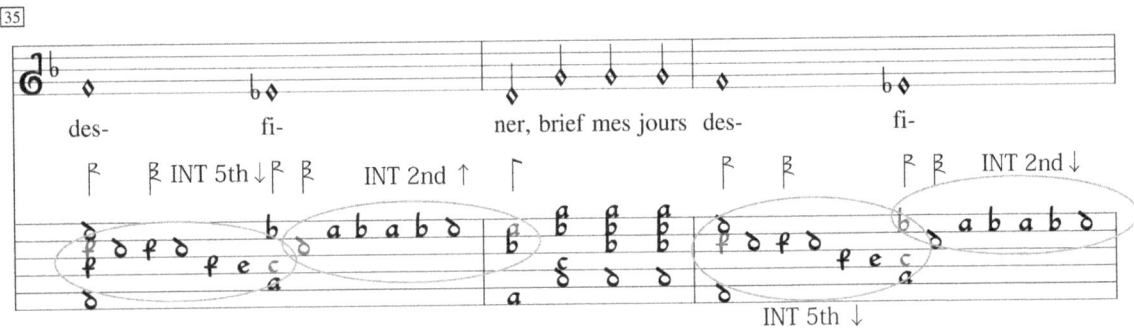

CHAPTER 9

GREENSLEEVES, ANON.

A Treble and Ground Duet

Source: Folger Dowland Ms., Ms. V.b.280 (formerly MS. 1610.1), f. 5.
    Folger Shakespeare Library, Washington, D.C.
    This little treble and ground duet is an excellent teaching piece. The very simple divisions are full of rhythmic variety, they lie under the hand easily and are also a well-written example of divisions on the *Romanesca* bass. The *Romanesca* bass had several forms, more often in triple time. (See Part 3: Method, for exercises on this ground.)
    The form used here is in duple time and is related closely to versions of the *Passamezzo antico*. The Spanish Vihuelists' favourite form of the triple time *Romanesca* was called *Guardame las vacas*.
Division types used:
    The predominant division types are *triad* and *static*. This gives the piece a very melodic feel. *Cadential* and *interval* figures complete the list.
    Two interesting anomalies can be found here:

- There are dissonances on the first beat of bar 38, reaching consonance only by the middle of the bar.
- If you look and listen, you will find some parallel fifths and octaves between the treble division and the bass of the ground. See bars 3–4, 11–12, 14–15, 18–19, and 27–28. You may well find that it does not sound wrong and you may not even have noticed them. Perhaps that was the case in the sixteenth century too!

The following score has annotations with invented *anchor notes* to show how the divisions were made. (We will also do this in *The Queen's Treble* by John Johnson later in the volume.)
    Upper tablature stave: Original treble part.
    Middle tablature stave: Suggested *anchor notes* line.
    Lower tablature stave: Ground (the same in each variation).

Playing with Patterns on the Lute. Nigel North, Oxford University Press. © Oxford University Press 2025.
DOI: 10.1093/9780197808764.003.0011

EXAMPLE *Greensleeves*, Anon. Treble and ground duet with anchor notes and annotations.

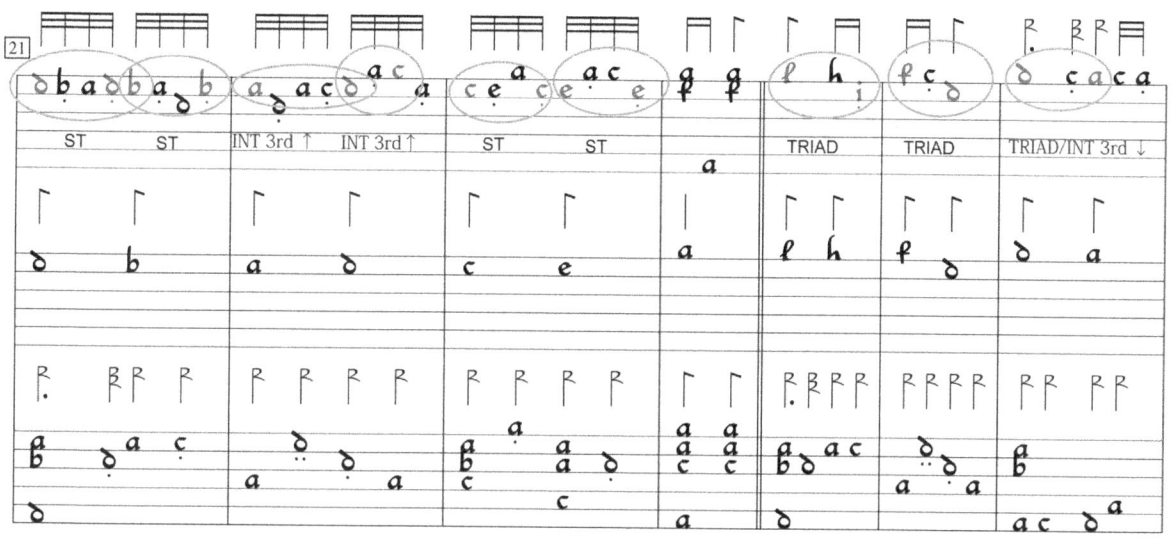

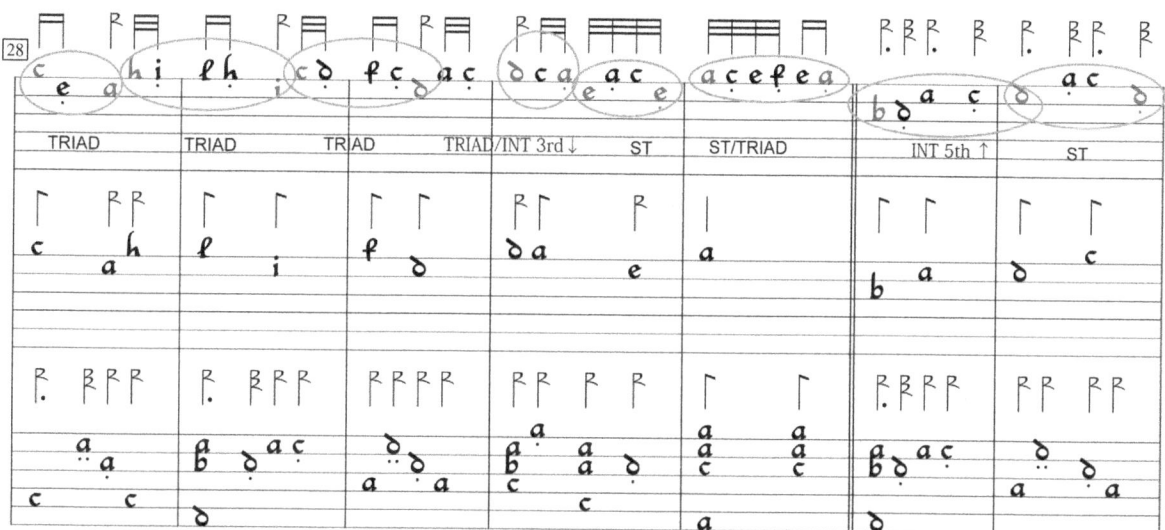

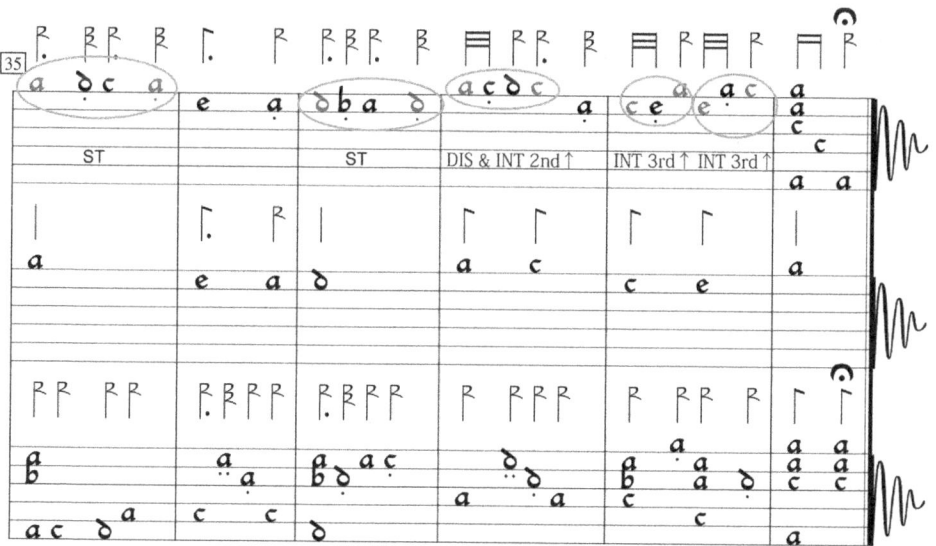

CHAPTER 10

PASSEMEZE (PASSAMEZZO ANTICO), ADRIAN LE ROY

A Briefe and easye instruction, London (1568)

(An English version of the original French, now lost: *Instruction*, Paris, 1557)

Advancing to solo lute pieces with inclusive divisions, the *Passameze* is one of several published by Adrian Le Roy in which a simple form of the *Passamezzo antico* dance is followed by one with divisions, and marked *plus diminuée* (or in English, *Passameze more shorter*). This is presented here in score, the simple and ornamented versions together for comparison. The original *Passameze* is the first practice piece in the book, following on from the *Instruction*, and is not an advanced piece. Like the *Greensleeves* duet presented earlier, it is simple and well written with good examples from which to learn. The divisions or diminutions that we find are not continuous but come in short bursts. They propel the music forward, add grace, and make it more *delightful*.

Division types used:

- *Intervals*: Ascending and descending intervals (2nd, 4th, 6th)
- *Static*
- *Triad*
- *Cadential* (only in bar 14)

Bar 15: A very common *filler* figure is found in the upper version, dividing on the final tonic. The lower version at the same place is an extended *triad* figure which goes up to the flat seventh and back, giving the hint of a 'blue' note for the seventh.

Playing with Patterns on the Lute. Nigel North, Oxford University Press. © Oxford University Press 2025.
DOI: 10.1093/9780197808764.003.0012

EXAMPLE *Passamezze (Passamezzo antico)*, Adrian Le Roy. Annotated French lute tablature.

CHAPTER 11

FANTASIA A DUI LIUTI, FRANCESCO DA MILANO

Castelfranco Ms. Extract

Intavolatura manoscritta per liuto del Duomo di Castelfranco Veneto
Fantasia di francesco da milano a dui liutti
Lute 1: *Tenore* f. 41
Lute 2: *Fantasia/Alio modo* ff. 51v–52

The opening of this *Fantasia* is very similar to that found in the *Contrapunto primo* by B(ernardo) M(onzino) in *Fronimo* (see Chapter 12). Francesco and 'B.M.' (Bernardo Monzino?) in *Fronimo* used standard harmonic and ornamentation figures to create the opening *exordium*. The success of these standard figures makes this *Fantasia* worthy of study. What is presented here is a short extract of a longer piece in which the first lute is the *tenore* and the second lute part has two *contrapunti* above; the *Fantasia* being simple, and the *Alio modo* more virtuosic, using an extra, faster level of division rhythm. A *contrapunto* in this form is like an Italian *treble and ground* duet. We will only consider the opening eight bars of each treble lute part.

Fantasia:
Bars 1 and 2 present material which is then imitated as a sequence, bars 3–4, 5–6, and 7–8. Each one follows the same course. Descending fifth, descending fourth (which could also be seen as two joining *triad* divisions or a descending 8ve), followed by a simple cadence. Beginning in G, the four cadences are on D, F, C, and back to G.

> Tablature stave 1: Original lute treble (*Fantasia* 1st version).
> Tablature stave 2: Invented anchor notes.
> Tablature stave 3: Original lute *tenore*.

Fantasia:

Playing with Patterns on the Lute. Nigel North, Oxford University Press. © Oxford University Press 2025.
DOI: 10.1093/9780197808764.003.0013

EXAMPLE *Fantasia a dui liuti*, Francesco da Milano. Bars 1–8, Lutes 1 and 2 with anchor notes.

Alio modo:

An excellent example of how to expand an original idea.

Bars 1–2: The basic two-bar material of the *Fantasia* is inverted, and has a very convincing repeated ascending fifth figure, also triad in form, leading to a normal fast *groppo* cadence to D.

Bars 3–4: Repeated down a fourth. The *groppo* is less fast and the voicing of the cadence is unlike the other three cadences. Cadence to F.

Bars 5–6: The figure is repeated a third higher with a cadence on C.

Bars 7–8: The figure is down another fourth with an expanded diminution leading to a cadence to G.

All cadences on D, F, C, and G are examples of a normal renaissance cadence, two voices a major sixth apart, expanding to an octave. Like the *Greensleeves* duet, this seems to have been conceived as a teaching piece and provides an excellent lesson.

Tablature stave 1: Original lute treble (*Alio modo*)
Tablature stave 2: Invented anchor notes
Tablature stave 3: Original lute *tenore*

Alio modo:

EXAMPLE *Alio modo*, Francesco da Milano. Bars 1–8, Lutes 1 and 2 with anchor notes.

CHAPTER 12

CONTRAPUNTO PRIMO, B[ERNARDO] M[ONZINO]

Fronimo dialogo, Vincenzo Galilei, Venice, 1584, pp. 178–179

Vincenzo Galilei published his book on the art of intabulation in two editions, 1568 and 1584. In the second and more well-known expanded edition of 1584, Galilei includes two of the most exquisite *contrapunti* in our repertoire. The following piece is the first of these two.

Types of divisions used:

- *Triad* and *static* figures are the most frequent.
- A new type featured is the *harmonic triad* and *imitative short figures*, often with repeated notes (see bars 19–23, 27–28, 36–38, and 40–41).
- *Cadential*: *Groppi* are the most common.
- *Interval*: Interval figures 2nd, 3rd, 4th, and 7th, and many 5ths.
- There is a noticeable absence of any 6ths being ornamented.

To help see which division types are being used, an invented line of *anchor notes* has been added (second stave). The *tenore* part (third stave) is (for the most part) in three voices, occasionally filling out to four. The *contrapunto* uses all three rhythmic levels, as demonstrated in bars 1–2.

Contrapunto primo, (Bernardo Monzino?) from *Fronimo* (1584):

Playing with Patterns on the Lute. Nigel North, Oxford University Press. © Oxford University Press 2025.
DOI: 10.1093/9780197808764.003.0014

EXAMPLE *Contrapunto primo* B(ernardo) M(onzino). *Fronimo dialogo*, Vincenzo Galilei, Venice, 1584, pp. 178–179.

CHAPTER 13

THE QUEEN'S TREBLE, JOHN JOHNSON (CA. 1545–1594)

A Treble and Ground Duet

Jane Pickering Lute Book, GB:lbm, Eg.2046, ff. 8v–9r.

If we only studied and imitated the art of divisions created by John Johnson, we would be in excellent shape! In studying this popular treble on a ground which is a version of the *Bergamasca*, we can see that Johnson's division technique is principally inspired by the harmony. *The Queen's Treble* has 14 variations on chords I–IV–V–I, using mostly *triad* and *static* figures. Some patterns may also be seen as *interval* divisions, and there is a total absence of *cadential* suspensions or *groppo* figures.

To the following score I have invented an *anchor note* line. Extracting *anchor notes* is just an interpretation, but in doing so, it is amazing to see that all those notes are *triad* notes which have a simple melodic logic all to themselves. When placed next to the *anchor notes*, the treble divisions are an excellent lesson. Part of Johnson's style and technique is to make each variation around one idea, usually predominantly rhythmic. For example:

- Division 1 (Bars 1–4): The rhythm of bar 1 with the dotted first beat is the principal subject of the variation. Bars 1–3 are the same rhythmically, but the melodic notes used on each chord vary, as does the contour of the line. Bar 4 gets a little faster, but bars 1–4 sound and feel naturally integrated.
- Division 2 has a rhythmic subject for all four bars, and this time the melodic shape of each bar begins on the third of each chord of the ground.
- Division 5 is much the same. The melody begins on the fifth of each chord and ends on the tonic of each. The rhythm is imitated in each bar.

There is one 'blue' note which shouts out so magnificently: Variation 13, bar 52. Johnson takes us to an E♭, which is the flat seventh over F (tablature *i* on the 1st course). The treble leaps there, not on the beat, but jumps to a dissonant note, breaking one of the general rules with great effect.

Range of the Treble

A total range of two octaves: the open 4th course (F) is the lowest, and tablature *l* on the 1st course (F) the highest. Tablature *h* on the 1st course, D, is the highest note, generally. This may be thought of as the *la* (6th note) of the soft hexachord (with *F* as the Ut).

Variations 6 and 7 venture up to high F (tablature *l* on the 1st course) as the fifth of the B♭ chord in both variations.

> Upper stave: Treble with division types annotated.
> Middle stave: An invented line of *anchor notes*.
> Lower stave: The ground (the same in each variation).

Playing with Patterns on the Lute. Nigel North, Oxford University Press. © Oxford University Press 2025.
DOI: 10.1093/9780197808764.003.0015

John Johnson, *The Queen's Treble*:

EXAMPLE *The Queen's Treble*, John Johnson. A treble and ground duet with added anchor notes.

CHAPTER 14

SIR JOHN SMITH, HIS ALMAIN, JOHN DOWLAND

A Varietie of Lute-Lessons, London (1610)

7-course lute, with 7 = D

This *Almain* is helpful in our studies of division making because bars 1–32 form a complete dance, which is then repeated with divisions (bars 33–64). So that the comparison between first and second times are easier to see, the following annotated score has:

Stave 1: Bars 1–32
Stave 2: Bars 33–64

In both staves, there are divisions made on a simpler version of the same phrase, so annotations will be found throughout the piece, on both staves! Dowland's tuneful and rhythmically varied division style is also well represented here. The tuneful aspect comes from so many *triad* figures. When taking a closer look, we can see that there are many figures which can count as either *triad* or *static*, or an alliance of both. Examples of this combination can be found in bars 14, 52, 53, 57, 59, and 61.

Dowland is also a master of long streams of equal notes which weave together several harmonies and melodic anchor notes. Bar 39 is a good example, and he uses that several times (bars 15 and 63). See also bars 62 and 63. Taking bar 53 as an original bar and bar 61 as its division, we can see a simple example of *doublers*:

Playing with Patterns on the Lute. Nigel North, Oxford University Press. © Oxford University Press 2025.
DOI: 10.1093/9780197808764.003.0016

Sir John Smith, his Almain, John Dowland:

EXAMPLE *Sir John Smith, his Almain*, John Dowland (1610).

RICERCATA PER VIOLA BASTARDA, E LAUTO

Aurelio Virgiliano, *Il dolcimelo* (c. 1600–1620), Libro secondo

Ricercari were often created as study-practice pieces, similar in didactic intent to nineteenth-century *études*. A ricercare in a *diminution* treatise seems most likely to be a vehicle for practicing the many types of division figures presented in that book. This present *Ricercata* was designated for either the *viola bastarda* or *lauto* (lute), perhaps indicating that the two instruments were similarly tuned, had an equivalent range, and were both considered equally effective in ornamentation. The *Ricercata per viola bastarda, e lauto* is written in staff notation, not tablature, and was probably primarily intended for the *viola bastarda*. As a lute piece written in staff notation, not tablature, it may well be a unique example from the surviving sixteenth-century repertoire. It is a single-line *Ricercata*, without chords. The pitches fit the A lute, and if you play it on an A lute the pitches will correspond with those of Virgiliano. Although unbarred, there are small dots under the stave which correspond with regular barring. I have created tablature with bar lines according to these dots. All right-hand fingering (index finger dots, etc.) is editorial. Of course, we have no unornamented original from which the divisions have been created, neither do we have a second lute part to outline the harmony. First, here is the complete solo without annotations, so that it may be played without the necessity of analysing the divisions.

Playing with Patterns on the Lute. Nigel North, Oxford University Press. © Oxford University Press 2025.
DOI: 10.1093/9780197808764.003.0017

EXAMPLE *Ricercata per viola bastarda, e lauto*, Aurelio Virgiliano (c. 1600–1620).

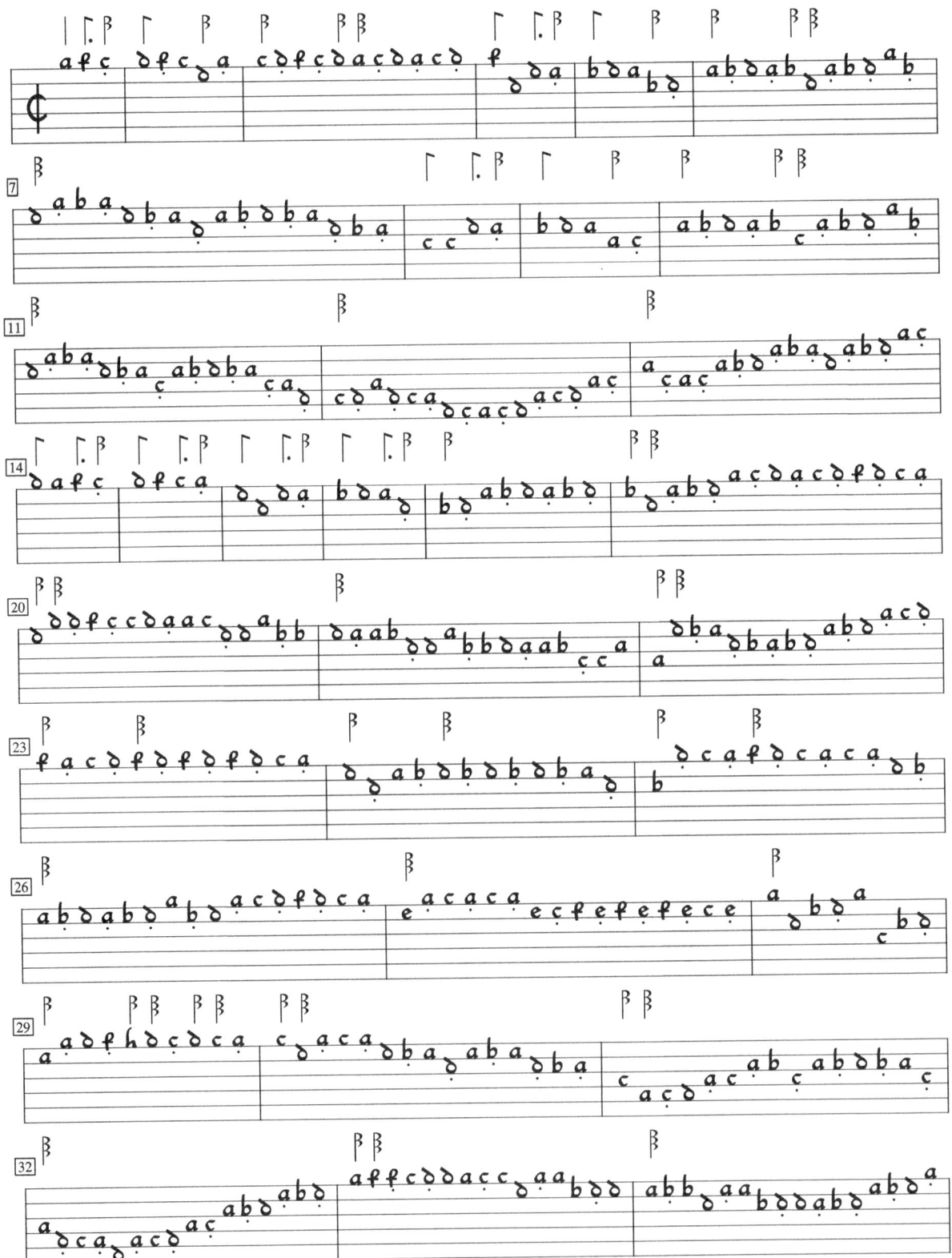

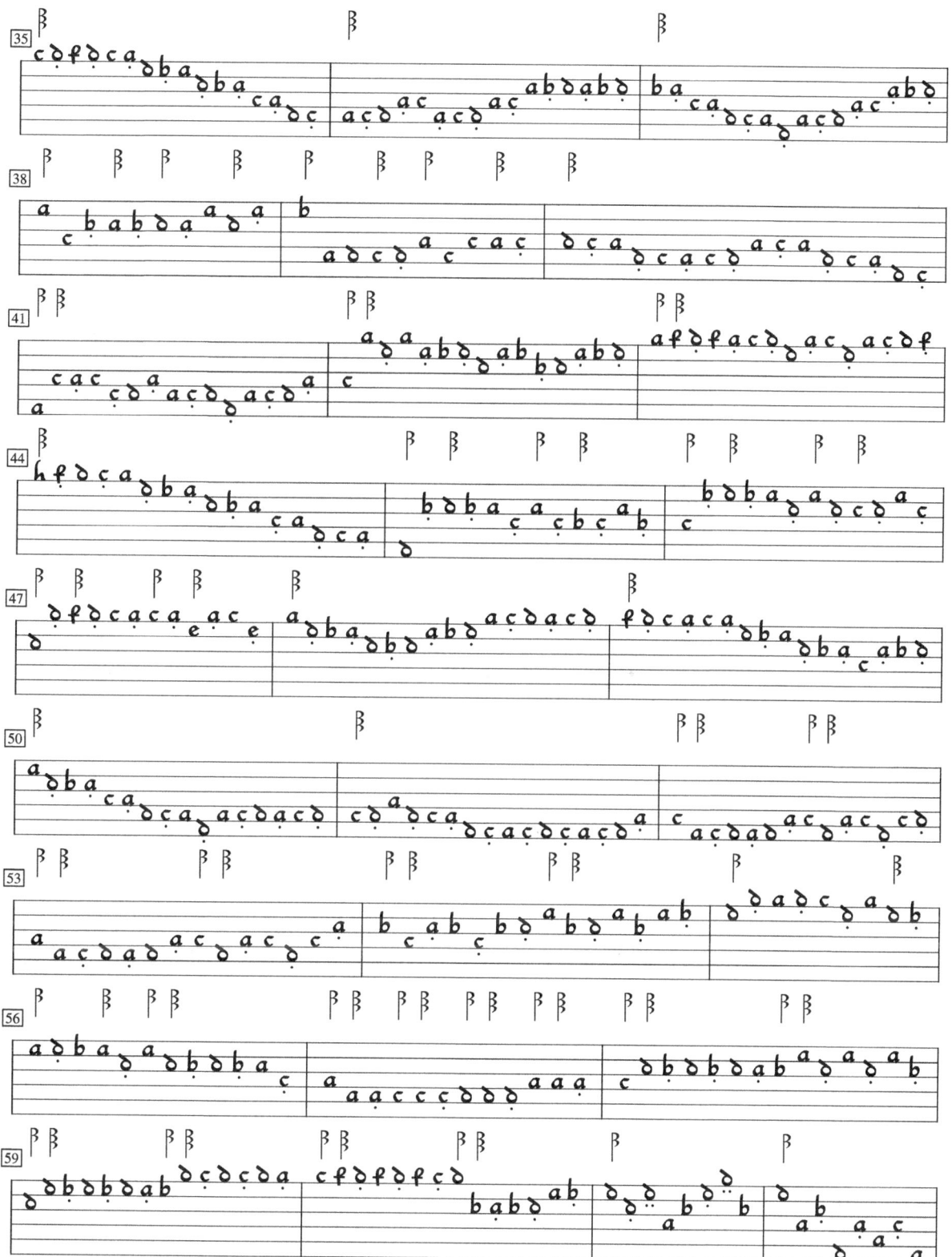

How can we study this piece, identify an unwritten, unornamented text, and see what divisions are used to embellish it? Many figures are easily understood and can take simple definitions, while others are creatively unconventional. When we compare it with previous works in the Tablature Case Studies, this *Recercata* has more rhythmic freedom and variety. For better comprehension, two techniques are worth studying and observing here.

- There are several passages with a sequence of a small triple-note division figure which then cuts across regular meter and barring. The number of notes always add up, in the end, to fit four quarter notes in each bar! Here are the bars concerned:

> Bars 20–21: Triplet sounding groups. Descending scale with each anchor note ornamented with a third below.
>
> Bars 33–34: Triplet sounding groups. Descending scale with each anchor note ornamented with a second above.
>
> Bars 74–77: Slow triplet sounding groups of *triad* arpeggios.
>
> Bars 78–79: Triplet sounding groups. Ascending scale with each anchor note ornamented with a third above.
>
> Bars 80–81: Triplet sounding groups of *triad* arpeggios.

- The second technique is one of imitation. In its simplest form, Virgiliano takes one division pattern and repeats by imitation at a different pitch level. One only has to glance at the annotated score that follows to see how often a sequence is made up of the same *interval* divisions. For example, bars 105–107 show an ascending fourth figure, 11 times! This shows us that repetition is one of the best ways to learn a pattern.

Often, it is the rhythm of the figure which is fully imitated, and the precise interval being ornamented is not always the same within a passage of imitation, but it will sound as though it remains constant. Consider the following passages:

Bars 11–12: An eight-note division repeated three times.
Bars 23–24: Repeated *cadential* figures with a *groppo*.
Bars 38–39: Repeated half-bar figures.
Bars 41–43: One bar pattern repeated over three bars.
Bars 45–47: Repeated *cadential* figures.
Bars 52–55: Repeated half bar figures, mostly ascending thirds.
Bars 58–60: Repeated half bar figures, almost *groppo* figures.
Bars 63–65: Groups of notes with three beats to a bar.
Bars 66–67: Descending scales of an octave.
Bars 68–70: Repeated *groppo* figures.
Bars 87–88: Groups of notes with three beats to a bar.
Bars 90–92: A half-bar group of notes repeated at six different levels.
Bars 94–95: Groups of rising fourths which sound in a triple meter.
Bars 99–100: A group of eight notes.

Here is the *Ricercata* in a second version. The extra stave has an invented line with *anchor* notes, sometimes as single notes, and other times as chords to define the harmonic structure. It is not for performance, but more as clarification of what may be behind the ornamentation. Many divisions are based on chords, not a melodic line.

Ricercata per Viola Bastarda, e Lauto, Aurelio Virgiliano (from: *Il Dolcimelo*)
Annotated score with anchor notes:

EXAMPLE *Ricercata per viola bastarda, e lauto*, Aurelio Virgiliano (from: *Il dolcimelo*). Annotated score with anchor notes.

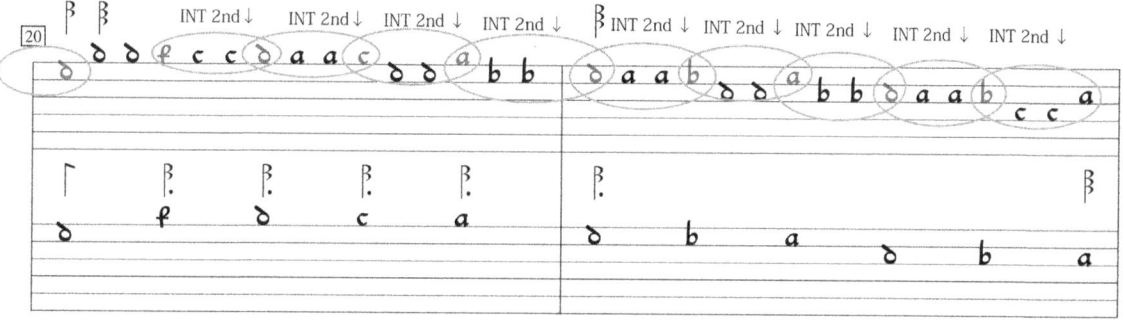

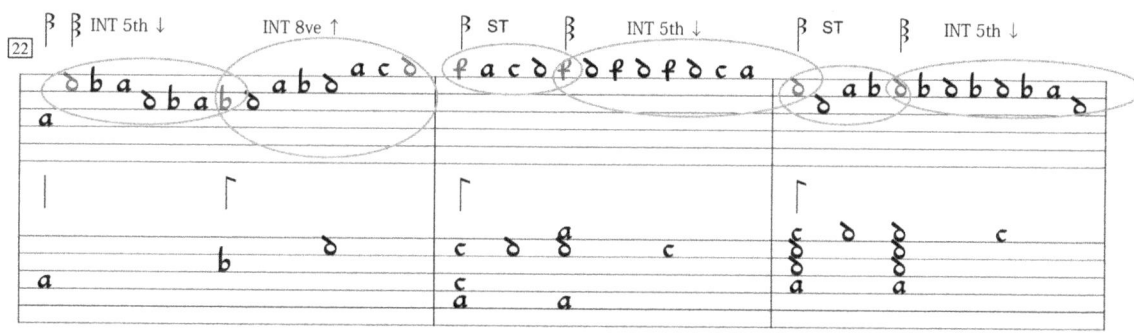

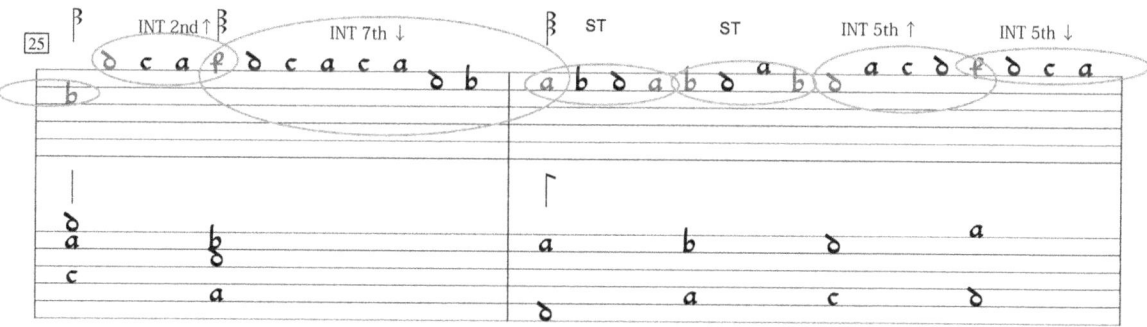

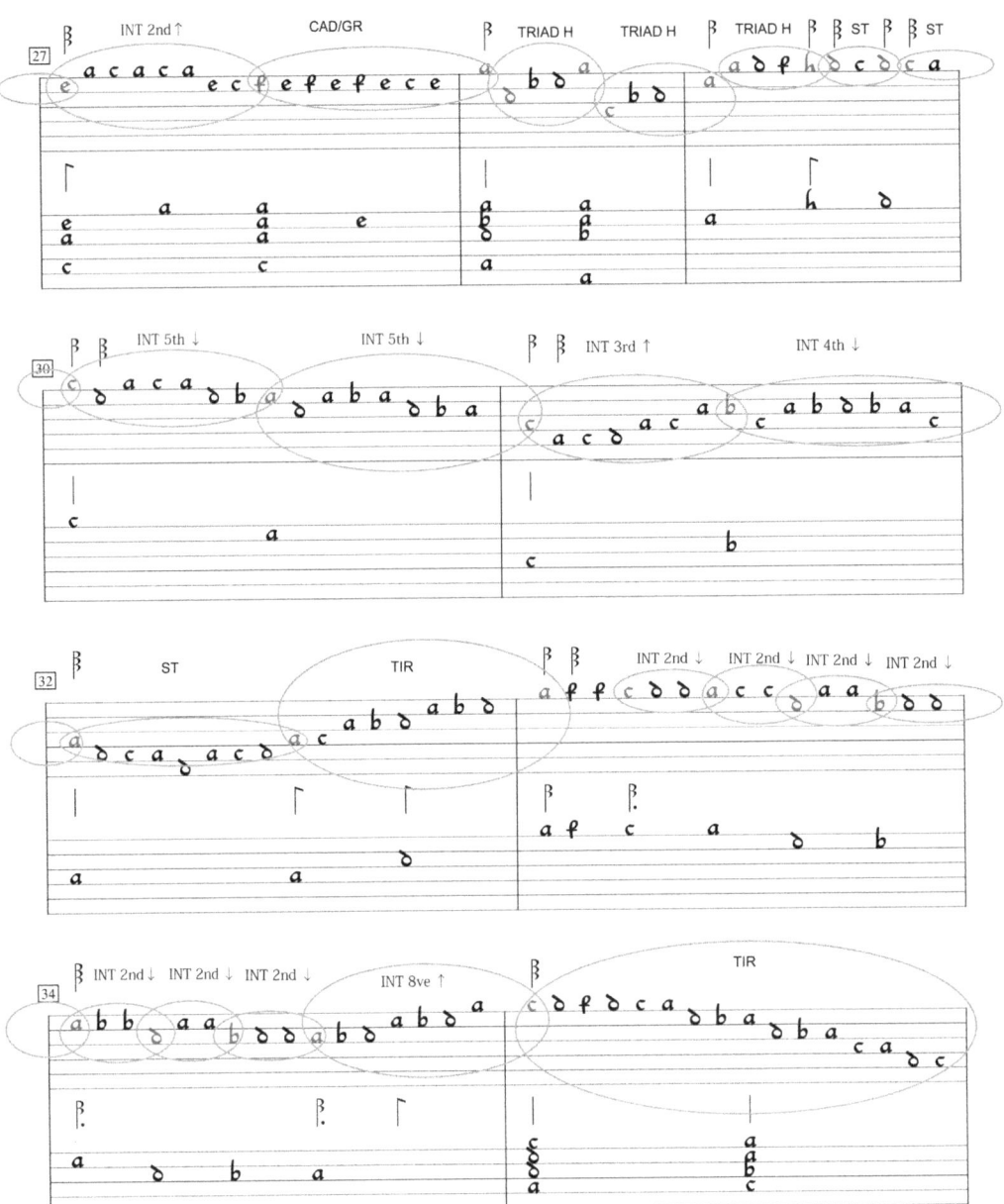

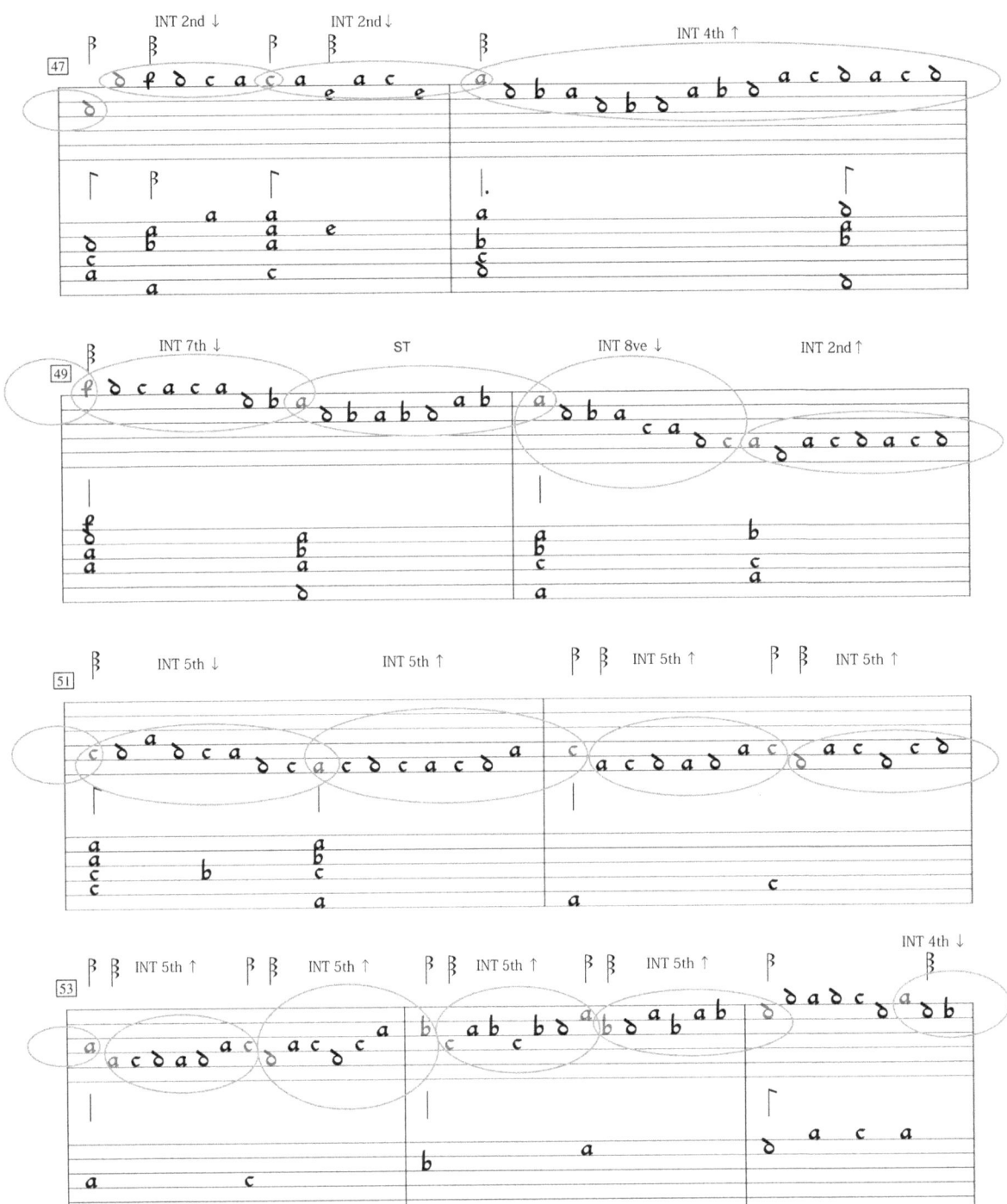

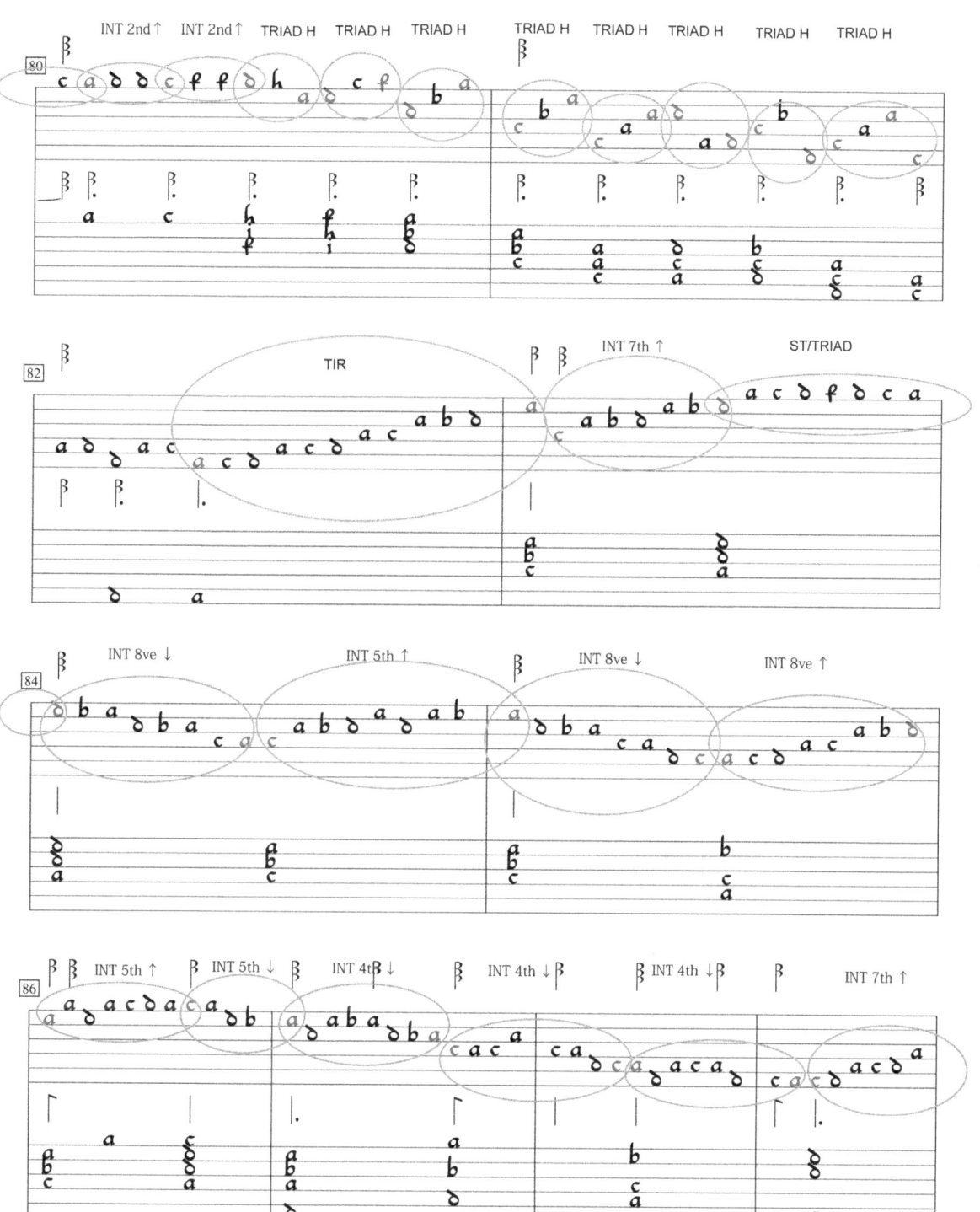

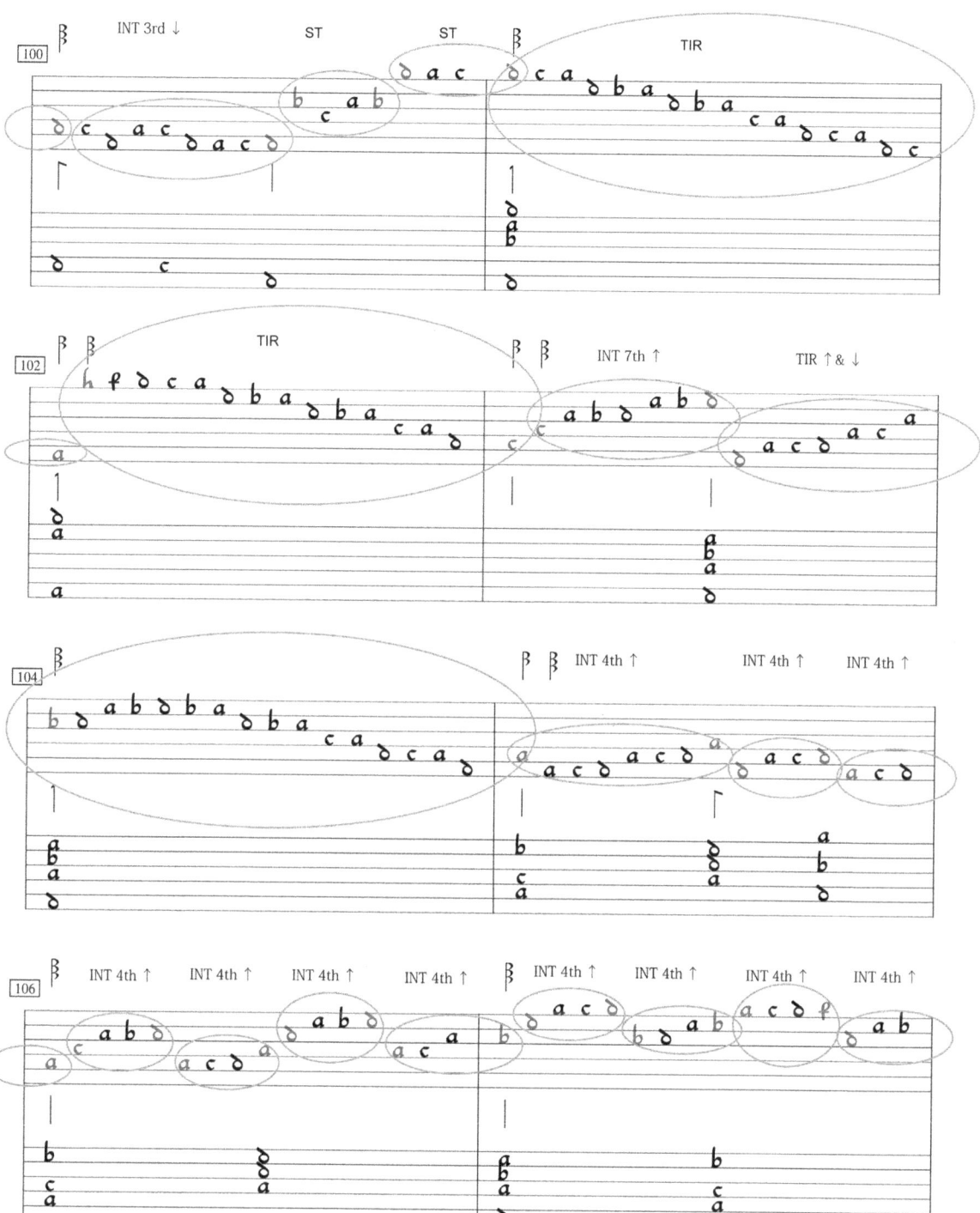

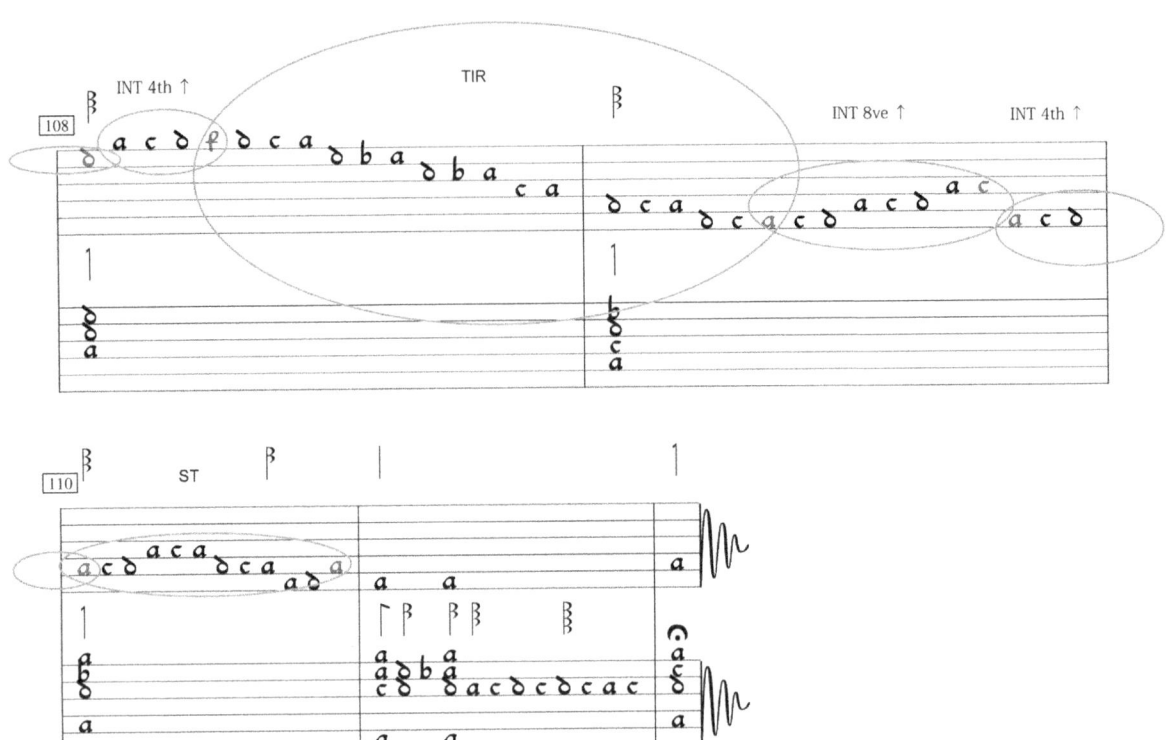

CHAPTER 16

CHANSON: *SUSANNE UN JOUR*, LASSUS

A *Contrapunto* Lute Duet in *Bastarda* Style by Giovanni Terzi (1593)

DI GIO. ANTONIO TERZI DA BERGAMO INTAVOLATURA DI LIUTO, Libro primo
Venice, 1593, pp. 38–42

This is a lute duet version of *Susanne un jour* (Lassus) in a *bastarda*-style *contrapunto* in which *a doi liutti in quarta* means for two lutes, tuned a fourth apart (both needing a 7th course). Solo lute intabulations of this chanson are plentiful. They are found in three pitches, G, F, and D (assuming a G lute). Six-course settings are mostly in G, with the range fitting perfectly from the open 6th course to the *l fret* on the 1st course. The lower the pitch, the more a 7th course at F or D is needed. The original notated vocal pitches of the chanson would equal a G lute playing in G, so it is understandable that many of the surviving intabulations have a final of G.

It is most likely that this duo by Terzi (originally in Italian tablature) is for two lutes tuned a fourth apart as follows:

> Lute 1 in G (*intabulation* of original 5-part madrigal)
> Lute 2 in D (*contrapunto* a 4th lower than Lute 1)

With lutes at those pitches, the chanson sounds in D, a fourth lower than the original, and the *contrapunto* second lute part is similar in range to a *viola bastarda*. However, for the sake of understanding the divisions, I have re-intabulated Lute 1 so that the two lutes are in equal tuning—both nominally in G!

(For those wanting to play a 4th apart, you will find original parts for G & D lutes in Appendix 2.) The two lutes could, of course, be tuned to one of two other popular combinations: lutes in C & G or lutes in A & E.

This *contrapunto* is more virtuosic than the Fronimo *contrapunto* (see Chapter 12) and is a *bastarda*-style *contrapunto* on a rich textured and well-known five-part chanson. *Susanne un jour* has survived in many versions. The original chanson was first published in 1560 and then reprinted until 1592, giving Terzi plenty of time to become familiar with the music before composing and publishing his *contrapunto*. Unlike the Virgiliano *Recercata* (see Chapter 15), we have the chanson intabulation as the real composition, and this provides all the *harmony* and *anchor notes* for us to study and understand the division writing of the second lute part. The *contrapunto* is very well written, and Terzi uses two aspects of the opening chanson theme throughout the piece. These two figures are:

Playing with Patterns on the Lute. Nigel North, Oxford University Press. © Oxford University Press 2025.
DOI: 10.1093/9780197808764.003.0018

Opening themes from the Chanson *Susanne un jour*

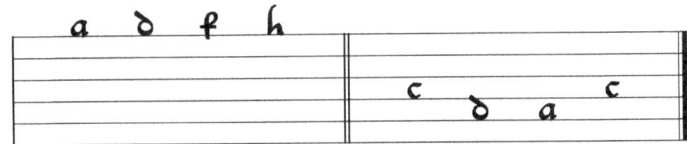

They are quoted here without rhythm signs, as Terzi varies the rhythms during the *contrapunto*. It is the pitches and intervals which are significant. A few examples show just how lute-like the motives are, and how often Terzi returns to these figures:

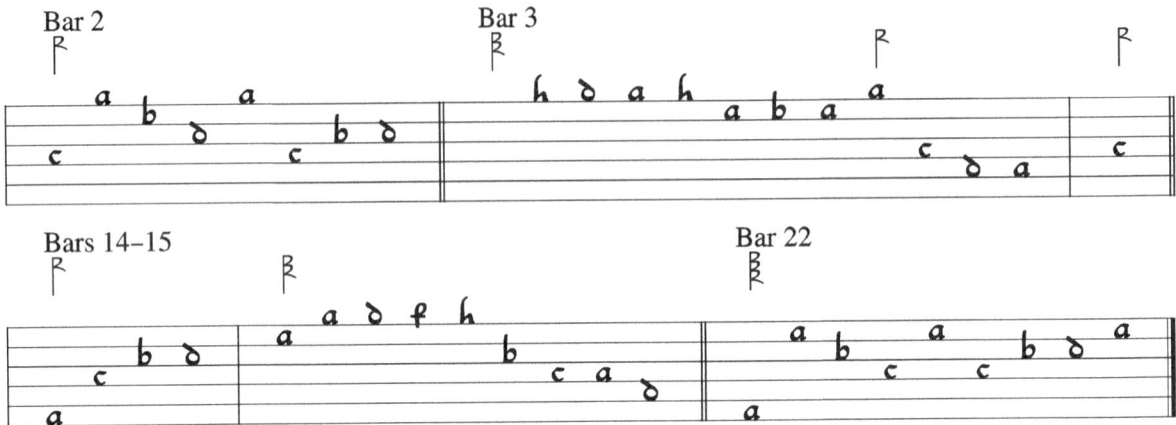

Both themes are *triadic* in nature. The soprano theme is a G minor triad with a passing fourth (C) and the bass is a C minor *triad* with no passing notes. It is, therefore, not surprising that Terzi uses many *triad* figures in the *contrapunto* divisions. We often find *harmonic triad* figures (notes of the triad, with and without passing notes), so that the *contrapunto* feels and sounds as though there are many arpeggios. As we will discover in Part 3 (Method: Interval Divisions), some interval figures of a fifth can be seen in two ways, both as *triad* figures and as intervals of a fifth.

Compared with the other works in the Tablature Case Studies, Terzi's *contrapunto* has a greater rhythmic variety, with interesting and unusual rhythms together with use of the complete range of the lute. There are divisions in the soprano, alto, tenor, and bass registers, and many long *passaggi* which go between these registers. Terzi uses the three levels of rhythm to full effect: the two basic levels of eighth and sixteenth notes, with the added third level of thirty-second notes.

At times, it may be difficult to truly define all divisions within the scope already set up in Part 1. I have used the term *tirata* to define a long scale in one direction (ascending or descending) which covers an interval of more than an octave, and one which moves by step. Terzi often employs two techniques in these situations. When connecting two chords with a long *connector/tirata*, and the interval in question doesn't fit a regular pattern, Terzi will suddenly double up the rhythms at the end, to get to the finishing line on the right beat—the last note of the division. Another solution, more normal, is to put a third into a scale which otherwise moves by step. Here are examples of these:

Bars 19–20, 30, 31, 32, 36, 43, 46:

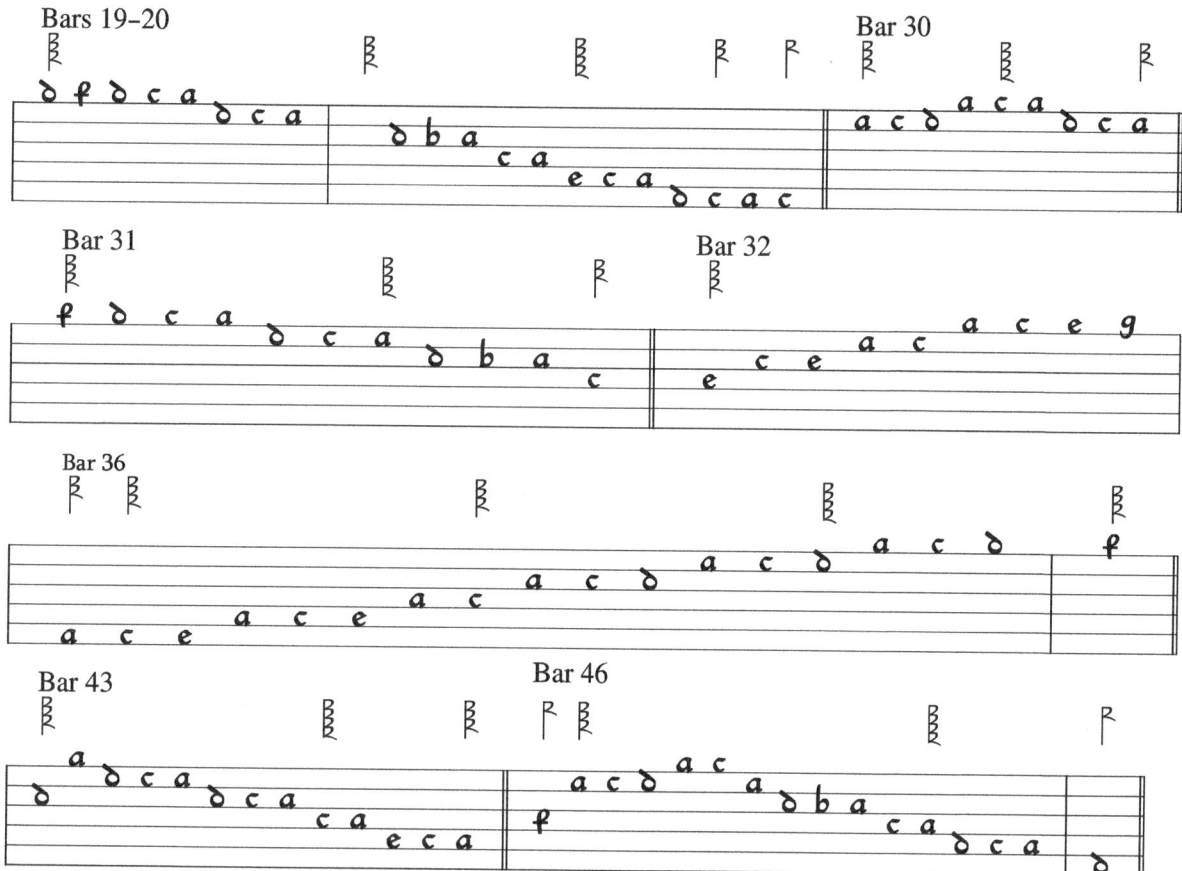

Imitation in the *contrapunto* is also present. For examples of this, see the following:

Bar 7, beats 3–4: The first eight notes are imitated a seventh higher.

Bar 13, beats 1–2: The D major *triad* is imitated by a G major *triad*.

Bar 20, beats 3–4: The first eight notes are then imitated an octave higher.

Bar 24, beats 3–4: Although slightly off beat, the first figure is imitated an octave lower.

Bar 33: The first long division is imitated a third lower.

Bars 41 and 42: In the first bar, the first half of the bar is imitated a fourth lower. In bar 42 it is the rhythm which is imitated three times.

Bar 46: The opening figure (ascending 5th, *triad* figure) is imitated five times.

EXAMPLE Chanson: *Susanne un jour*, Lassus. Examples of imitation in Terzi's Lute Duet.

We can also see the use of a standard bass figure, usually found at cadences. This figure is often found in diminutions written for bass voice, *viola bastarda*, and so on. Examples of these from bars 14, 25, 35, and 57:

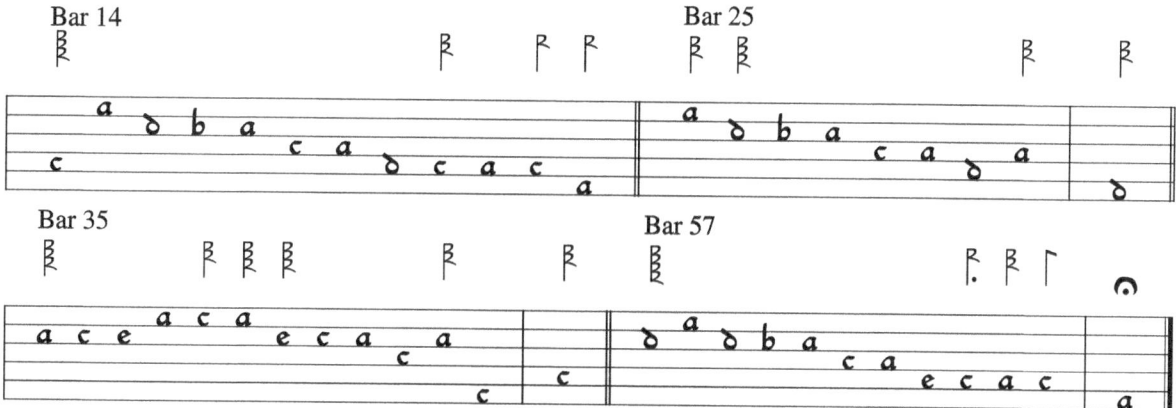

Apart from the abundance of *triad* divisions, all intervals are much used, with the exception of a sixth! There are many occasions of a long series of *triad* divisions and sometimes we find two or three figures of the same interval in succession. A good example of this can be found in bar 51, beat 3–bar 52, beat 2: a sequence of ascending fifths at different levels.

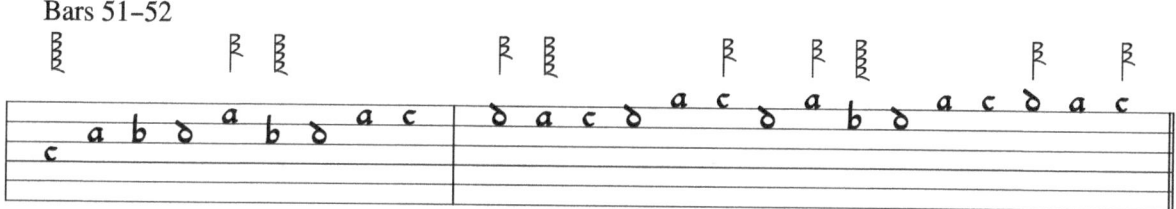

Many of the long *passaggi* and *tirate* are really *connectors*: a division (usually by step) which joins two chords with *anchor* notes from two different voices. To understand the use of this basic division technique, we can look at bar 27. The division is a constant stream of sixteenth notes. Considering the whole bar in four steps:

Step 1: The tenor C of the first chord (tablature *d* on the 3rd course) divides to the soprano G of the second chord (tablature *a* on the 1st course.)
Step 2: The soprano G on which we landed then descends to the tenor A of the third chord (tablature *a* on the 3rd course).
Step 3: This tenor A then descends a fifth to a bass D (tablature *c* on the 5th course) and then leaps an octave to connect with the next chord and cadence.
Step 4: A standard *groppo* in the soprano leads to a resolution in bar 28.

This is normal procedure for *contrapunto* writing and shows us how useful a *connector* diminution can be and how natural it sounds. Here is the bar with each step isolated:

Here follows an annotated score of the two equal lute parts together with Lute 1 transposed up a fourth so that we can imagine two G lutes. (The Lute 1 transposed into G minor is very similar in its intabulation to several surviving solo intabulations at that pitch.) There is a repeat sign, like a *petit reprise*, found in the middle of bar 53 which is optional. If you wish, Terzi returns to that sign to repeat bars 53 to the end.

EXAMPLE Chanson: *Susanne un jour*, Lassus. Terzi's Lute Duet in an annotated score for two equal lutes.

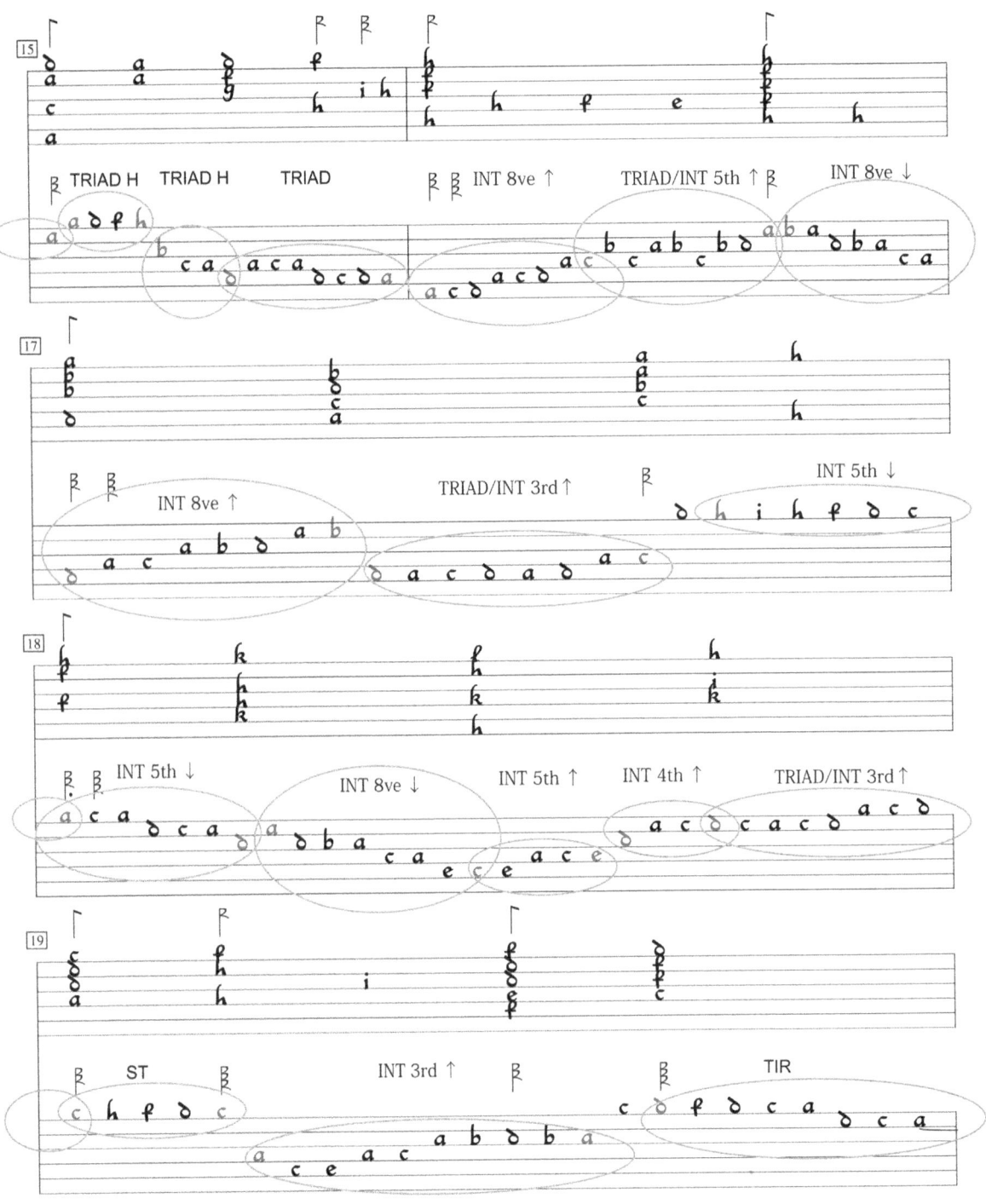

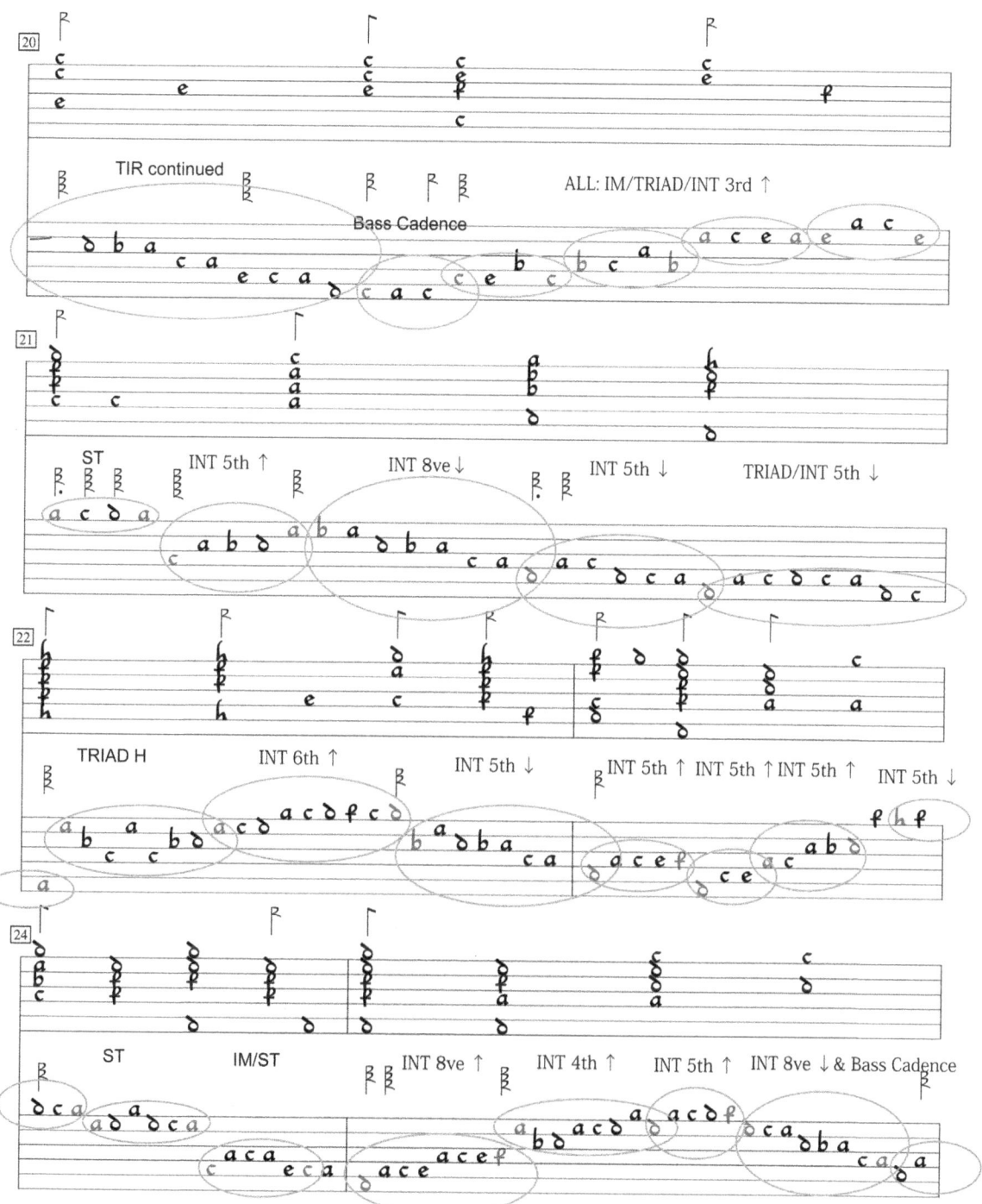

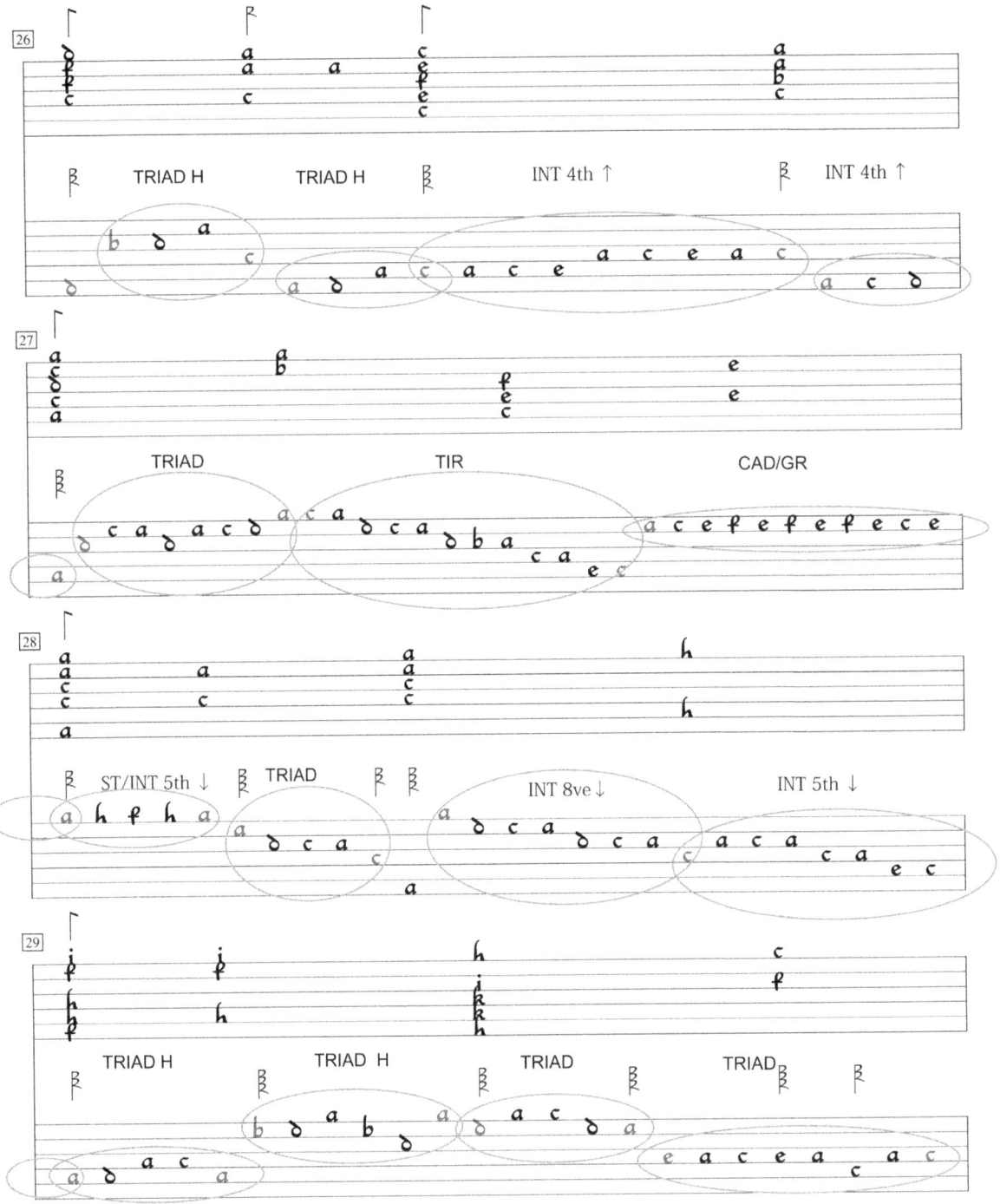

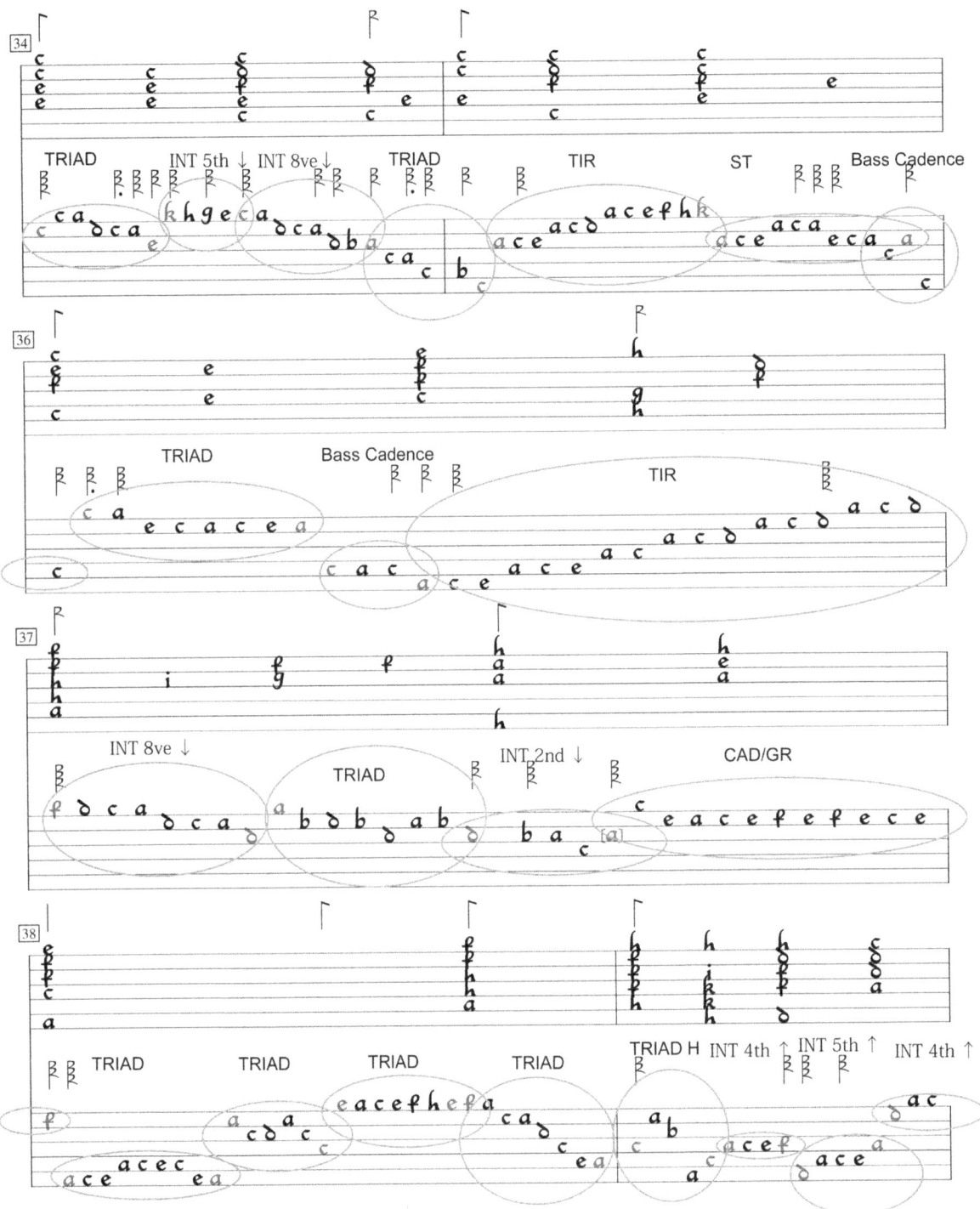

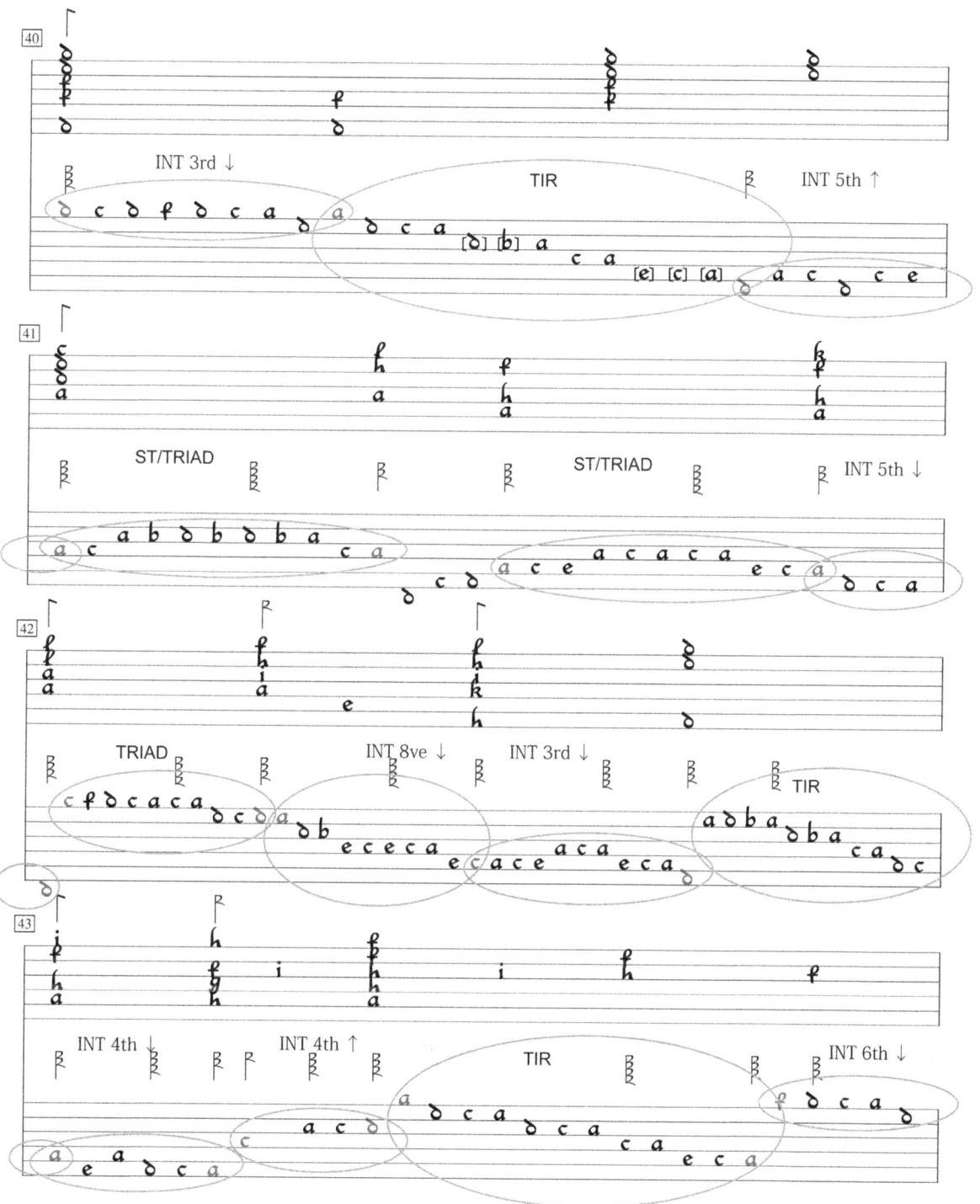

Bass Cadence

PART 3
METHOD

In Chapters 17–20 you will find a variety of Explanations, Examples, and Exercises. The most important division figures or patterns, defined in Part 1, are explained with examples which can then be practiced with exercises.

Chapter 21 contains three guided lessons in building patterns. Step by step, we can build a simple, complete division on a short figure or make a simple piece into one with embellishments.

Chapters 22–28 follow with a series of complete melodies, pieces, and grounds to use for division practice. All presented as Explanations, Examples, and Exercises.

CHAPTER 17

CADENCES

Cadences are one of the most natural places which we can ornament with a division. We will study three of the most common sixteenth-century cadences, with examples and exercises.

17.1. Cadence Type 1

EXPLANATION AND EXAMPLES

In the sixteenth century, the most normal cadence was identified by two voices moving outwards from an interval of a major sixth to an octave. It was not necessary to approach the cadence with a suspension, but it was a common practice. There are two versions of this cadence, both with three bass notes. The first version is shown in the following four-part example. In bars 2 to 3, the bass moves down a whole tone, E to D, and the upper voice ascends by a semitone, C♯ to D. Seen in figured-bass terms, the suspension and resolution shown in (b)–(d) are on the 7–6 above the second bass note.

- (a) shows this basic cadence without suspension.
- (b) the same with a suspension and resolution in bar 2.
- (c) with a simple interval division in the upper voice of the first bar, and a *groppo* figure in bar 2.
- (d) shows the same, with a full *groppo* figure in bar 2.

The second version has the bass of bar 2 descending by a semitone. The interval between the two voices at bar 2 is still a major sixth, moving outwards to an octave in bar 3.

Playing with Patterns on the Lute. Nigel North, Oxford University Press. © Oxford University Press 2025.
DOI: 10.1093/9780197808764.003.0020

The same four steps as above, with the alternative bass:

Taking a tonality with D as a final, here are six common division patterns for this first cadence. Observing these and practicing them will lead you to recognize cadences and find variants for your divisions. Bar 2 of each example contains a *groppo* figure. A *groppo* was an articulated trill with a final turn: 3 pitches involved. With a D final, that would be a 'trill' of C♯ and D with a turn at the end to include the note B. Variant 4 represents what may be considered the normal *groppo*. Variants 5 and 6 have doublers at the end of the trill.

Examples of Variant division figures for Cadence 1:

EXAMPLE Cadence 1 with six variant division figures.

- Cadence Type 1: Exercises

Using the following cadences in various tonalities, practice all with the six variants above.

EXAMPLE Cadence 1 in various tonalities, to practice with the six variant division figures above.

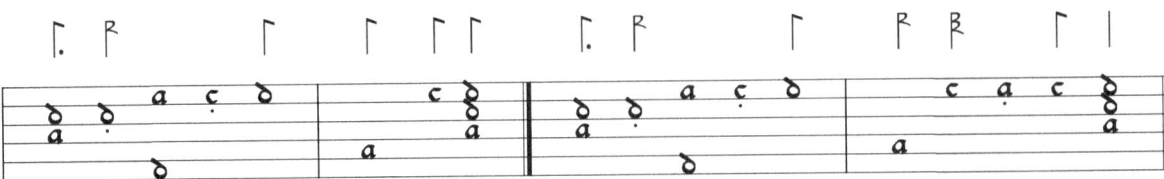

17.2. Cadence Type 2

EXPLANATION AND EXAMPLES

This is related to Cadence Type 1, with similar melodic patterns for the divisions. In figured-bass terms, this is a 4–3 cadence, not a 7–6. Harmonically the structure is I–IV–V–I. The 4–3 refers to the intervals above the penultimate bass note of each cadence, in bar 2. Here is an unornamented version of the cadence with its approach and suspension, followed by a simple division in bar 2.

Examples of Variant division figures for Cadence 2:

EXAMPLE Cadence 2 with six variant division figures.

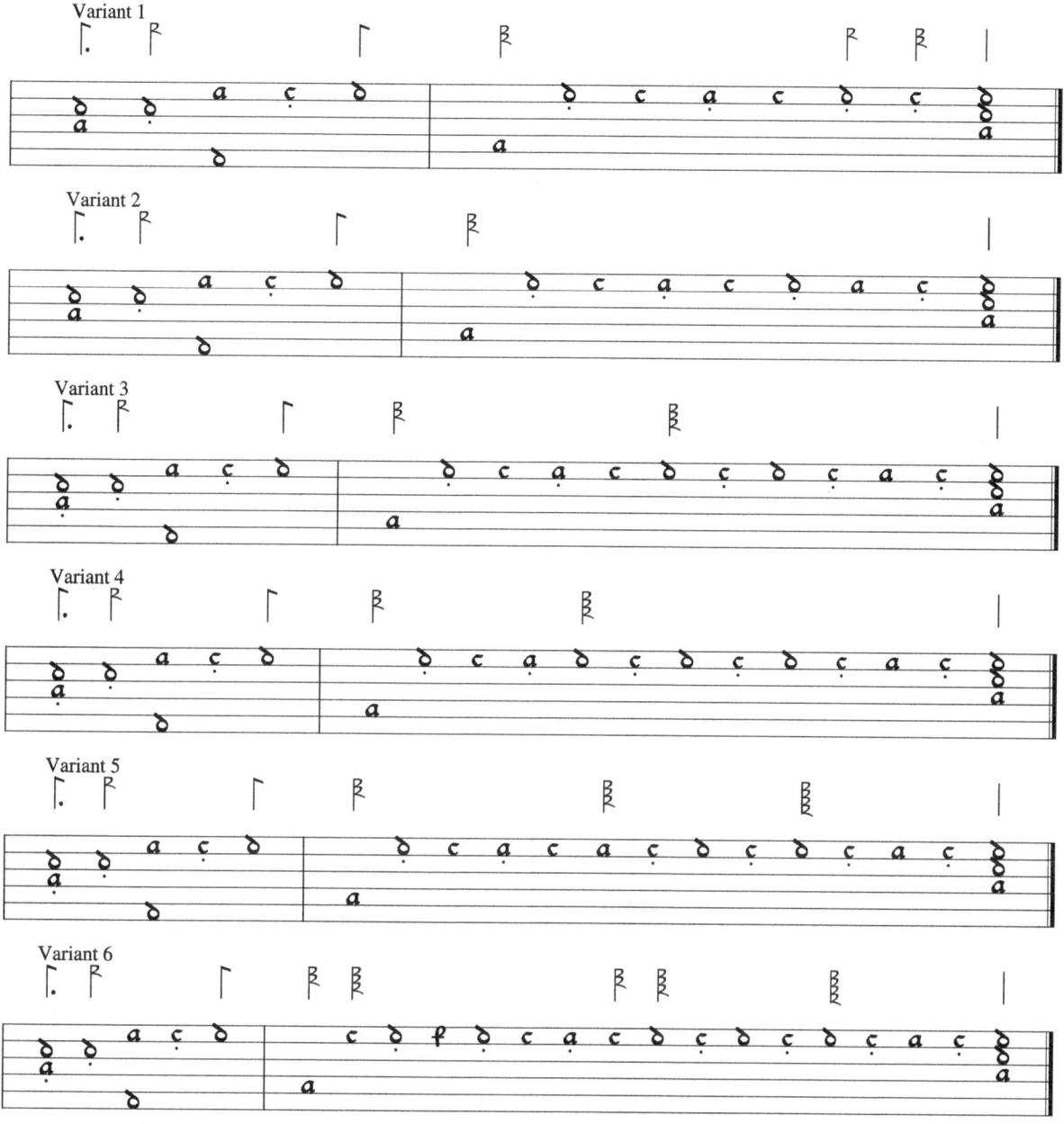

• Cadence Type 2: Exercises

Using the following cadences in various tonalities, practice all with the six variants above.

EXAMPLE Cadence 2 in various tonalities, to practice with the six variant division figures above.

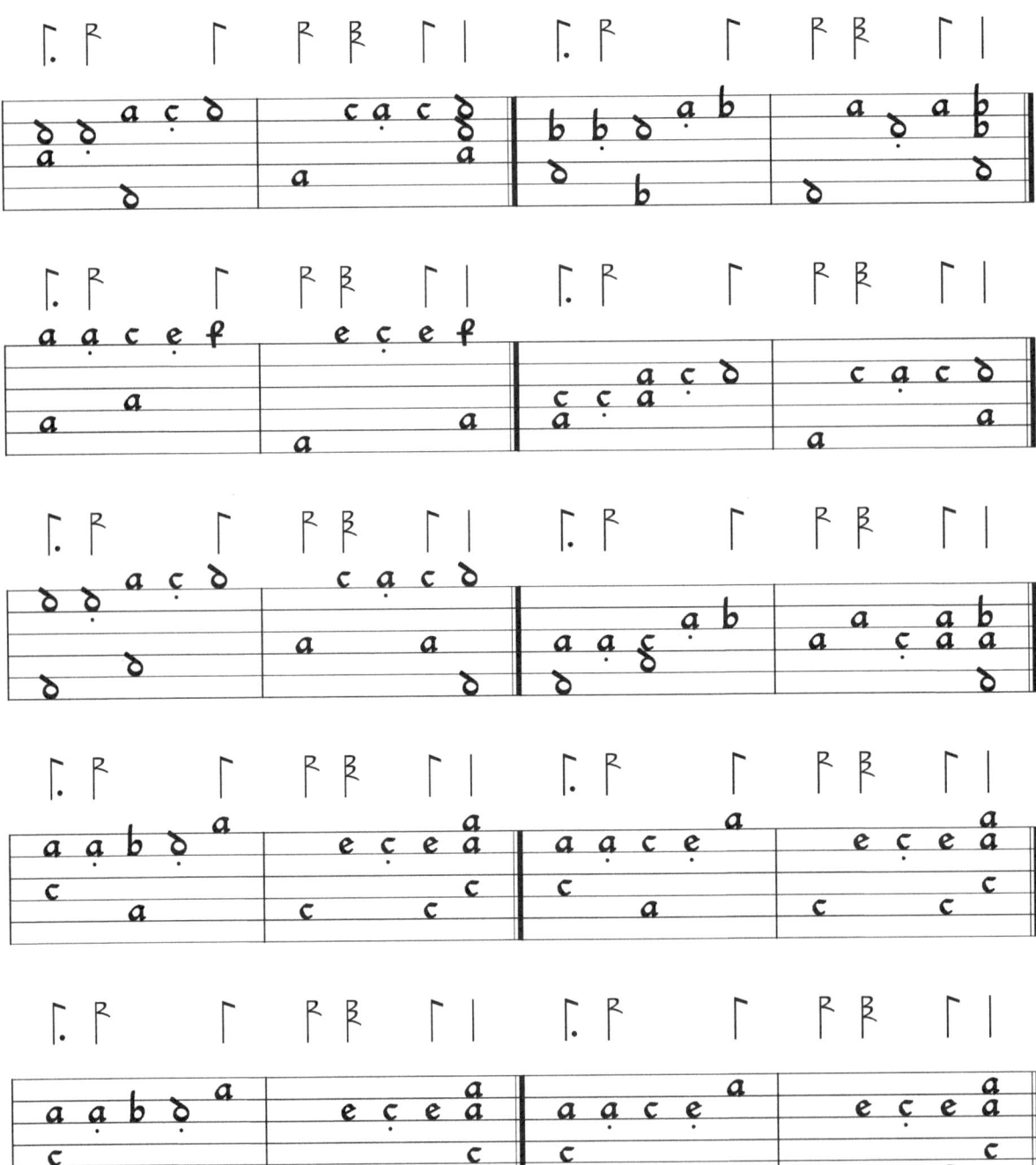

17.3. Cadence Type 3

EXPLANATION AND EXAMPLES

This cadence is often found in the supplementum or the extra, closing phrase after the official final cadence of a piece. Using chords IV to I, it can also be understood as a plagal cadence. Here is a simple example, with a G final.

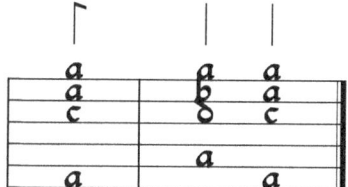

Examples of Variant division figures for Cadence 3:

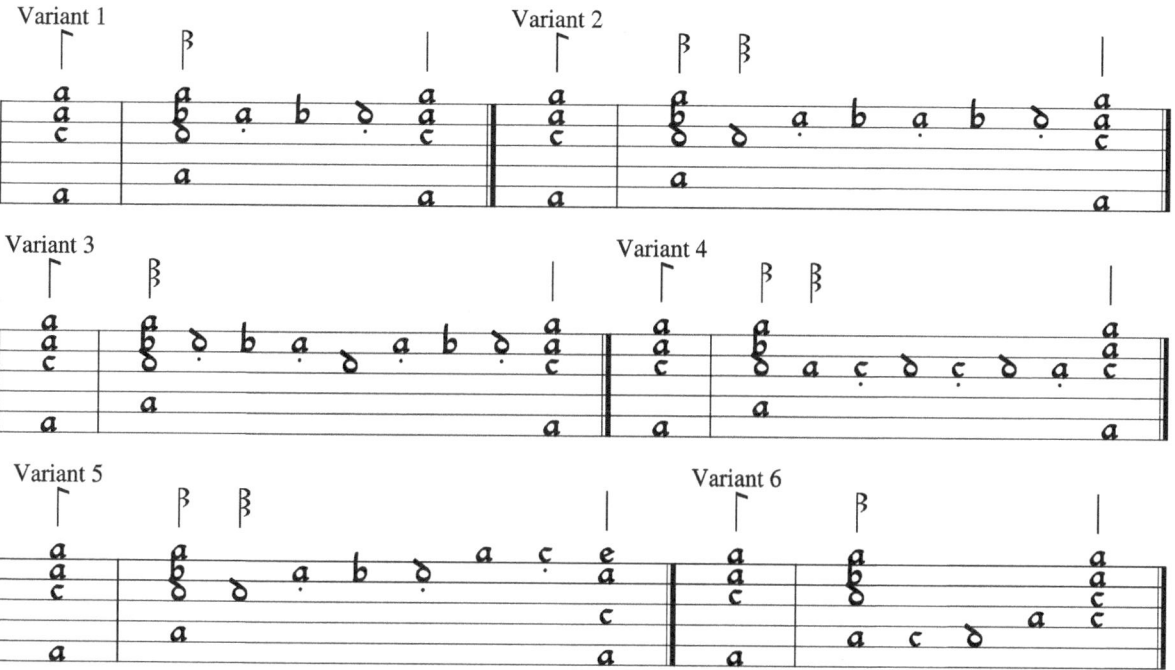

- Cadence Type 3: Exercises

Using the following cadences in various tonalities, practice all with the variants above. In these exercises, the three notes of each key which would be the most likely to be ornamented with a division can be seen in grey. The first nine examples on lines one and two show the second chord with the third of the chord suggested for division. In the last five examples, on line 3, it is the octave of the second chord which is suggested for a division. In all examples, the simple bass division of an ascending fifth is possible, as shown in Variant 6.

CHAPTER 18

TRIADS

Explanation and Examples

Most *triad* divisions are melodic and move by step. They are very common and primarily made from the three notes of a *triad*. Practicing *triad* divisions can help give a strong sense of how to proceed by step with alternating good and bad notes. We can become accustomed to thinking of the *triad* notes as anchor notes, which are the *good* notes and usually plucked with the RH thumb. The connecting notes (most commonly the 2 and 4 between the 1–3–5 of the triad) are *bad* notes and would normally be played with the RH index finger.

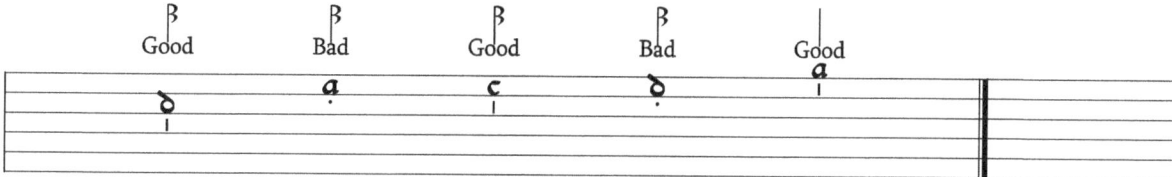

We can think of *triad* divisions in four distinctive forms.

18.1. Simple

These are divisions with the consonances (1–3–5) as the good notes and 2 and 4 connecting them as bad notes; moving by step and the occasional third.
The good notes are all part of the triad. The division can begin on the 1, 3, or 5.
Range: 5 notes only, occasionally including the leading note a semitone below the tonic.
Examples of *simple triad* divisions:

18.2. Extended

Simple triad divisions can be extended to include additional notes above 5, or below 1. *Triad* figures will fall easily under the hand.

 Good notes: 1, 3, 5.
  Bad notes: 2, 4, 6, and 7.
  Range: 6 or 7 notes, sometimes as many as 10.

Playing with Patterns on the Lute. Nigel North, Oxford University Press. © Oxford University Press 2025.
DOI: 10.1093/9780197808764.003.0021

Examples of *extended triad* divisions:

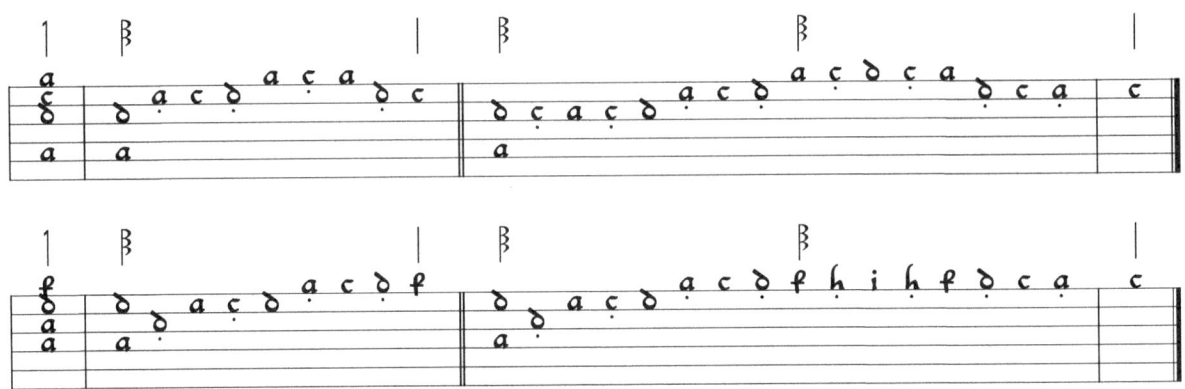

18.3. Octave Extensions

These are divisions which originate from triads but also extend past 1–3–5 to cover the whole octave. All good notes are still on the beat and consonant with the triad.

Good notes: 1, 3, 5, 8.
    Bad notes: 2, 4, 6, 7 and 7 an octave lower (or the leading note below the tonic).
    Range: 8 or 9 notes.

In the following examples, the first division is just between 1 and 5 from D. The second division is a common octave *interval* division, ascending. The third division is a simple octave *interval* division, descending.

    Examples of *octave extended* triad divisions:

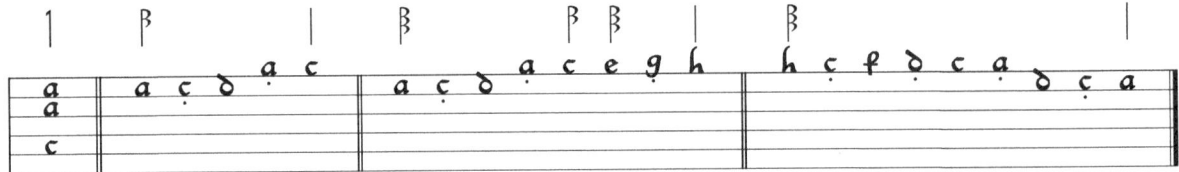

18.4. Harmonic Triad

These are figures which do not move by step, but principally use the chord notes, 1, 3, and 5, with the occasional passing note of 2, 4, or 6, and which sound like arpeggiation. In the Terzi Lute Duo version of *Susanne un jour* (Lassus) (Part 2: Tablature Case Studies), we find many examples of *harmonic triad* divisions. In general, they were more in use towards the end of the century.

Examples of *harmonic triad* divisions (all from Terzi, bars 8–10):

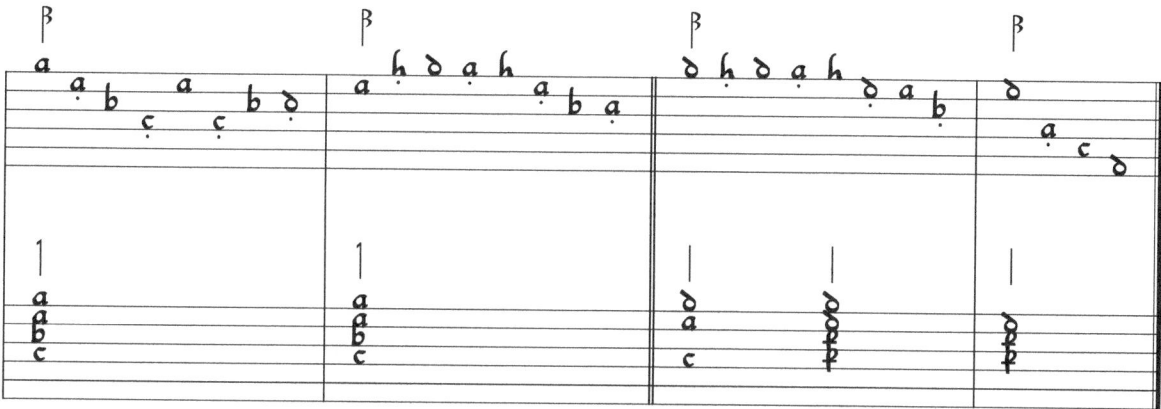

Examples of *harmonic triad* divisions mixed with *simple* and *extended triad* figures:

18.5. Frère Jacques

EXAMPLES AND EXERCISES

For a simple beginning exercise, I have found the ancient children's song and round, *Frère Jacques*, to be very helpful. (Some sources say this song was composed by Jean Philip Rameau in the 1720s, but it might be much earlier than the eighteenth century.) For our purpose, it has a small range, is based mostly on *triads*, with much step-wise motion, and gives us a template for trying out many basic division figures.

Here is the melody in F:

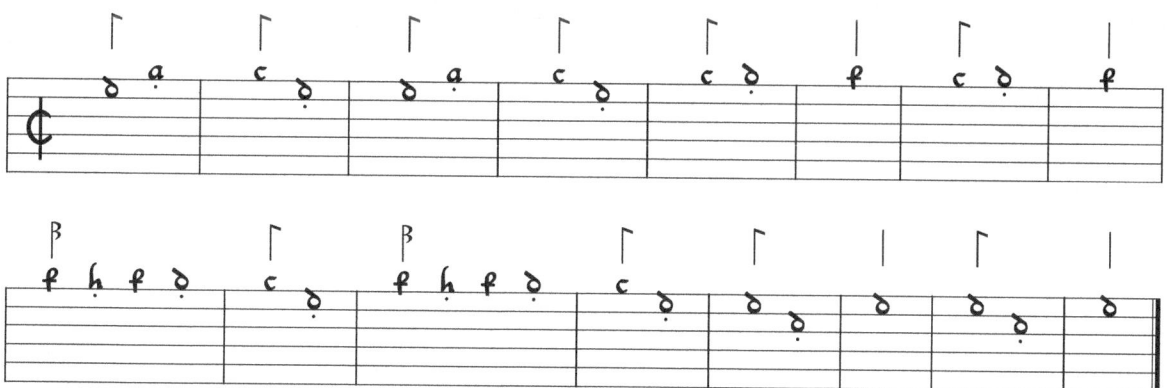

- Notice the ascending seconds in bars 1–8. They are all simple *triad* figures, using 1, 3, and 5, with 2 and 4 to connect.
- Descending seconds in bars 9–12: they are simple *triad* figures, with one extension to 6, otherwise 5–4–3–2–1.
- In the cadence, bars 12–16, the original tune lacks a *cadential* suspension, but we may still find a way to include a division or a *groppo*.

The anchor notes are sketched out here; one bar of anchor notes for each four-bar phrase:

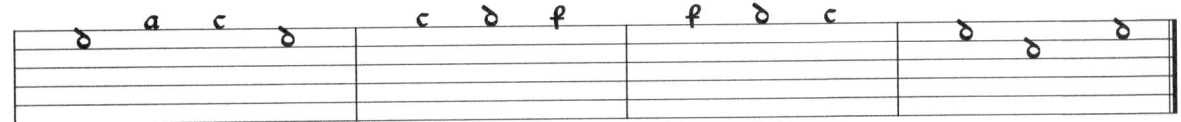

- First phrase, followed by simple division examples:

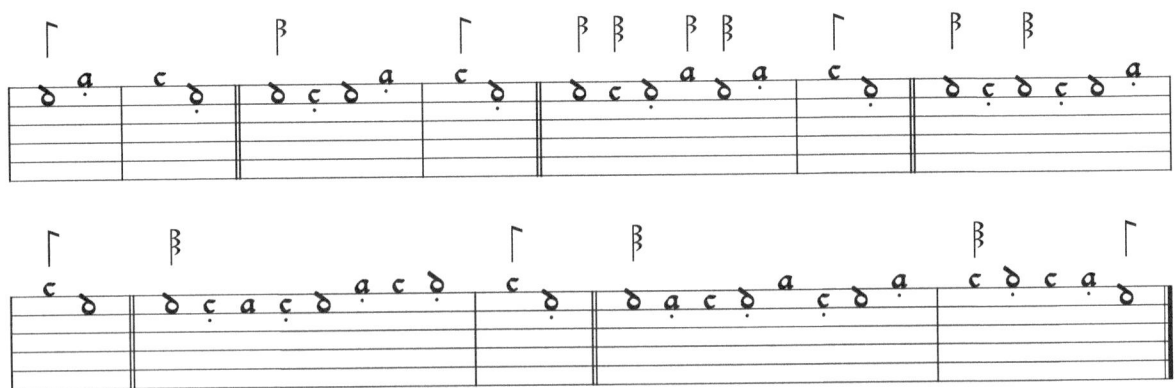

- Second phrase, followed by simple division examples:

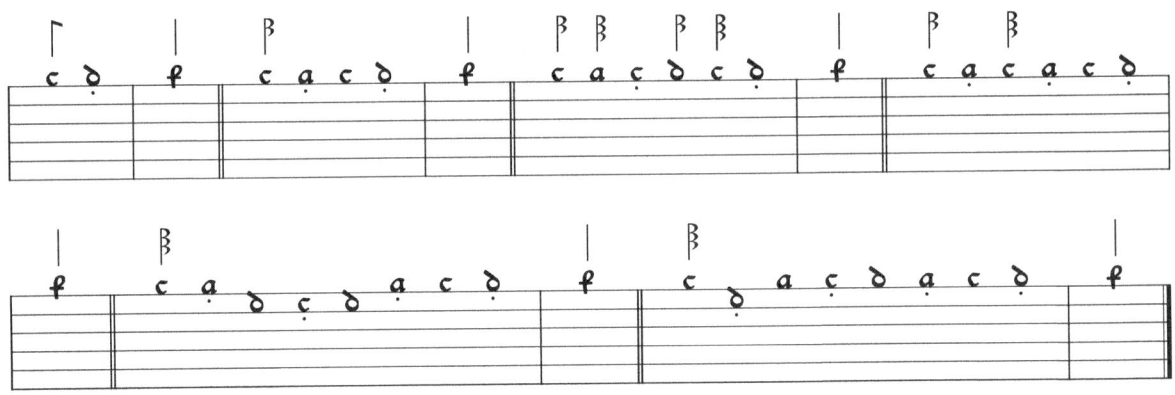

- Third phrase, followed by simple division examples:

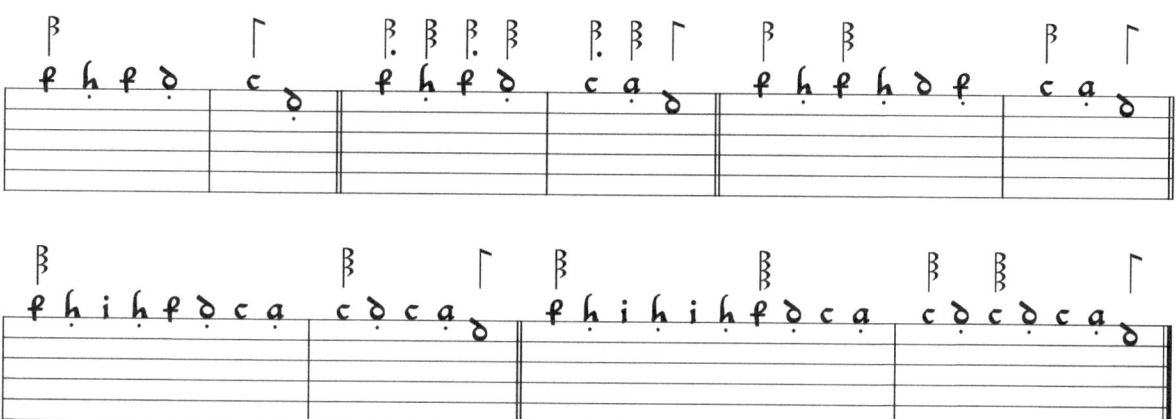

- Fourth phrase, followed by simple division examples:

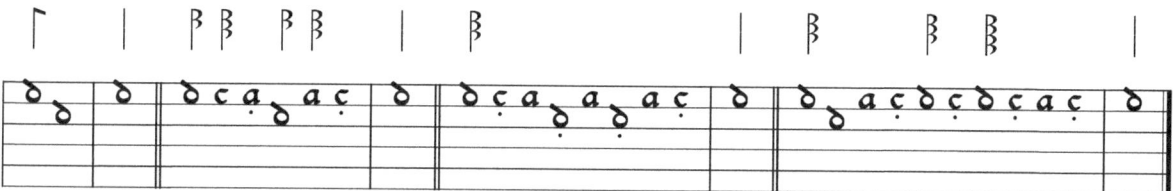

Exercises on Frère Jacques

To practice simple triad divisions, you will find in the following exercise several versions of *Frère Jacques* in a variety of tonalities. Two methods of practice are recommended:

- Read from the tablature and systematically add in the variants while all the time looking at the tablature score of the anchor notes. You can also compose some examples and write them out in tablature on the spare stave.
- Alternatively, take one key at a time and play from memory and by ear, so that your fingers and ears begin to connect.

EXAMPLE *Frère Jacques* in four tonalities for division practice.

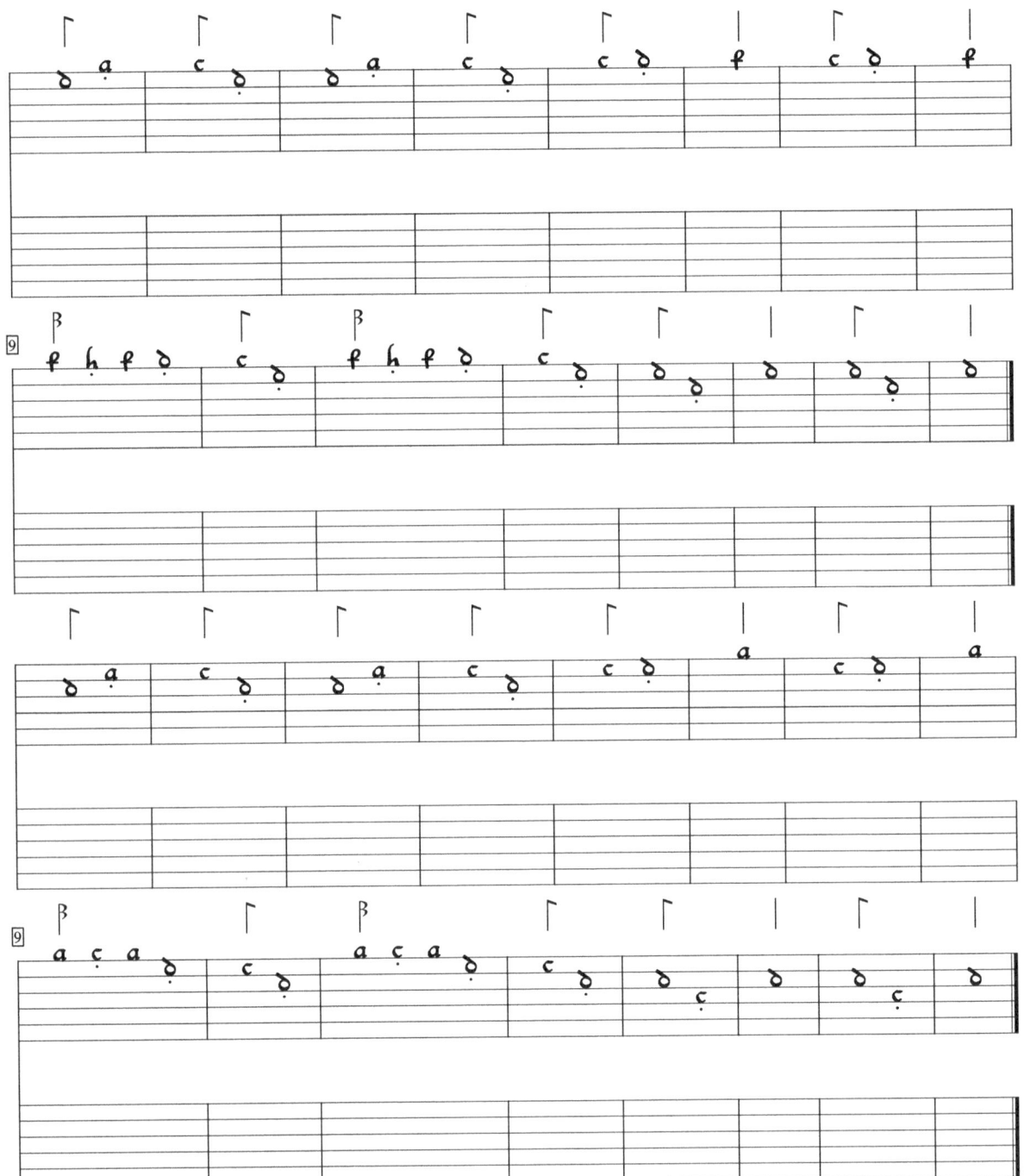

18.6. *Triad* Divisions (Simple): Exercises

SIMPLE

In the first *triad* exercises, we will practice simple patterns which move by step between 1 and 5. This will help train the fingers and connect them with our ears!

Here are our anchor notes, with the chords to show the implied harmony. It is a sequence of pairs of descending notes which are all the root notes of each triad. In each pair, the first chord is minor, the second major.

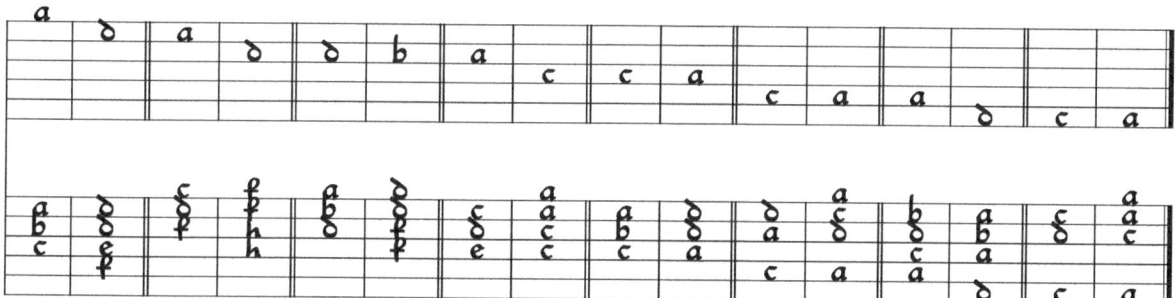

On these pairs of anchor notes, we can practice some patterns. In the first exercise, the whole sequence is written out. The variants which follow only show the first pair.

The first pattern, ascending:

A new pattern with variants:

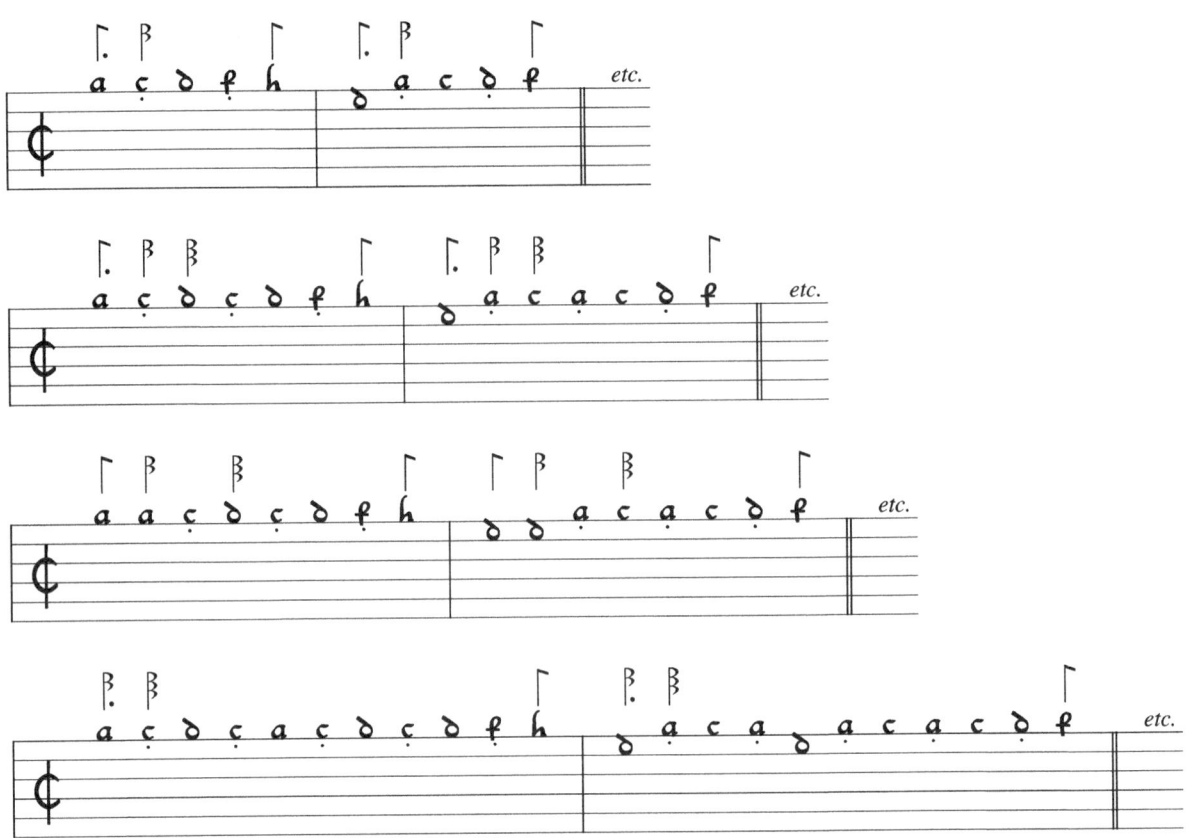

With these five notes in our fingers, we can continue practicing *simple triad* figures, but now both ascending and descending and starting on various notes of the *triad*, not just on 1:

EXAMPLE *Simple* triad figures, ascending and descending and starting on various notes of the triad.

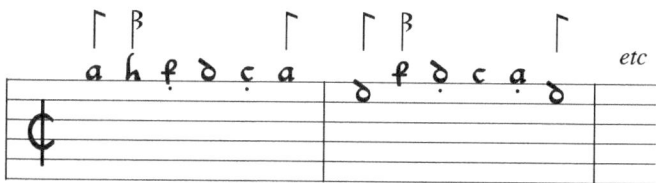

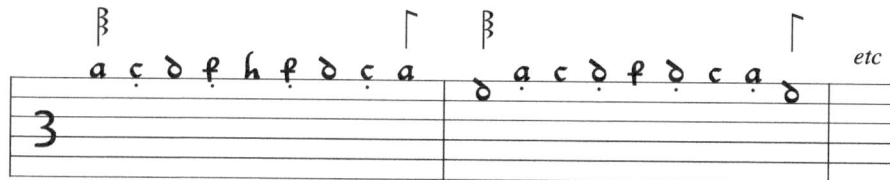

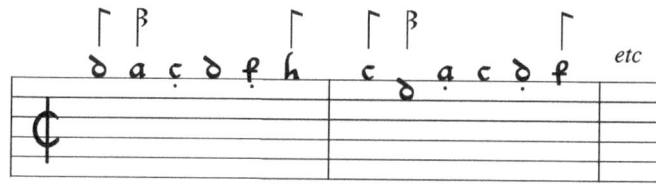

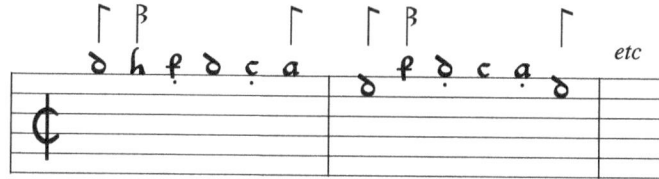

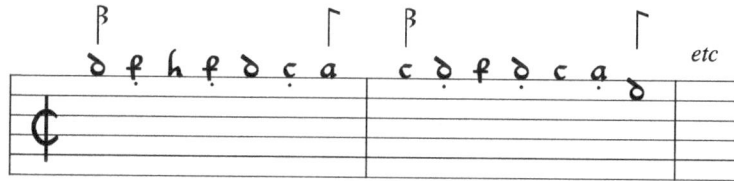

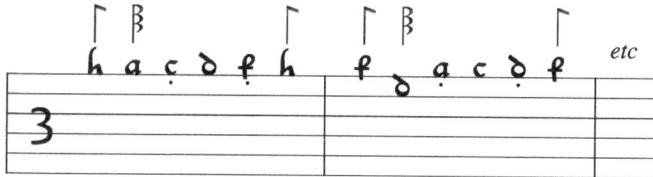

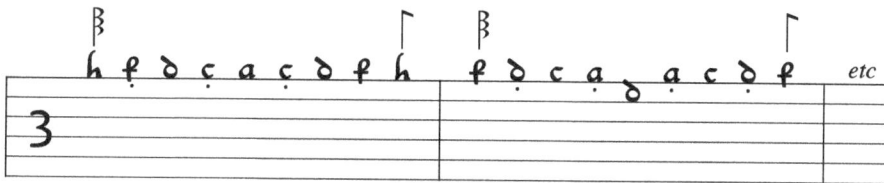

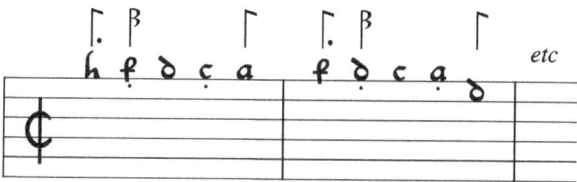

Here is a second anchor note sequence, for practicing *simple triad* figures which are descending fifths:

EXAMPLE A second anchor note sequence, for practicing *simple* triad figures which are descending fifths.

With the variants to practice on this sequence:

18.7. *Triad* Divisions (Extended): Exercises

EXTENDED

Here is another anchor note sequence with pairs of chords for practicing *extended triad* figures. The top stave shows the sequence of chords, the lower stave the individual anchor notes of those chords.

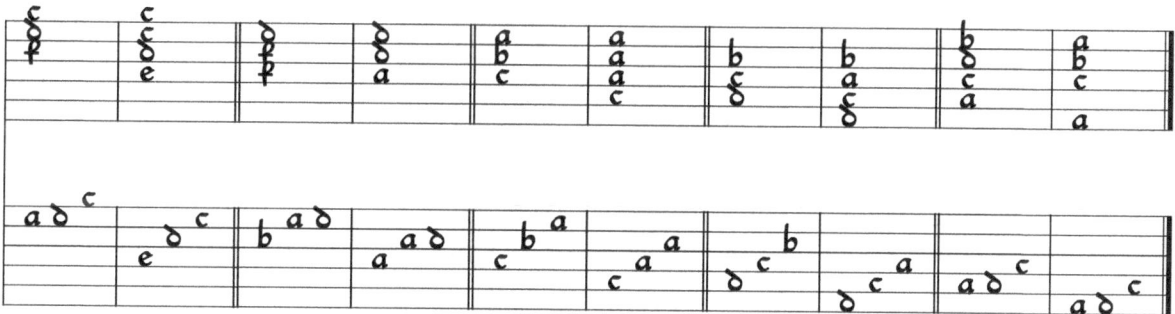

On this sequence, you can now practice the following variants.
The first has a range of six notes, beginning on 1:

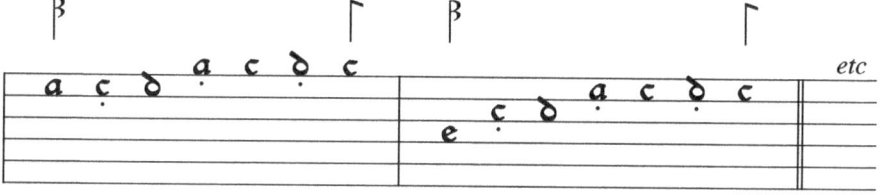

The next three variants, in triple meter, have a wider range of notes and directions:

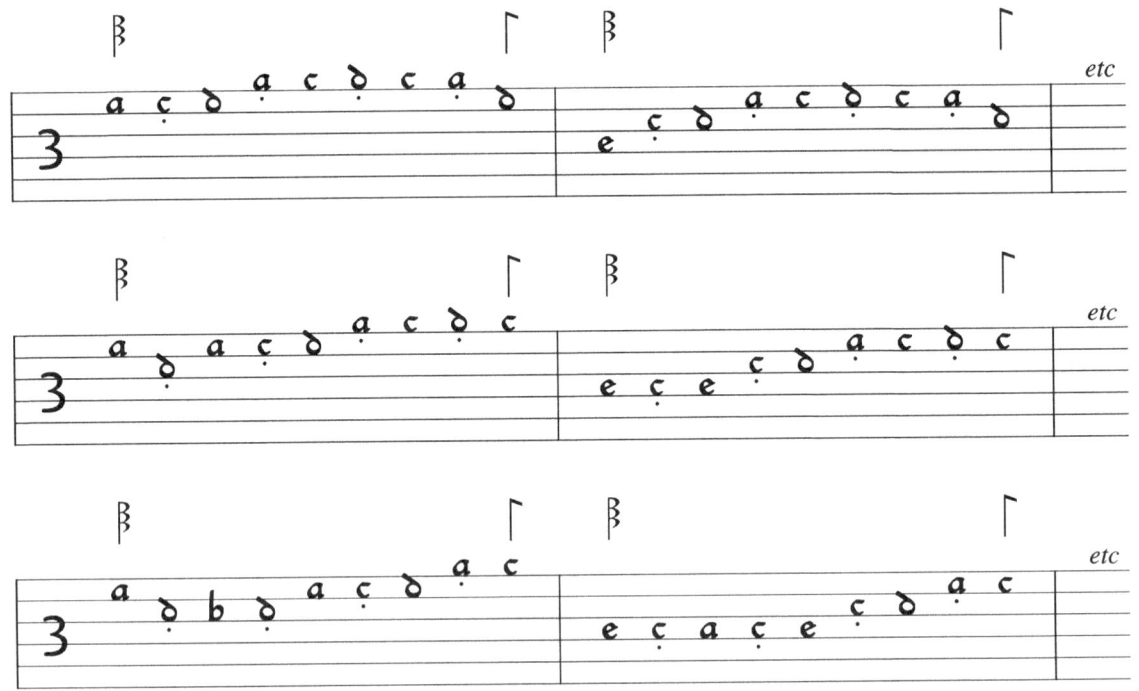

The final four variants all begin on the third of the chord:

18.8. *Triad* Divisions (Octave Extended): Exercises

OCTAVE EXTENDED

As these *triad* figures are basically octave scales, we will practice those in Chapter 20: Intervals. Here, we can take one very common and practical pattern. The first line shows the anchor notes, a descending scale. The second line is one pattern, and the third is almost the same but with a different rhythm. Practice and memorize!

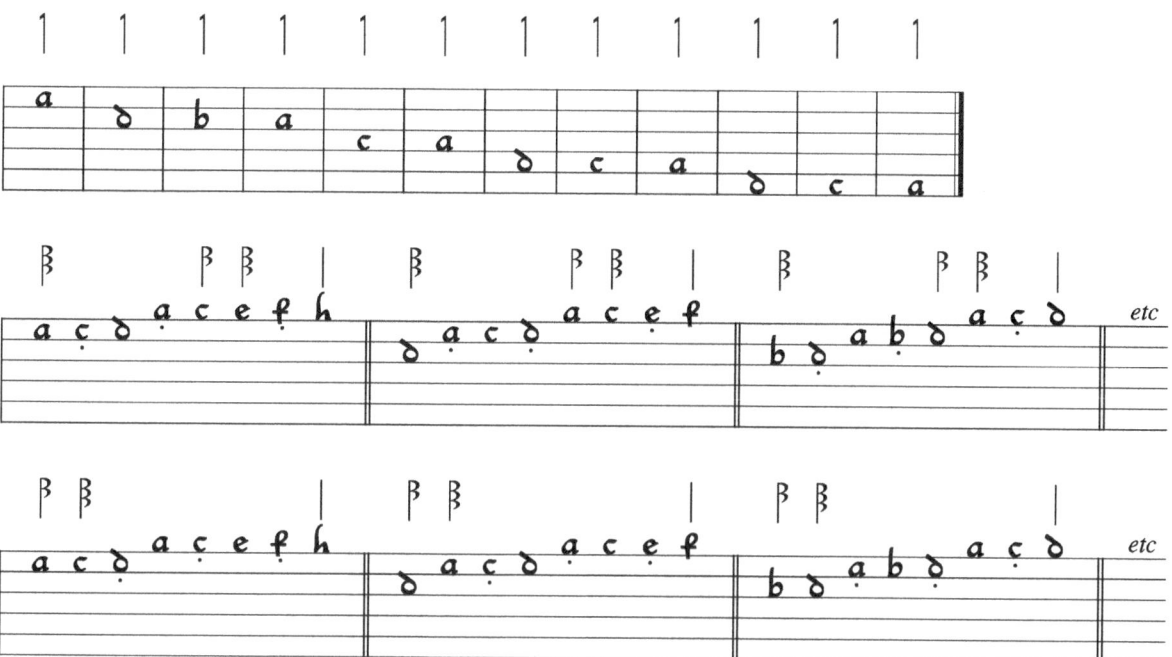

18.9. *Triad* Divisions (Harmonic): Exercises

To practice a few harmonic *triad* patterns, here is a sequence to use for anchor notes and harmony:

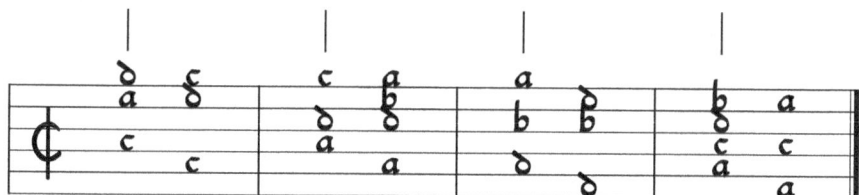

Here are three variants to practice. In Variant 1, all the divisions are harmonic and use only chordal notes, in a pattern. Variant 2 is still harmonic except at the end of each bar, bars 1–3, where there is a connecting note. Variant 3 is harmonic in the first part of each bar and then uses a descending octave scale which leads to the next bass note.

Now take the sequence and use it to invent your own harmonic *triads*, sometimes mixed with melodic patterns.

EXAMPLE The four-bar anchor note sequence, for your own division practice.

CHAPTER 19

STATIC

A brief survey of the Tablature Case Studies (Part 2) will show that static divisions are very common. It will be helpful to repeat its definition here. A *static* division is one which:

- Starts and ends with the same note.
- Centres around the written, or main note.
- Can even include repetition of the written note.
- A *cadential groppo* is often used as a static division on the final tonic.
- It is often used to represent one note to sustain it.

19.1. *Static* Divisions: Exercises (1)

Here are three simple scales in tenths to practice with some variant patterns below: divisions are to be added to the upper voice.

Scale 1:

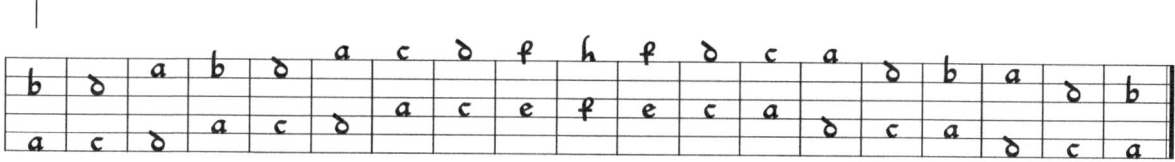

Scale 2:

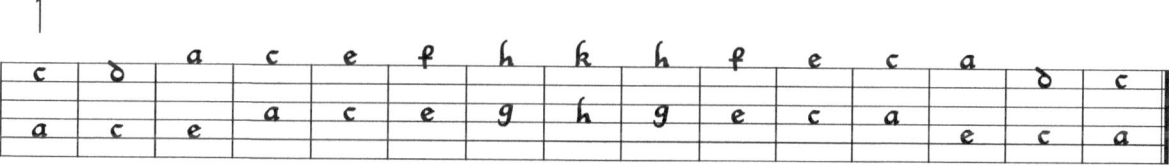

Scale 3:

Four variant patterns can be practiced on each of the three scales. Triple and duple time figures vary a little:

Playing with Patterns on the Lute. Nigel North, Oxford University Press. © Oxford University Press 2025.
DOI: 10.1093/9780197808764.003.0022

Variant 1:

Variant 2:

Variant 3:

Variant 4:

19.2. *Static* Divisions: Exercises (2)

As mentioned previously, a *groppo* is often used as a *static* figure on a final note or chord.

In this example, the anchor notes are in grey and there is a simple *static* division without *groppo* for each chord:

We can now practice a *groppo* figure on each chord and final note:

CHAPTER 20

INTERVALS

Divisions of intervals may be seen in at least two forms: simple and compound.

20.1. Simple Interval Divisions

- The first and last notes define the interval and may be considered as *anchor notes*.
- The notes of the division move by step only.
- The range of the division fills the interval between the two anchor notes with nothing outside that range.
- The divisions move in one direction and do not circle around or go further than the last anchor note.

Here are examples of a third, fourth, and fifth, ascending and descending, in duple and triple meters:

The number of notes needed for a *simple* interval division is always a different number from the interval number. For example, two notes which define a fifth (e.g., C–G) need only three more notes to make a complete interval division.

Playing with Patterns on the Lute. Nigel North, Oxford University Press. © Oxford University Press 2025.
DOI: 10.1093/9780197808764.003.0023

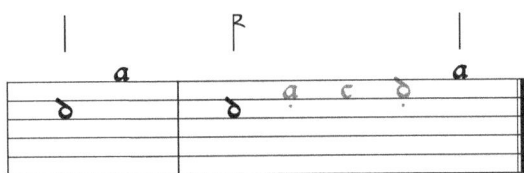

The number of steps between the two anchor notes is always two less than the number of the interval. Here are some examples of *simple* divisions of different intervals. Each interval is shown in two forms: the anchor notes defining the interval, followed by a simple pattern showing the extra notes needed in grey.

20.2. Compound Interval Divisions

- The first and last notes define the interval. They can be considered as anchor notes which may also represent the original composition.
- The notes between the anchors, the connecting notes, may go up or down in a variety of ways.
- The division will proceed mostly by step but may have one or more larger intervals which must be *consonant* with the harmony.
- Repetition or circling back can extend a *simple* interval division to a *compound* interval division.

Here are some examples of an ascending fifth interval, with a few variants of a compound interval division:

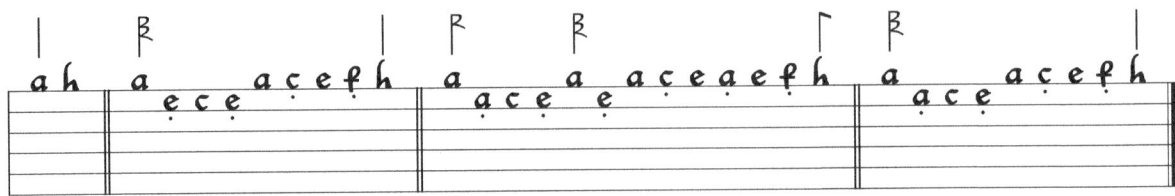

Let us look at two well-known pieces from our sixteenth-century repertoire:

- *Pavin 6* by Alfonso Ferrabasco (*A Varietie of Lute Lessons*, Robert Dowland, London, 1610)
- *Passamezze*, Adrian Le Roy (see Part 2: Tablature Case Studies)

We will consider bar 1 of the Ferrabosco *Pavin*. In the following example,

> Stave 1 = first time.
> Stave 2 = the repeat with the divisions, for observation.
> Stave 3 shows the interval anchor notes.

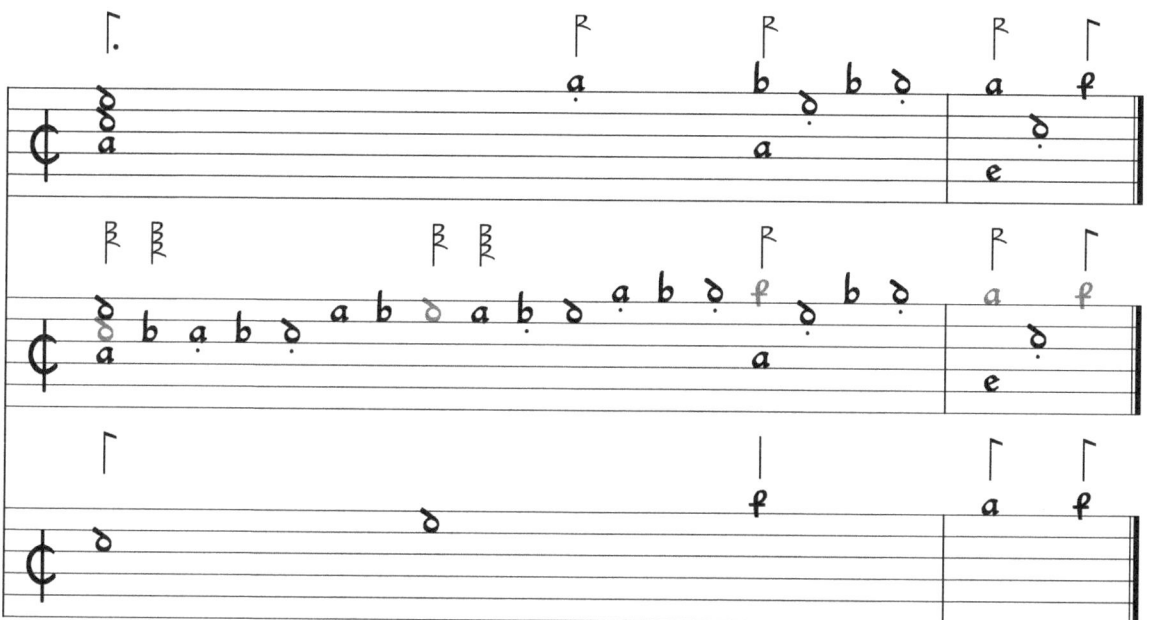

All five anchor notes are shown in grey.

> Bar 1: The first interval is an ascending fourth, marked in grey.
> Bar 1: The next interval is an ascending fifth.

They sound the same because the rhythm is imitated, but the compound division figures are different, to accommodate the different sizes of intervals. They sound the same and illustrate how valuable and useful compound interval figures are.

If we look more carefully, we can see that the first division descends a third before ascending a fifth; beats 1–2.

The second division also jumps down a third at the start but then ascends a seventh in a *simple* way; beats 2–3.

By combining these two interval divisions in bar 1, tab *d* on the third course, beat 1, ascends an octave to tab *f* on the first course, beat 3.

Here are the three stages described, in tablature:

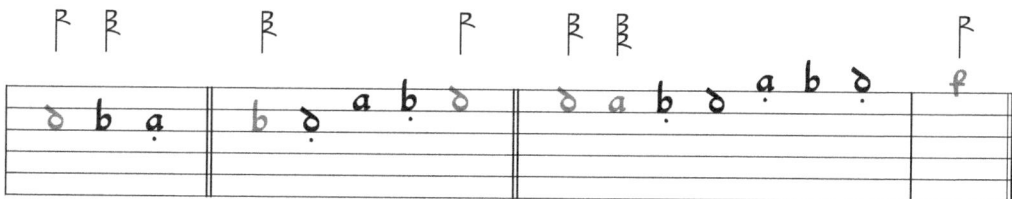

The second example is from the *Passamezze* from Adrian Le Roy (see Part 2: Tablature Case Studies). In this extract, bar 6, the upper stave shows the unornamented version, and the lower stave the version with divisions.

Bar 6, *Passamezze*, Adrian Le Roy:

We can see this as an interval division of an ascending fifth (middle voice of the chord, tab *d* on the third course to tab *a* on the 1st course), which then goes one note higher and circles around to return to the first note. The following example shows this sequence:

- Interval of a fifth.
- Simple division moving by step.
- Extending to the sixth.
- Circling around at the top of the scale, before descending to where it began (tab *d* on the 3rd course).

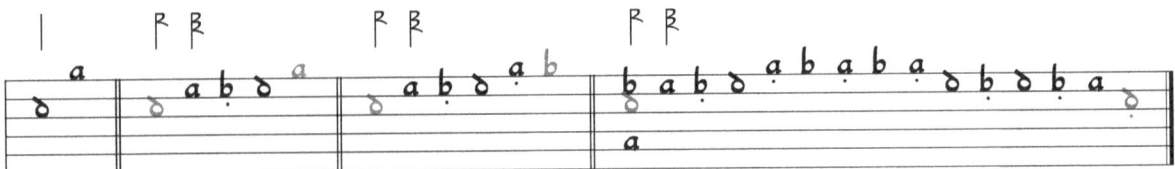

On the way down, there are two groups of four notes which do not descend directly, while covering an interval of a sixth. This type of solution is a very common *compound interval* pattern.

20.3. Scales and Octaves: Exercises

Our first interval division practice will be with scales. One of the most common patterns is centred around the octave, ascending and descending. It is very useful to become acquainted with octaves. Ascending and descending, the most common rhythmic patterns are:

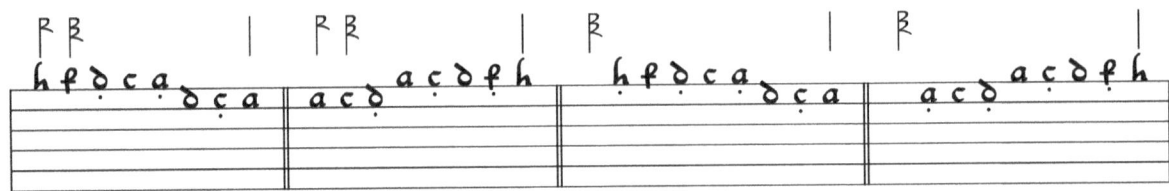

These are all *simple* interval divisions. As a *static* division, in which the first and last notes of a pattern are identical, we can also use one of these patterns:

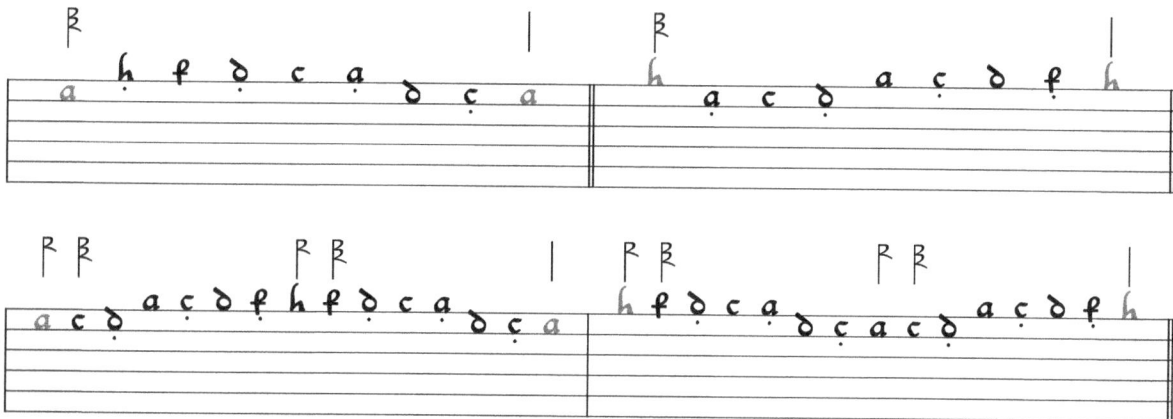

INTERVAL EXERCISE

Using this octave scale of anchor notes:

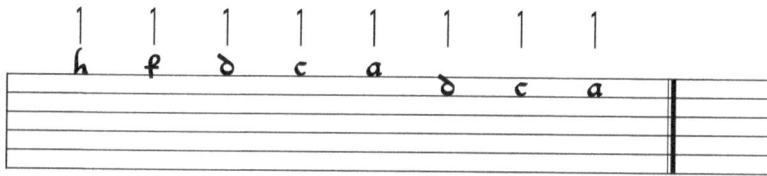

Practice descending and ascending octave patterns. The anchor notes of the scale are in grey in this example.

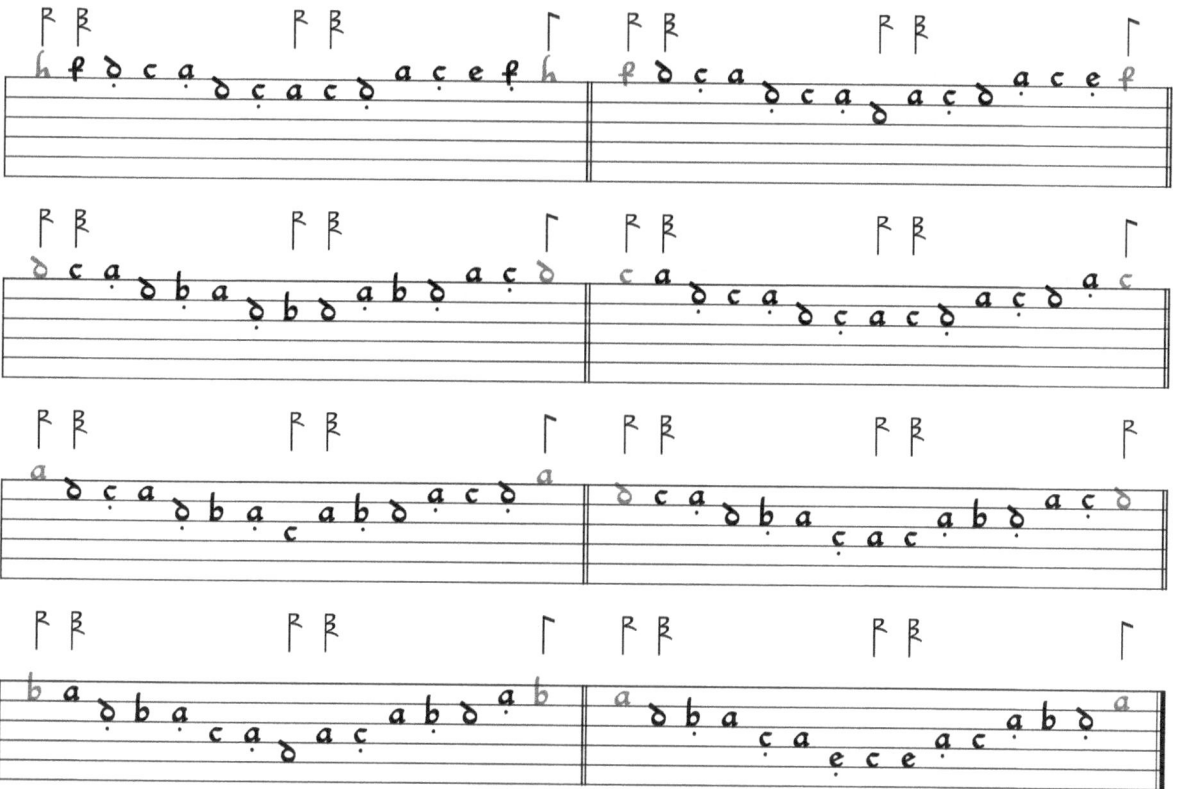

The ascending seventh is another figure used in much the same way as an octave. If we look at this excerpt from the pavan *Solus cum sola* from John Dowland, we see his favourite way of using a division of a seventh to connect anchor notes—he doubles the first lowest note of the scale. The divisions on beats 1 and 2 are ascending sevenths; beat 3 sounds the same but is a compound figure of only a fifth. Anchor notes are in grey on staves 1 and 3.

Upper stave, bar 7 (1st A section).
Middle stave, bar 15 (2nd A section with divisions).
Lower stave, anchor notes.

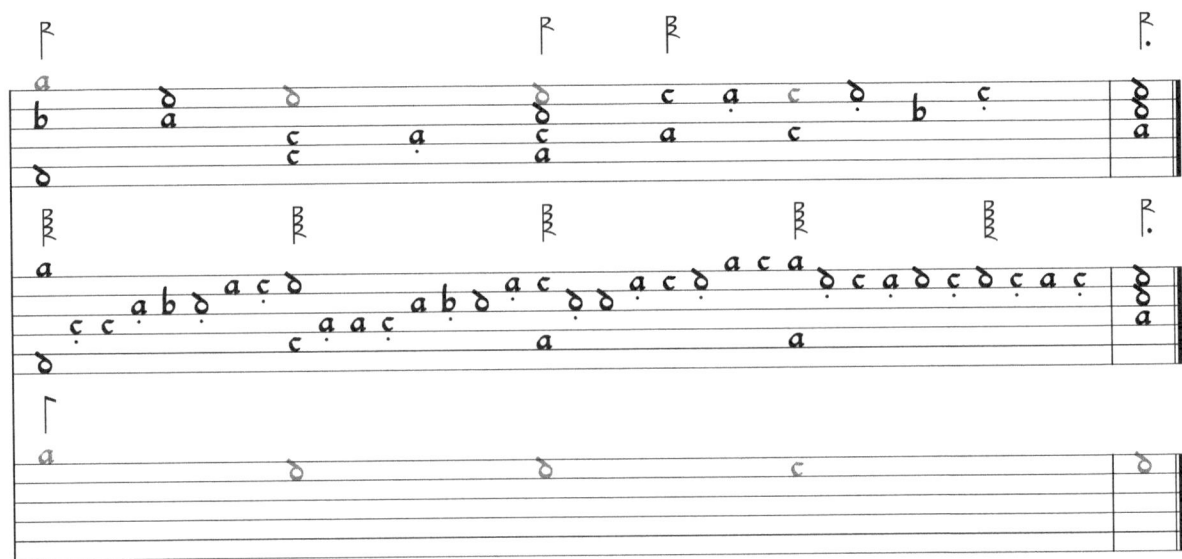

INTERVAL EXERCISES

To practice using a descending octave together with an ascending seventh, we can take the same scale as used previously (anchor notes are in grey) and decorate it thus:

Five variants on the same scale with anchor notes in grey:

EXAMPLE Five variants on the same scale above, with anchor notes in grey.

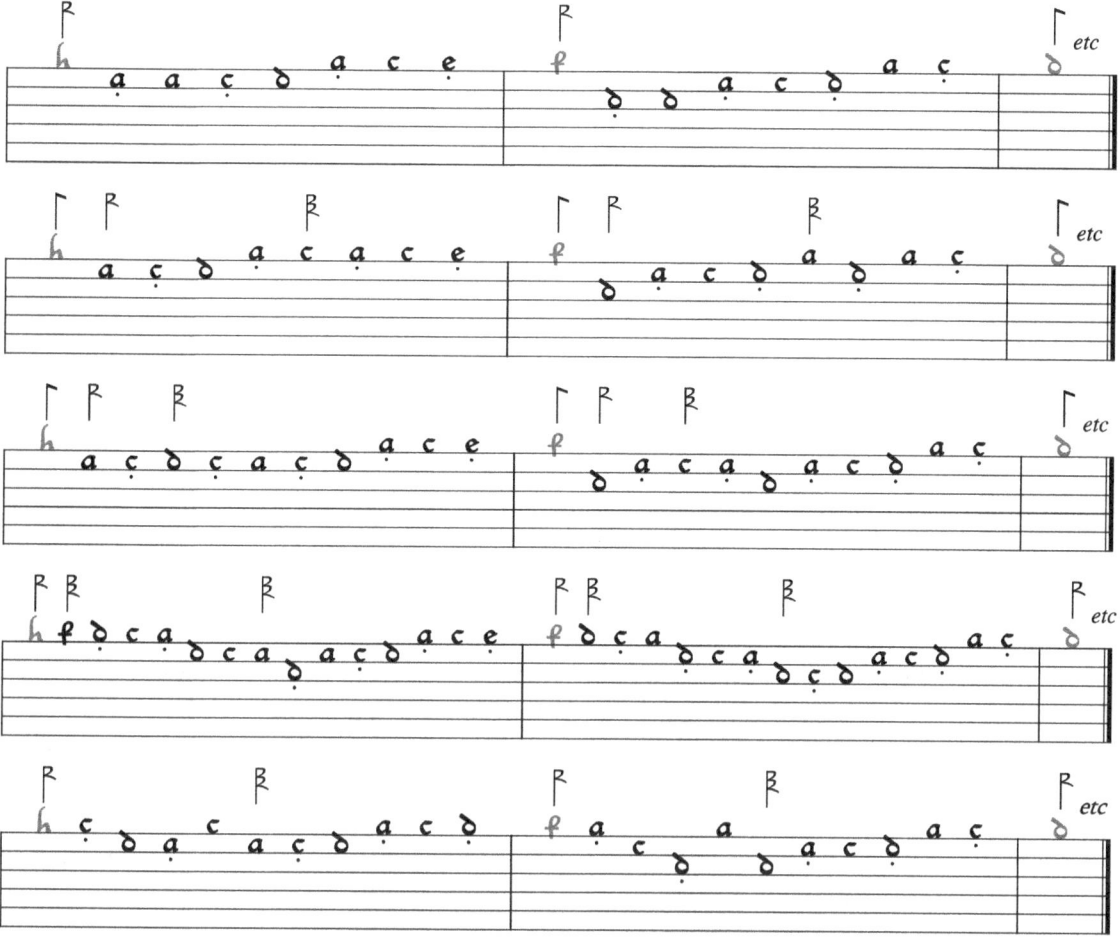

Now, working with an ascending octave scale:

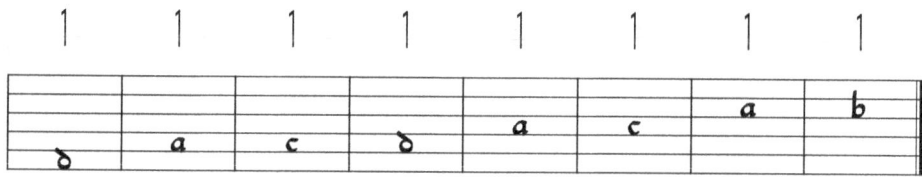

We can decorate this scale with another descending seventh pattern:

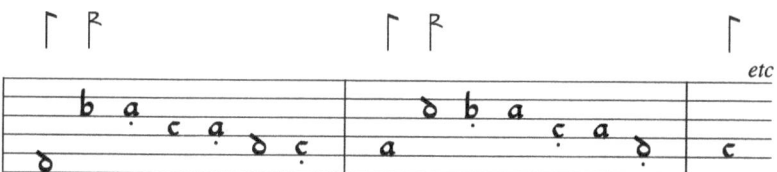

The next scale and division pattern for octave practice takes a common figure which was still in use in the eighteenth century and will be recognized from Mozart's famous sonata in C major, *Sonata facile*, K 545, 1st movement, Allegro. Going from the first to the last note in each bar, we can see this as a *static* division figure. It may, however, feel as a division which descends by step when we hear the first notes of each bar as *anchor notes*. We can practice it on this descending scale of *anchor notes* used earlier:

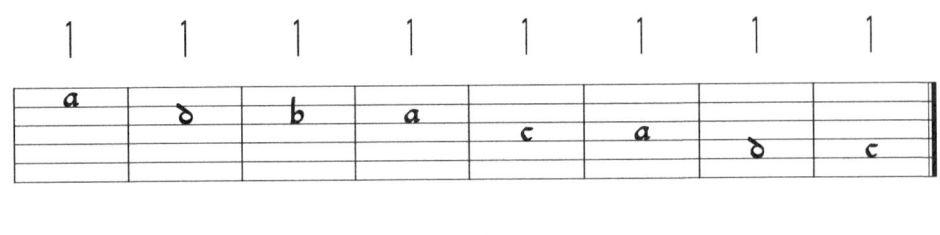

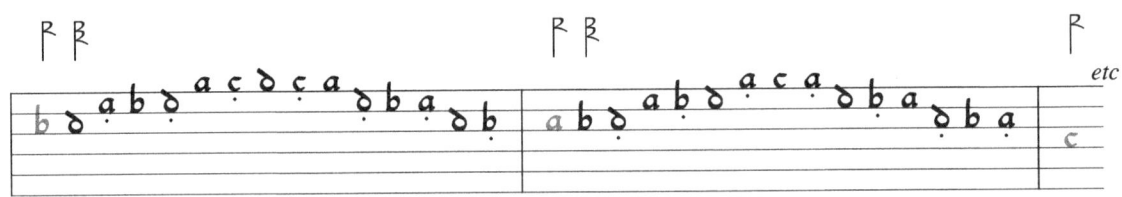

ASCENDING THE OCTAVE

Several of the late sixteenth-century diminution manuals for wind and strings (see Appendix 1 for a list of sources) mention the good practice of going an octave higher at cadences. Presumably, this was to add a clear, audible, and thrilling decoration to a final cadence. Here is how to do it! The division patterns change according to the harmony.

In the first example pattern, the division begins on the tonic note, ascends an octave with a common rhythmic pattern which takes us immediately to a *groppo cadential* figure. The harmony underneath is I–V–I, with a 4–3 suspension on V.

First pattern:

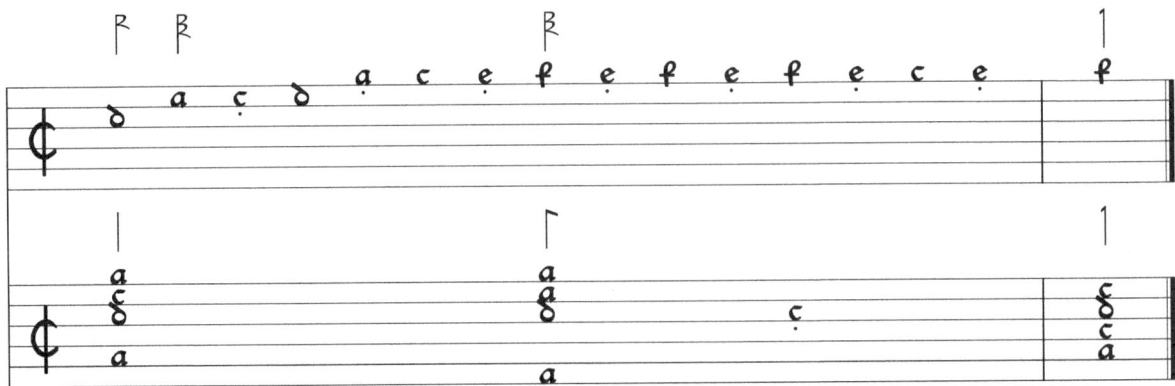

In the second pattern, the division begins on the third of the chord on V, ascends an octave, and then proceeds into a *groppo cadential* figure. The harmony underneath is V–I with a 3–4–4–3 *cadential* suspension on V.

Second pattern:

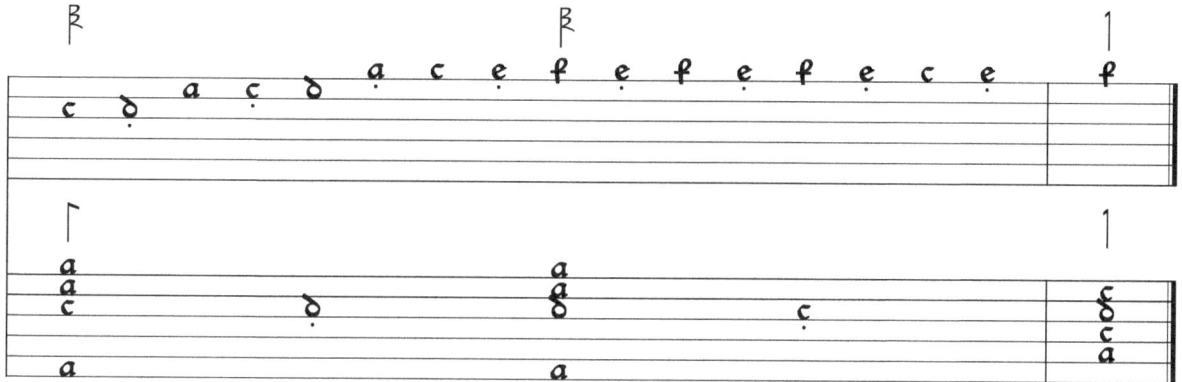

In the third pattern, like the first, the division begins on the tonic note, ascends an octave with a different common rhythmic pattern, arrives on the leading note, and then proceeds to a *groppo cadential* figure, with a *doubler*. The harmony underneath is I–V–I, with no *cadential* suspension.

Third pattern:

In the final pattern, the harmony underneath is I–V–I, with no *cadential* suspension.

The division begins on the third of the chord on V, ascends the octave, arrives on the leading note, and then proceeds into a *groppo cadential* figure.

Fourth pattern:

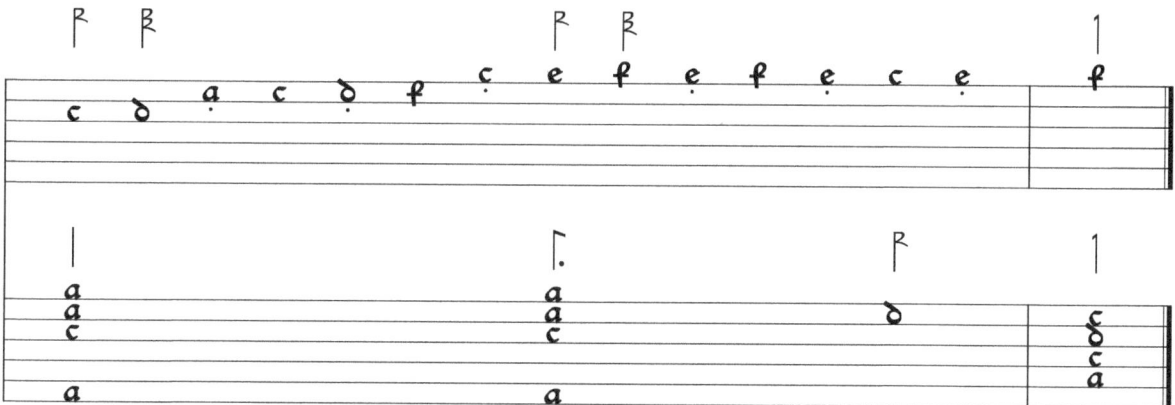

EXERCISES

The preceding four patterns can be practised with the following chord progressions and are extremely valuable to have at one's fingertips as part of a division pattern repertoire. In each exercise, the upper stave gives the harmony, the lower stave the anchor notes of the division, in grey.

Pattern 1:

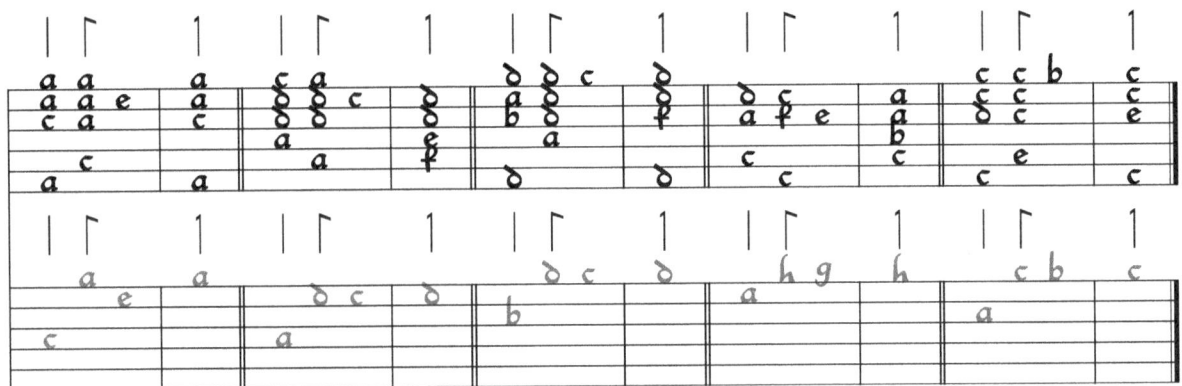

Pattern 2:

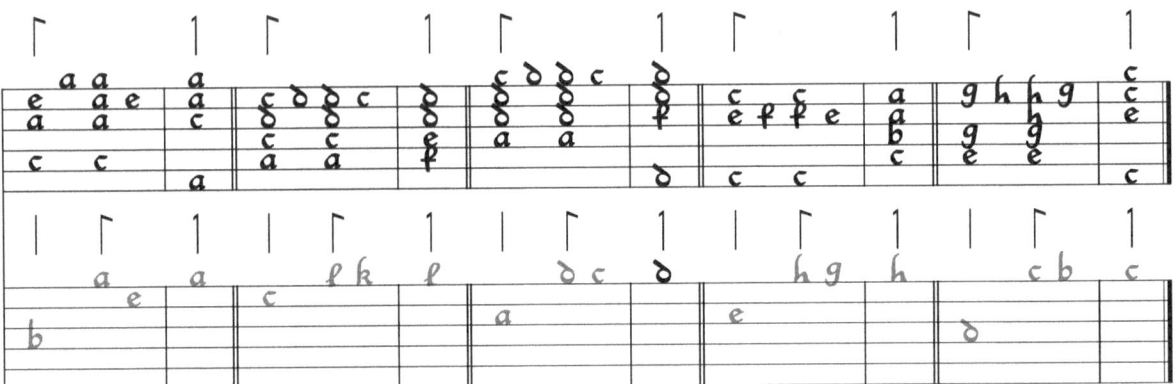

Pattern 3:

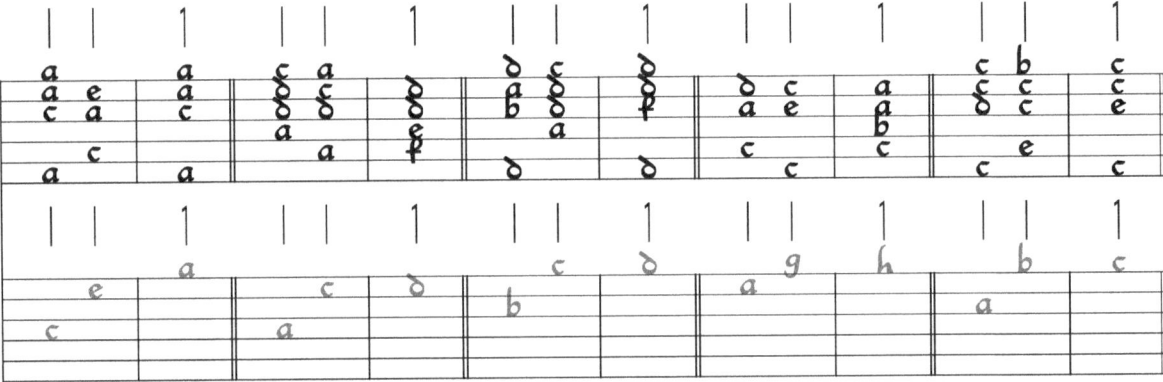

Pattern 4:

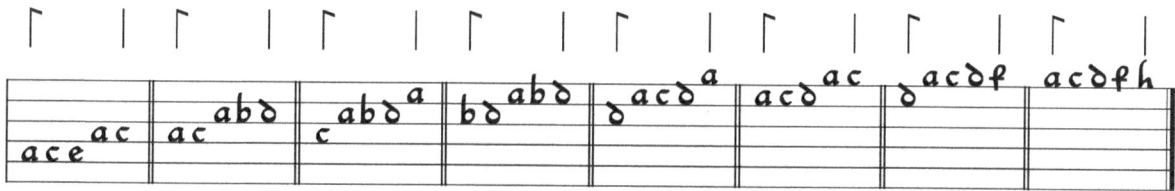

20.4. Ascending and Descending Seconds

ASCENDING SECONDS: EXERCISES

Here are eight short scales, which can be used to practice the variants which follow. I would suggest making these part of a morning warm-up routine.

The following variant patterns all begin by going beneath the main note. Anchor notes are in grey. The example of each pattern is shown from the fifth scale, starting from middle C (tab *c* on the 3rd course), but all patterns can be played on all eight scales, starting from the fifth course.

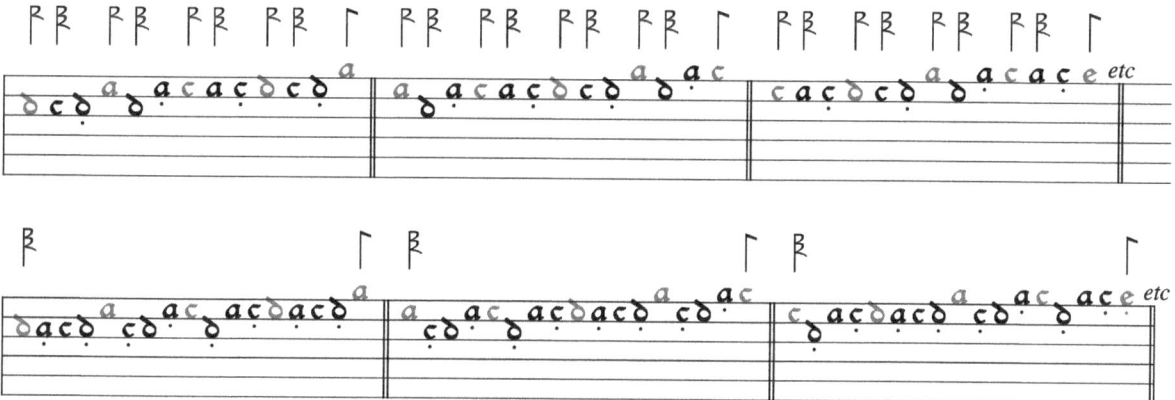

The eight scales remain the same as above:

The following variants all begin by going above the main note. The anchor notes are in grey.

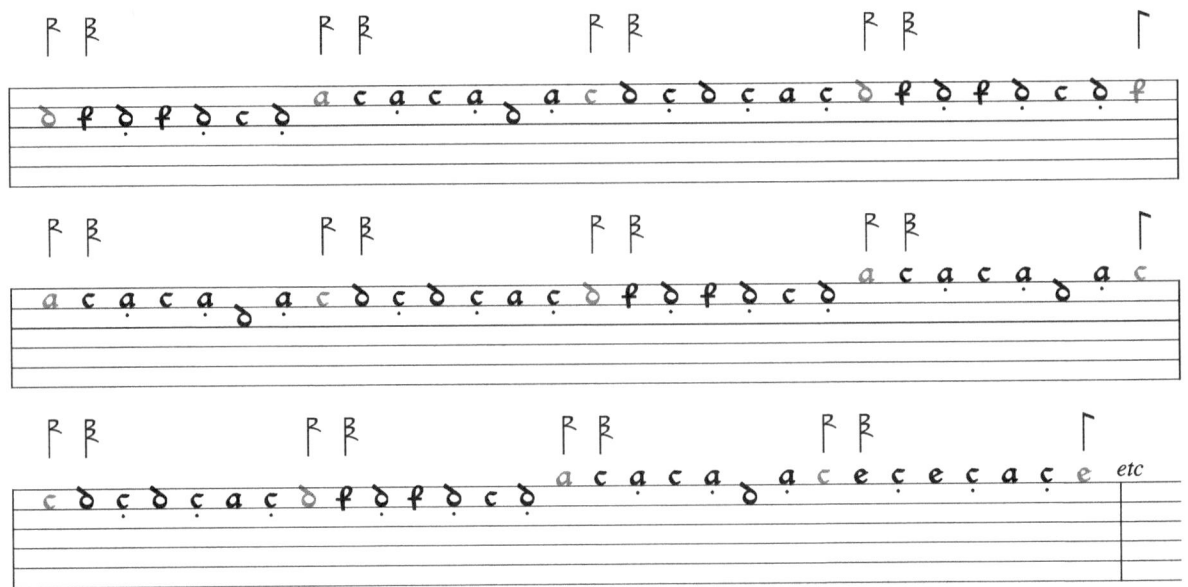

DESCENDING SECONDS: EXERCISES

Using this first scale of anchor notes, use the following 12 variants to practice patterns for descending scales.

Pattern 1 is presented here complete, with anchor notes in grey:

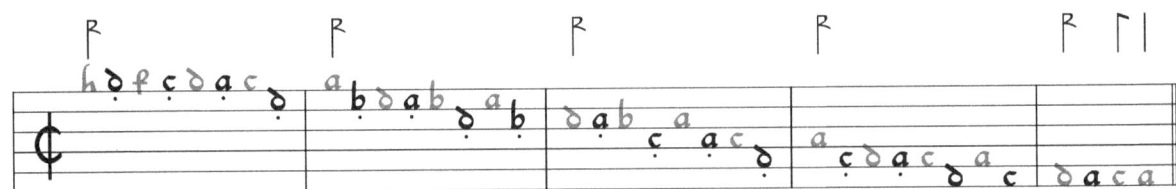

Patterns 2–12 show only the beginning of each new pattern, and the final pattern (12) begins a third lower due to its range:

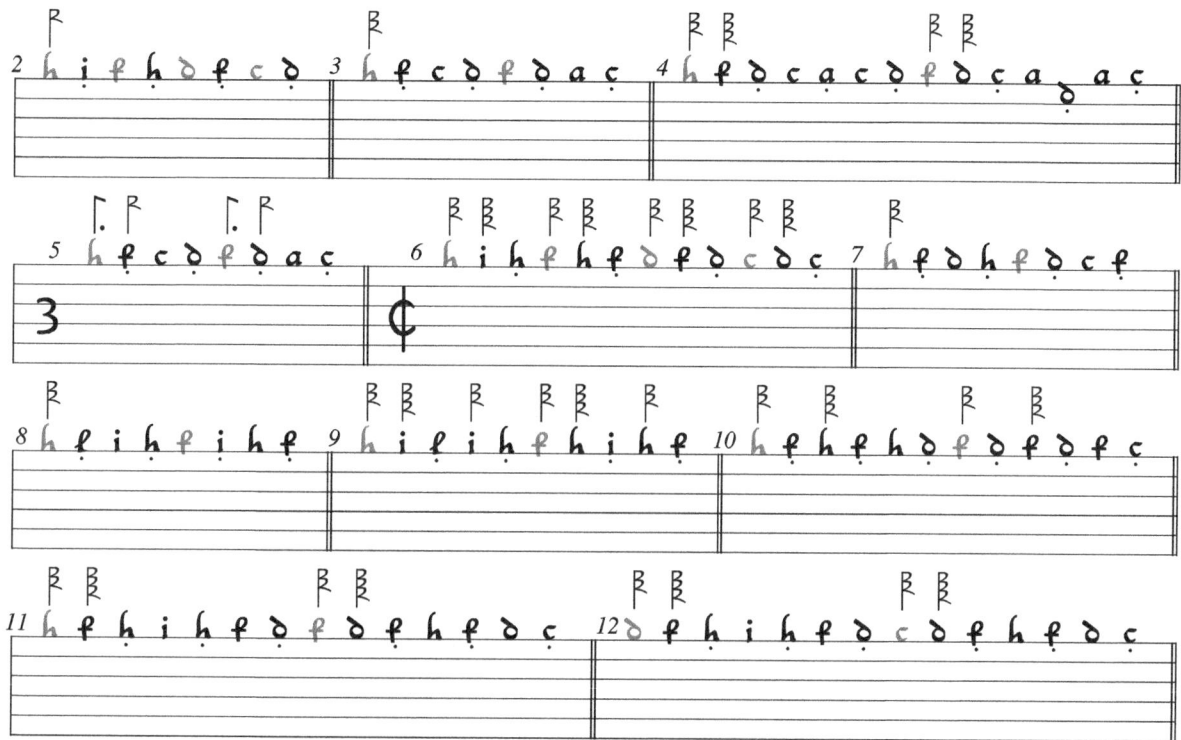

20.5. Ascending and Descending Thirds

ASCENDING THIRDS: EXERCISES

Patterns which divide thirds, ascending and descending, are much used. As a basic *triad* is made up of two thirds, you will also find that some of the following patterns may also be seen as *triad* figures. Here are three sequences of anchor notes which ascend by thirds.

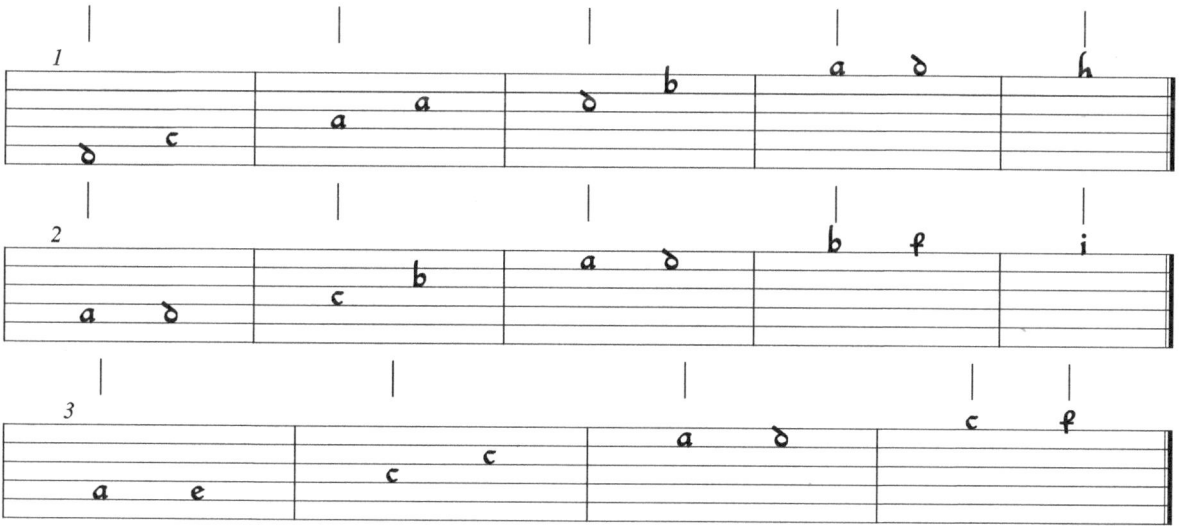

As an example, here are the three sequences with the first basic division pattern fully written out. Anchor notes are in grey.

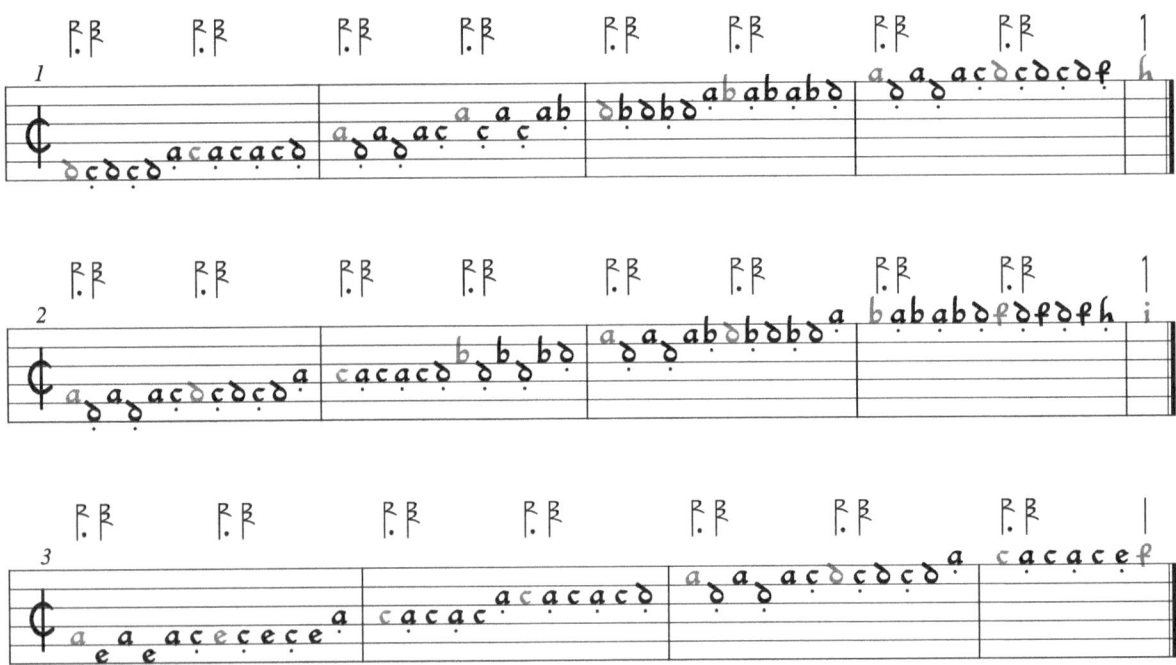

All the following variant patterns can be practiced on all three sequences. The first anchor note with each division pattern is given here:

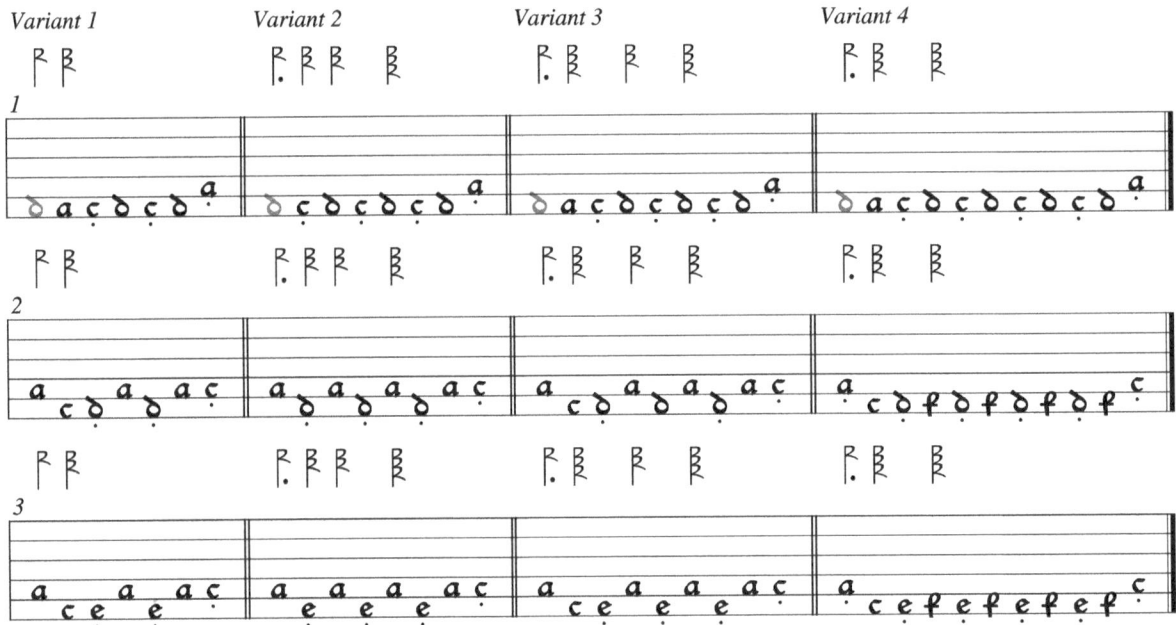

SEQUENCE 4 WITH VARIANT PATTERNS

Here follows a descending sequence of pairs of ascending thirds:

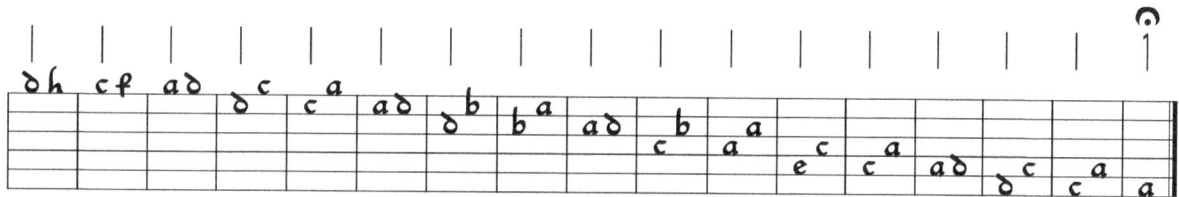

Variant 1 is shown in full, with grey anchor notes.

In variant patterns 2–9, only the first two measures are provided here, but they can be played in full. Anchor notes are in grey:

EXAMPLE Variant patterns 2–9 with anchor notes in grey.

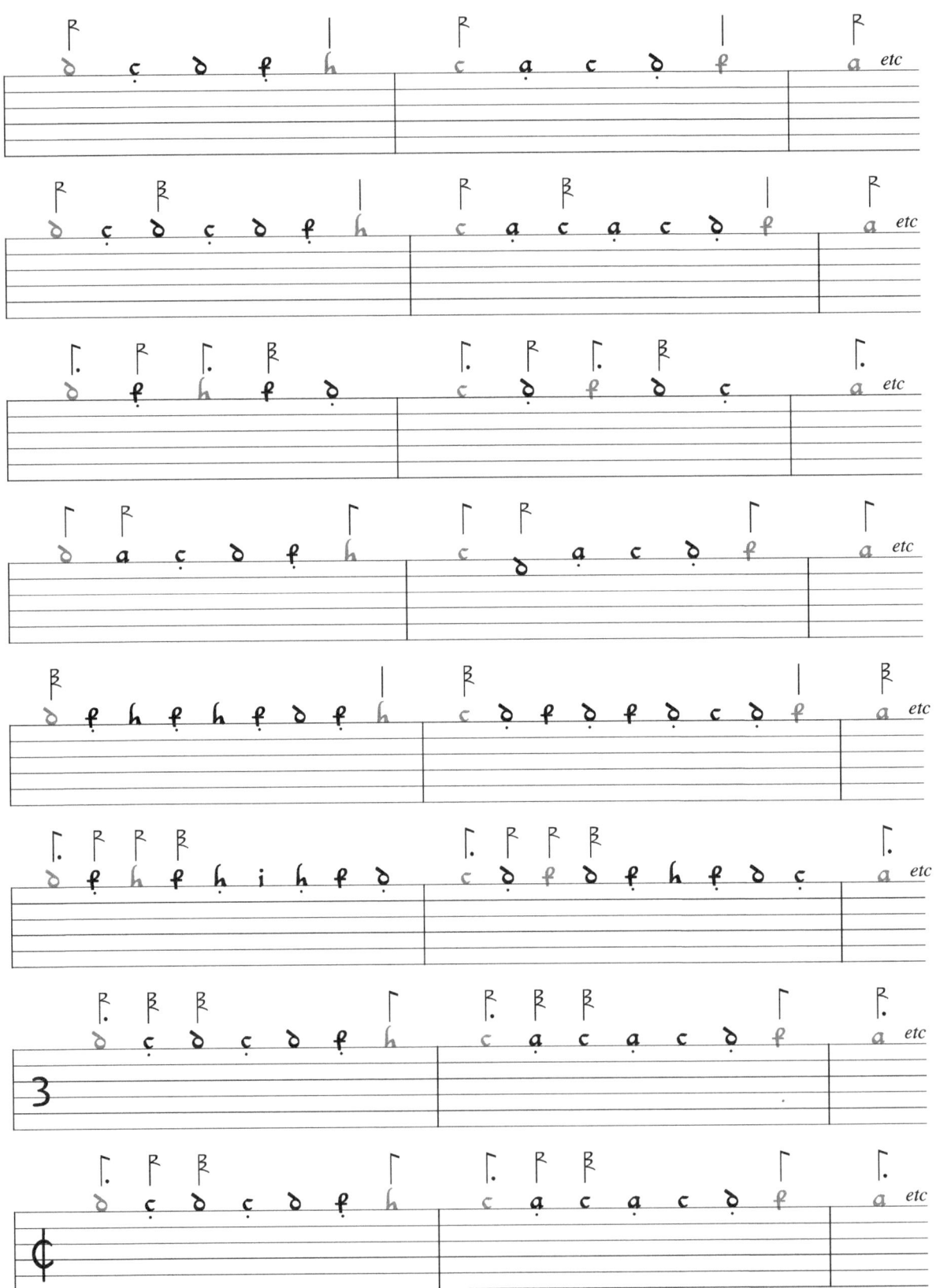

EXAMPLE: ASCENDING THIRDS

The final ascending thirds pattern is most useful and is often used. Considering it as part of a *triad* division, it can be understood in two contexts. In all cases, the division descends a fourth and then turns around and ascends a sixth to end on a note a third above the starting note.

Version 1: Beginning on the fifth of the first chord and ending on the third of the second, here is an example. Lower stave, the unornamented sequence; upper stave, the division figure with grey anchor notes:

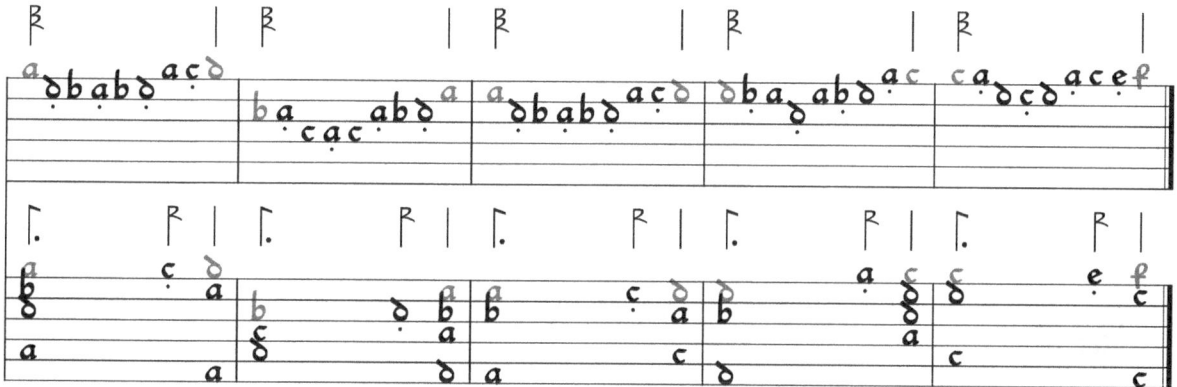

Version 2: A *triad* without a change of harmony with the division going from the third to the fifth of the chord:

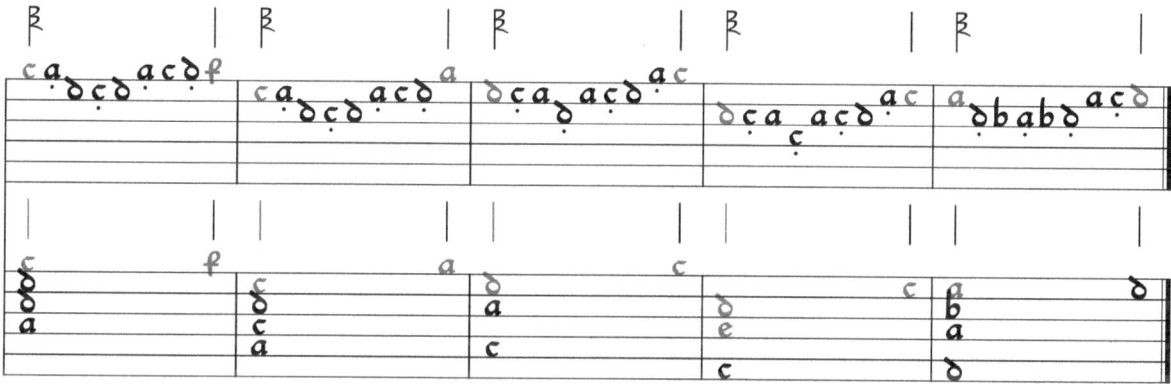

Exercise: A sequence of anchor notes:

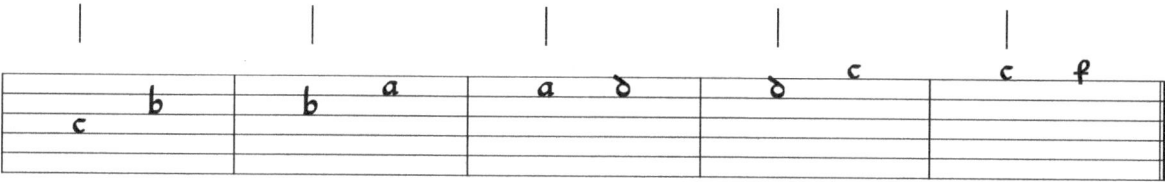

This can be practised in the two forms described previously:

Or even continuously:

DESCENDING THIRDS: EXERCISES

Exercises

We will take four sequences of descending thirds, and practice variant patterns on these sequences.

Sequence 1 and 2. Upper staves are the scales, lower staves the simple divisions:

EXAMPLE Sequences 1 and 2, descending thirds, for practicing variant patterns on these sequences. Upper staves
are the scales, lower staves the simple divisions.

Using these two sequences, you can practice the following variant patterns:

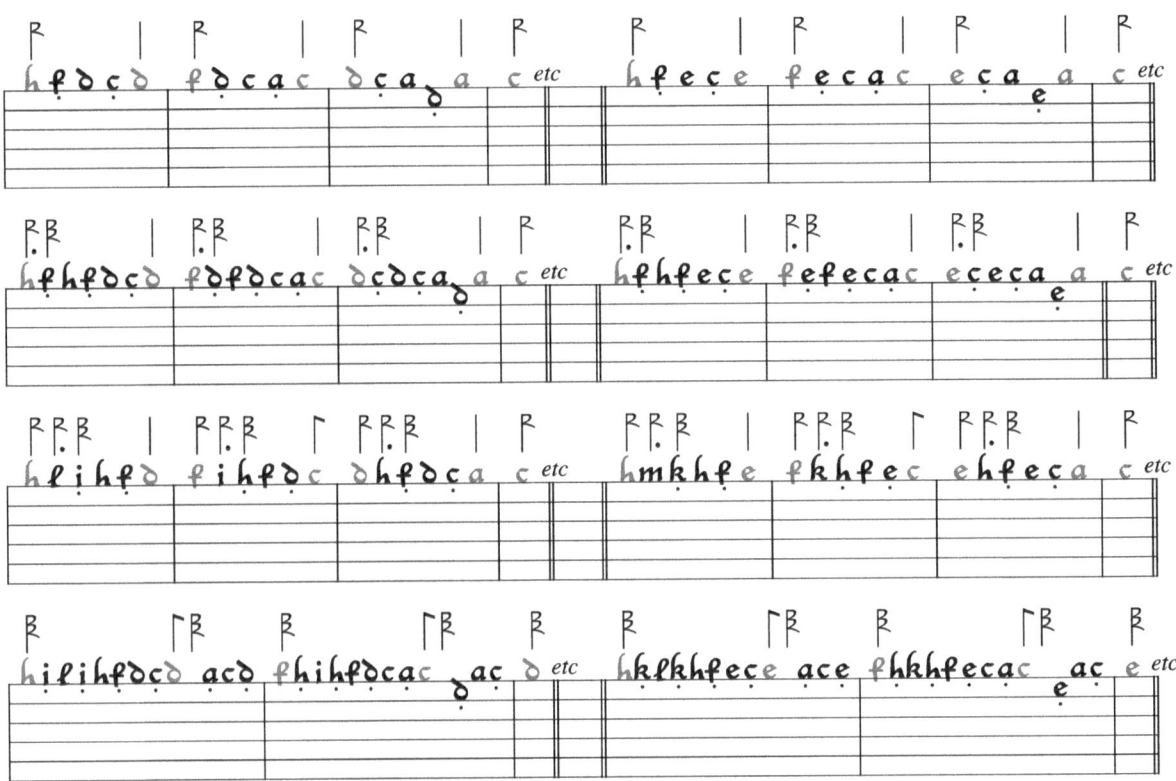

Sequences 3, 4, and 5 are shorter and made up of pairs of descending thirds:

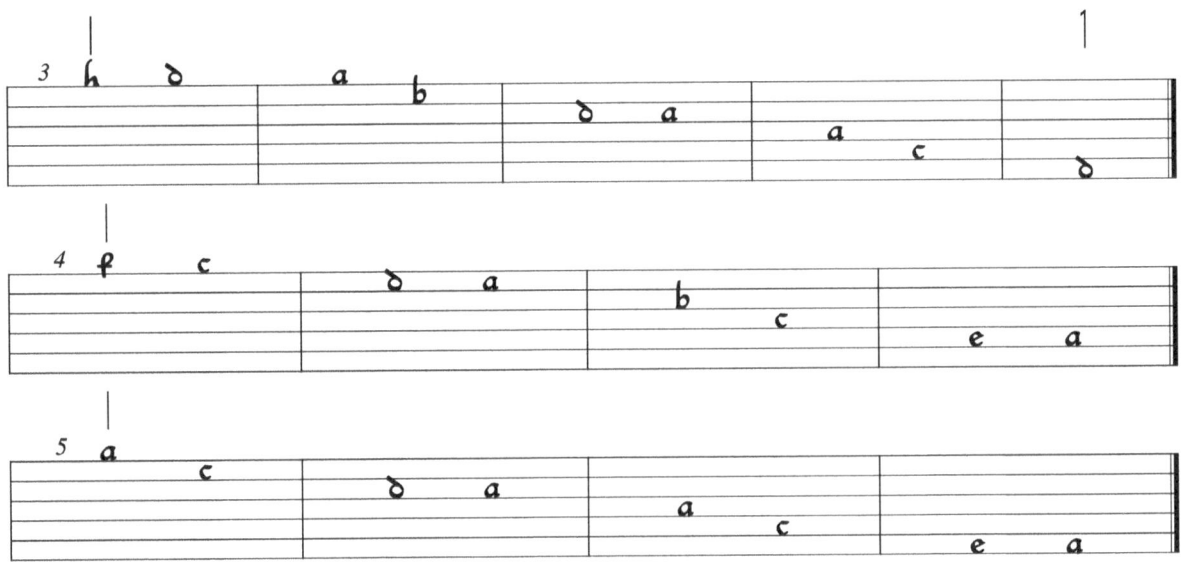

Using these three sequences, you can practice the following variant patterns.

Pattern 1 is written out in full, for all three sequences. All anchor notes are shown in grey:

Pattern 1:

Patterns 2–5 are presented with only their first bars. All anchor notes are shown in grey:

Pattern 2:

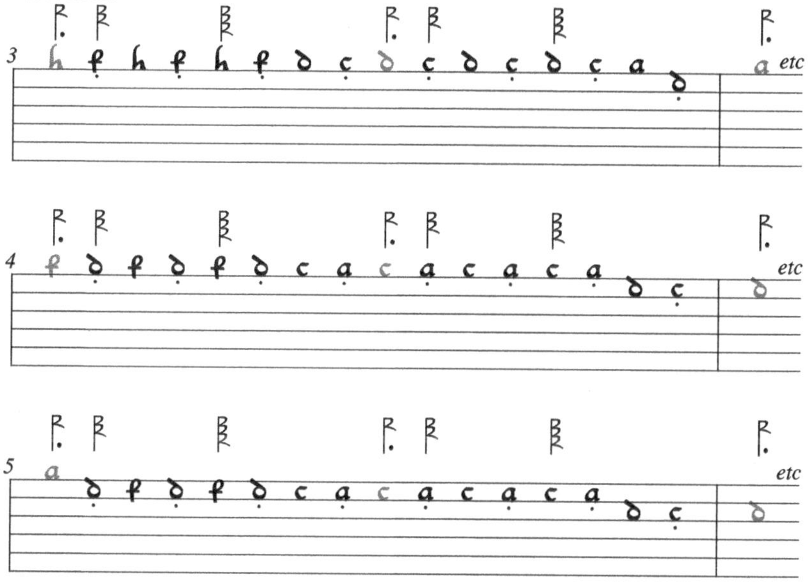

Pattern 3:

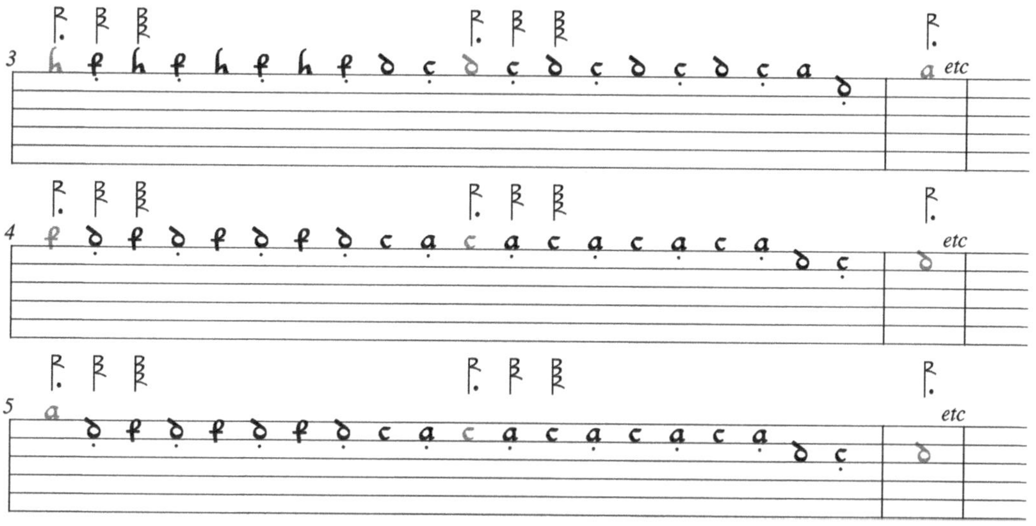

Pattern 4:

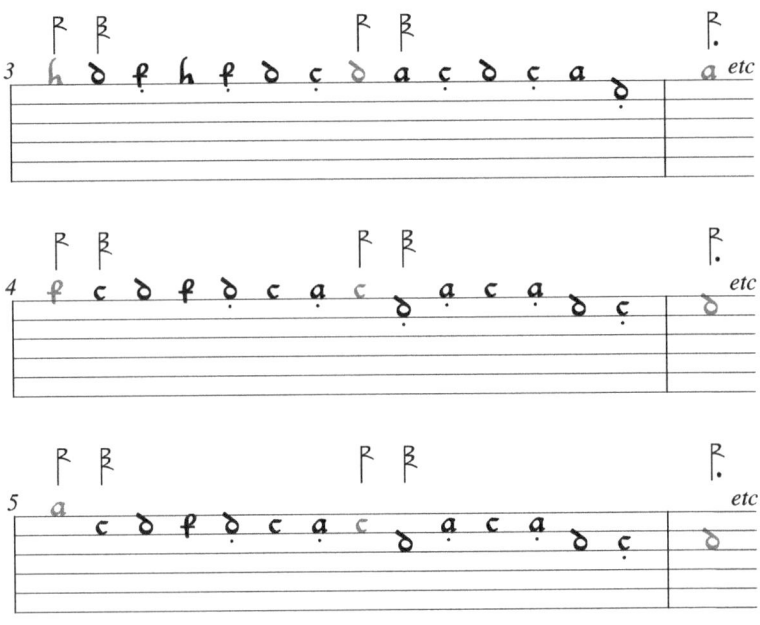

Pattern 5:

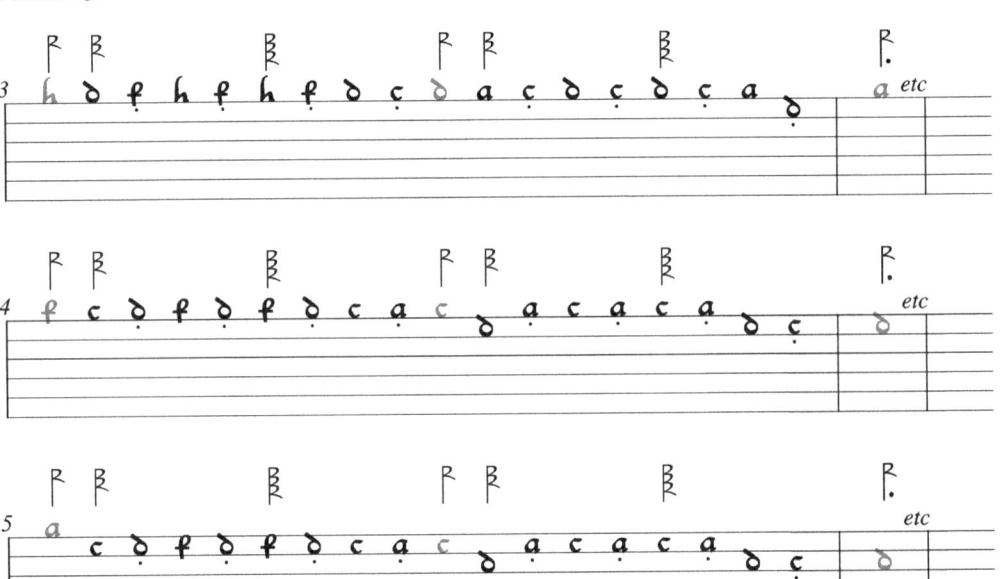

20.6. Ascending and Descending Fourths

EXPLANATIONS AND EXAMPLES

The interval division of a fourth is best first understood in the context of a chord, between the tonic and the fourth below that tonic. For example, as a *simple* interval division of G–D, or D–G, as represented here in the context of a chord of G. First, we see the intervals and how they fit into the chord, and then a *simple* division, descending and ascending:

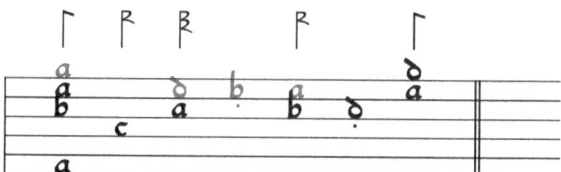

The next example shows a *cadential* division (here to a final on C) with a *simple* division. This is one of the most common uses for a descending fourth division:

A descending fourth is familiar to us from the opening of John Dowland's *Lachrimae Pavan.* This melodically descending fourth often indicated *melancholy.*

Lachrimae Pavan, John Dowland:

A similar figure can be found in many cadences. At the final cadence of *Fantasia #31* from Francesco da Milano, the tenor voice has the descending fourth. In the first example we see the original tablature (lower stave) with *anchor* notes of the tenor voice (upper stave). In the second example we can see the tenor voice with divisions (upper stave).

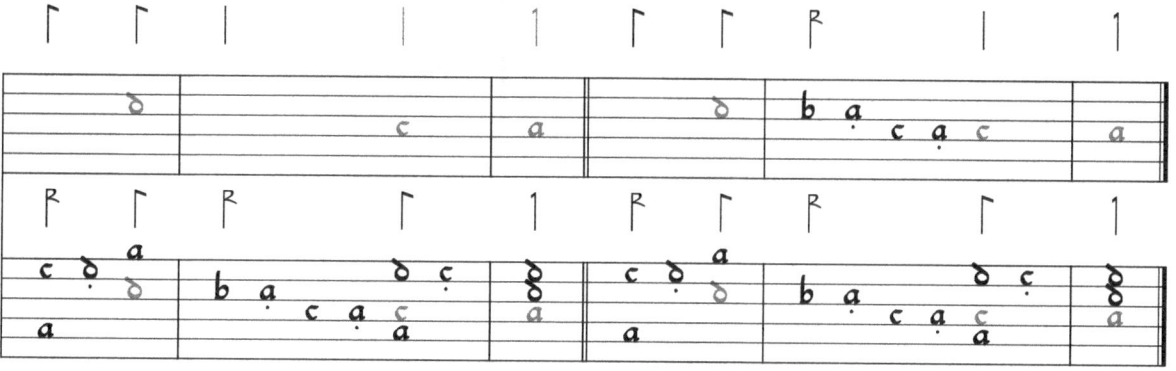

In *Lady Laiton's Almain,* Dowland demonstrates the most normal use of the ascending fourth in a *simple* division. In the following example, we see the opening phrase (lower stave, 1st time; upper stave the repeat with divisions):

Lady Laiton's Almain, John Dowland:

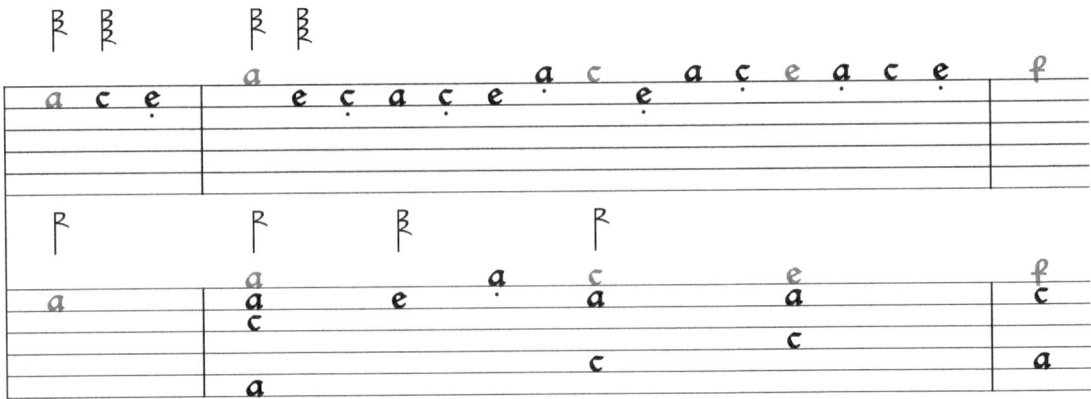

A normal division of the up-beat to the down-beat of the first bar is an ascending fourth. Bar 1 sounds as though there are several fourths, but Dowland uses other division figures. Seen one way, we have a *static* figure:

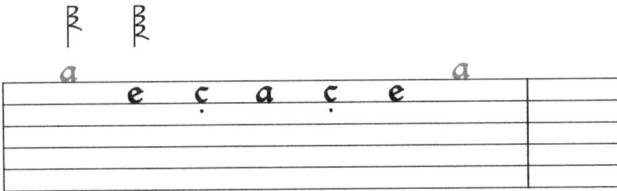

Alternatively, beats 1–2 are a *compound* interval division, ascending a second to the third beat (tab *c* on the 1st course). The first four notes descend a fourth, but are followed by a rising fifth, dividing the melody by ascending only a second:

On beats 3–4, the division figure descends a third before ascending by a fourth. The fingers will feel a fourth, but the overall division is only an ascending second!

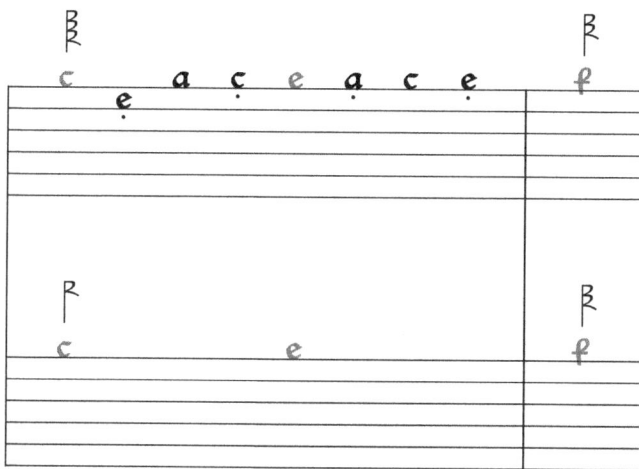

EXERCISES: DESCENDING AND ASCENDING FOURTHS

Scale One, for Descending Fourths:

   A sequence of descending fourths, which rise a third and then descend again. Here is the scale with the anchor notes in grey, with a *simple* division:

Four variant patterns to practice with this scale:

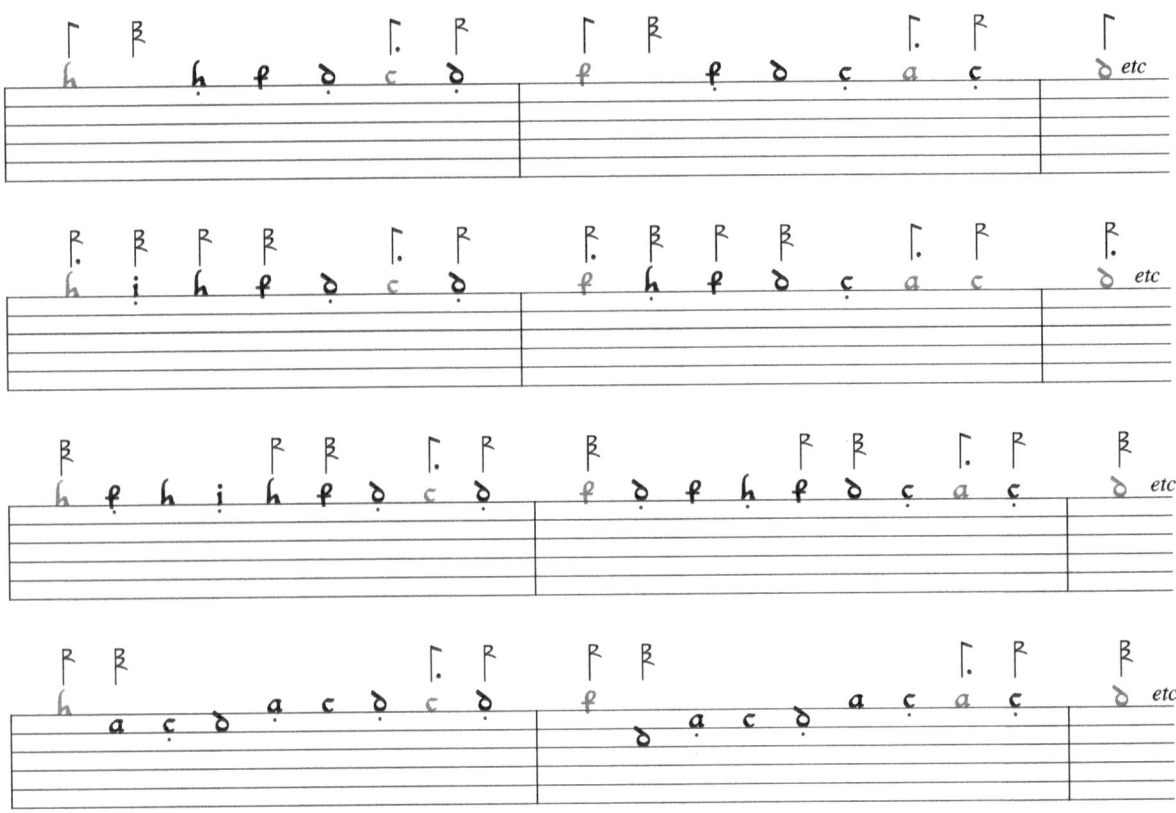

Scale two, for ascending fourths: A sequence of ascending fourths, in which we ascend a fourth, and then descend a third for the next level. Here is the scale with the anchor notes in grey, with a *simple* division:

Four variant patterns to practice with this scale:

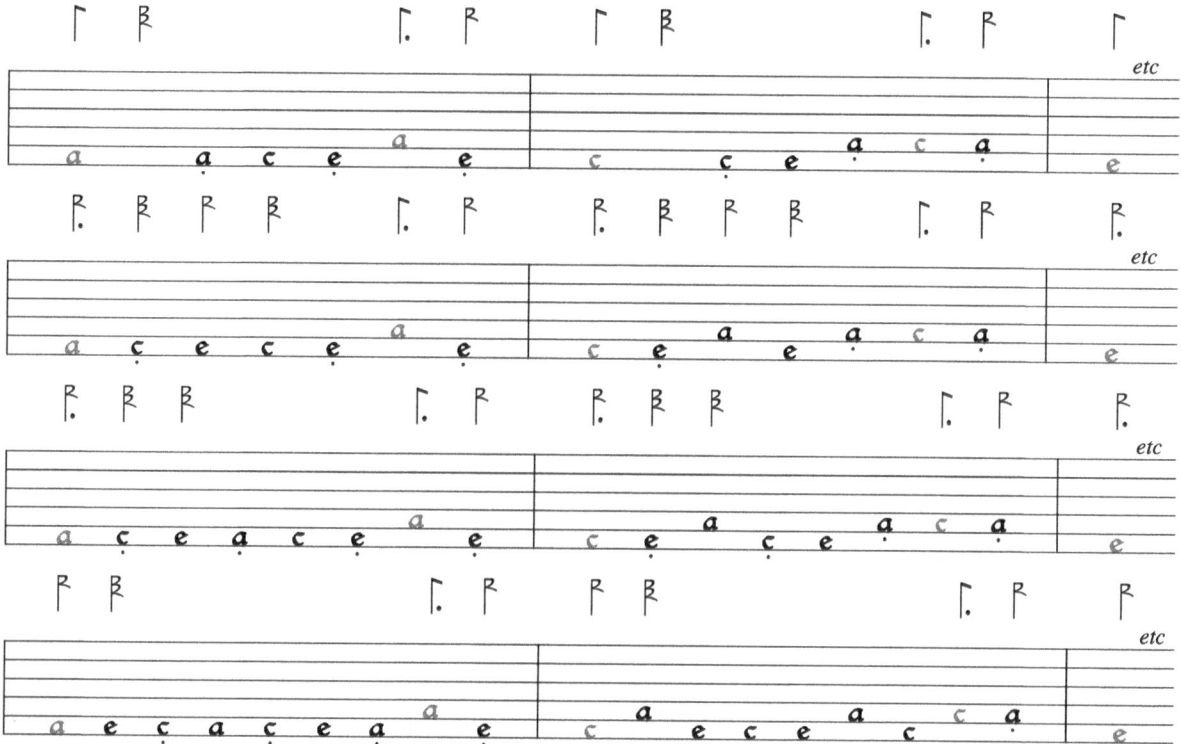

20.7. Ascending and Descending Fifths

EXPLANATIONS

As the interval of a fifth is mostly found as part of a *triad*, we can practice fifths in that context (look back at the exercises and explanations in Chapter 18). There is, however, one *cadential* formula which is commonly used and most worthwhile practicing. The melodic line is usually found in the *cantus* or tenor at a cadence:

This pattern can be understood as a *simple* descending fourth or descending fifth. The anchor notes are shown in grey:

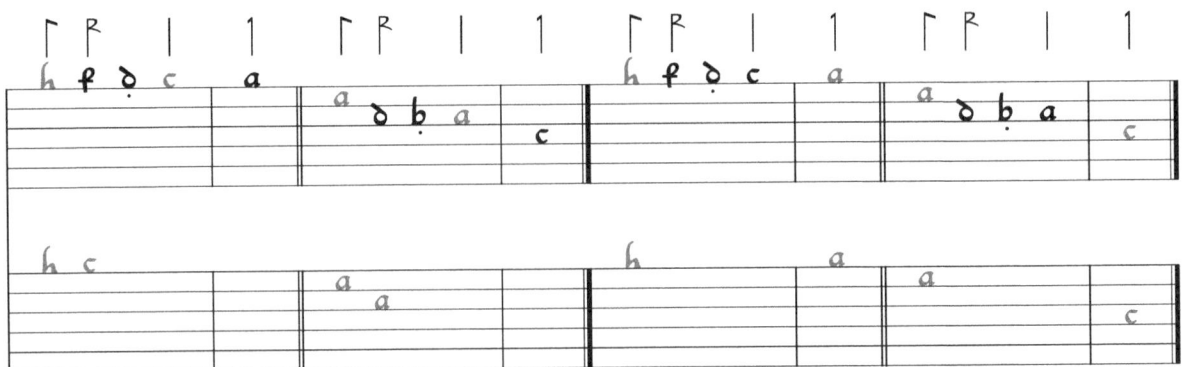

It can be treated with *simple* and *compound* figures:
The descending fourth:

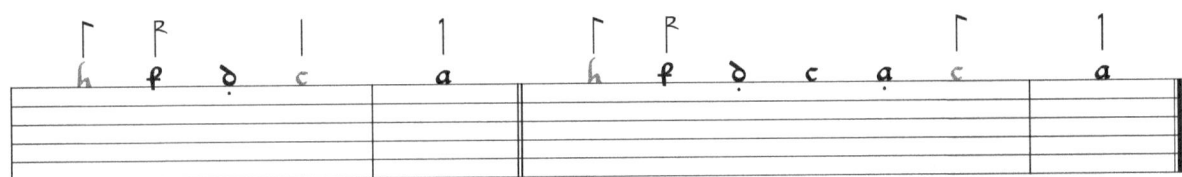

The descending fifth extends the interval being divided until the final note:

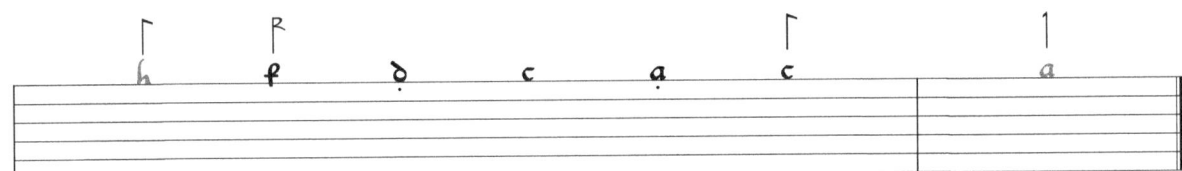

It can also ascend a minor third before descending. This results in a very common *cadential* pattern:

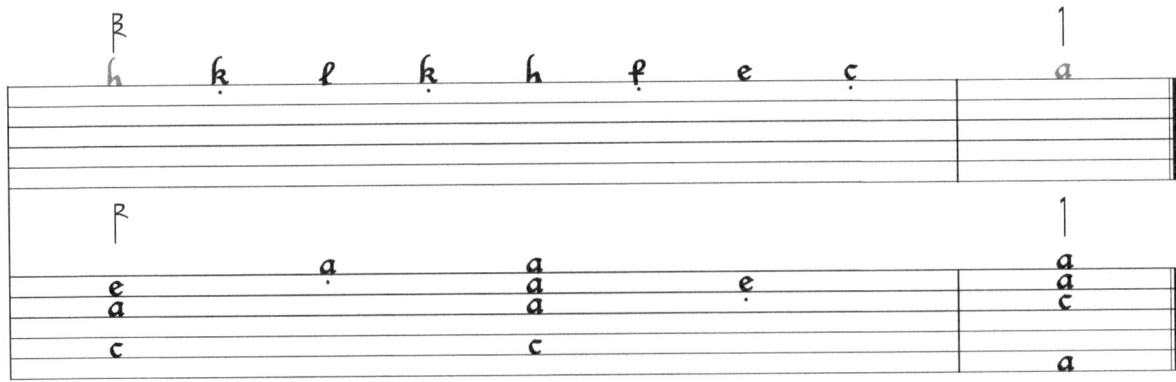

DESCENDING AND ASCENDING FIFTHS: EXERCISES

Here is a sequence which combines the last two descending fifth patterns.

The first key is fully written out, with grey anchor notes and harmony underneath:

The following four keys have harmony and grey anchor notes, waiting for the divisions to be filled in:

EXAMPLE For division practice of descending fifths.

A second sequence, in four parts, for ascending fifths. Each bar ascends a fifth and then descends a second for the next bar.

Here are the anchor notes:

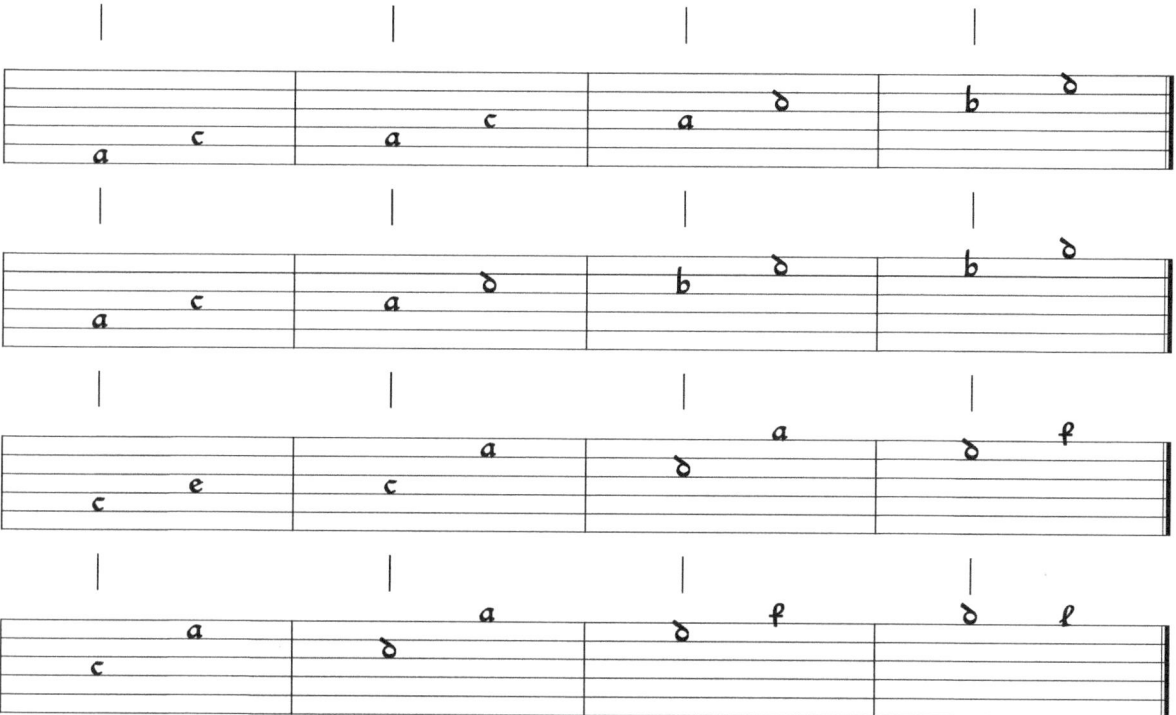

The first division is a *simple* pattern. Here is the first part of the sequence, with grey anchor notes:

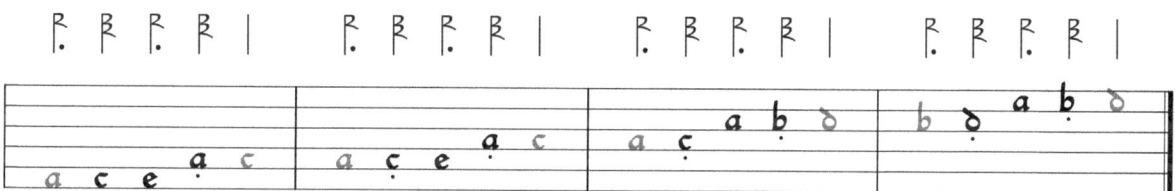

The second pattern shows how we can mix harmonic with melodic divisions.

The first note descends a fourth and then returns to ascend by step in a *triad* division to the fifth of each chord. Here is the second part of the sequence, with grey anchor notes showing the *triads* used:

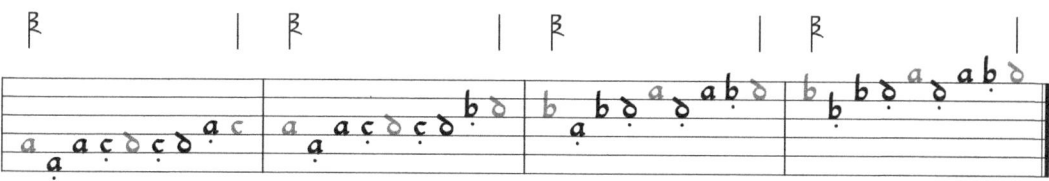

20.8. Ascending and Descending Sixths

EXPLANATIONS

Divisions on the interval of a sixth are not very common. One can look through all the pieces in Part 2: Tablature Case Studies to see how rare they are. The most helpful way of understanding their context is within a *triad*, major or minor.

A sixth exists between the third of a chord and the tonic above:

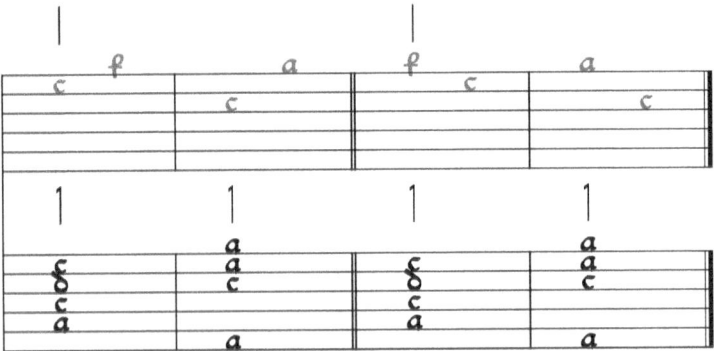

Or the fifth of a chord and the third of the chord above:

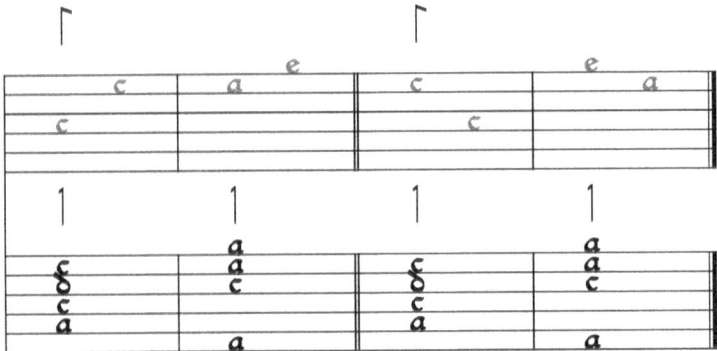

To see these intervals in context, we can look at two original pieces. Francesco da Milano, *Fantasia #30*, has a sequence which uses *simple* divisions of ascending sixths. The lower stave is an extract from the *Fantasia*; the upper stave outlines the implied *anchor notes*, all of which are marked in grey.

Francesco da Milano, *Fantasia #30*, extract:

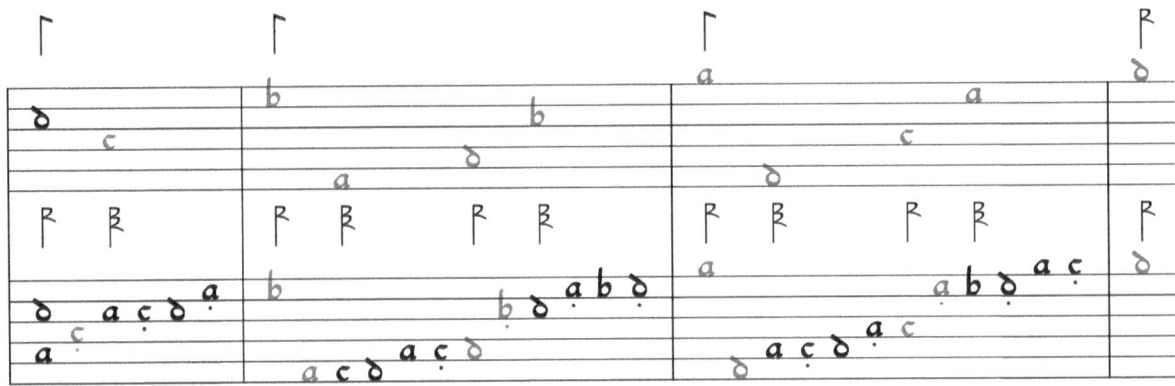

The second example comes from *Zouch his Maske.* An anonymous setting found in the *Folger-Dowland Lute-book*, (US-Ws) Ms.V.b.280 (*olim* MS 1610.1), f. 8r.
In the following example:

Upper stave: Bars 1 and 2, first time.
Lower stave: Bars 9 and 10 which are embellished version of bars 1 and 2, with implied anchor notes in grey.
In bar 1 we see a sixth treated to divisions. The third of the chord to the octave of the chord.
In bar 2 we see a normal extended *triad* division spanning an octave, but this can also be heard as dividing the same *anchor* notes found in bar 1.

ASCENDING AND DESCENDING SIXTHS: EXERCISES

In this first scale sequence for practicing ascending and descending sixths, the upper stave shows the bass with the two *anchor notes* above. The lower stave shows the division patterns. Each bar has ascending and descending sixths. The ascending sixth pattern descends a step before ascending as if it were a seventh. (The pattern of an ascending seventh is now quite familiar to us.) The intervals above the bass are a third of the chord to the octave.

The descending sixth pattern goes by step with the same rhythm as the ascending sixth. It mirrors the ascending pattern by going one step above the starting note before descending by step as if it were a descending seventh! The intervals above the bass are a third of the chord to the fifth below.

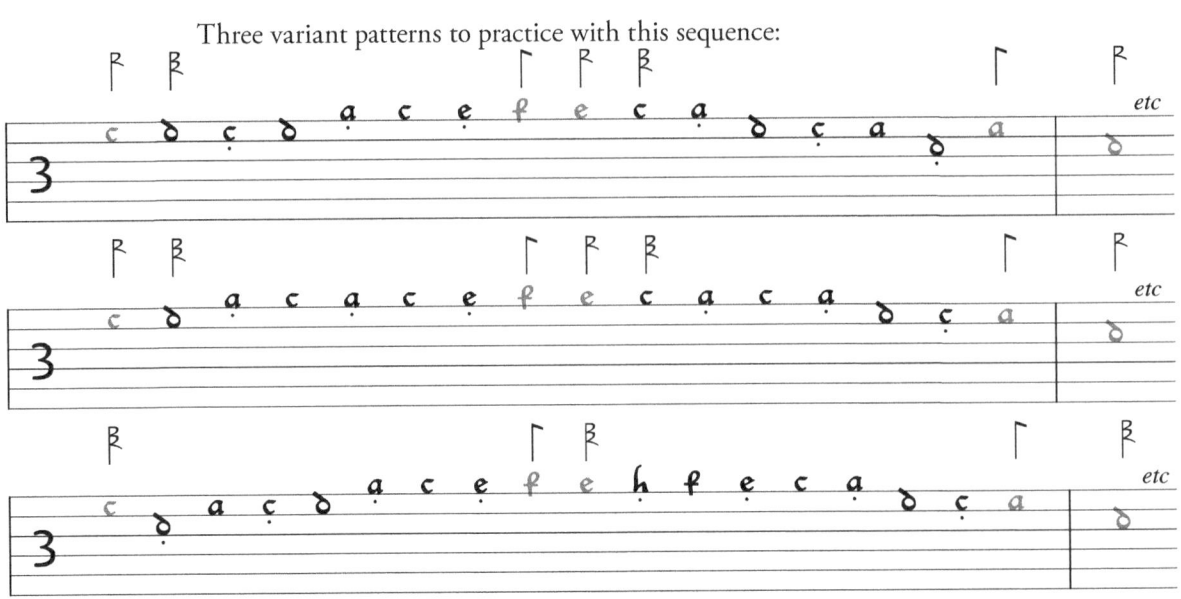

Three variant patterns to practice with this sequence:

Now we can reverse the whole sequence.

Descending from the octave of the chord down to the third.

Ascending from the fifth of the chord up to the third above.

Three variant patterns to practice with this sequence:

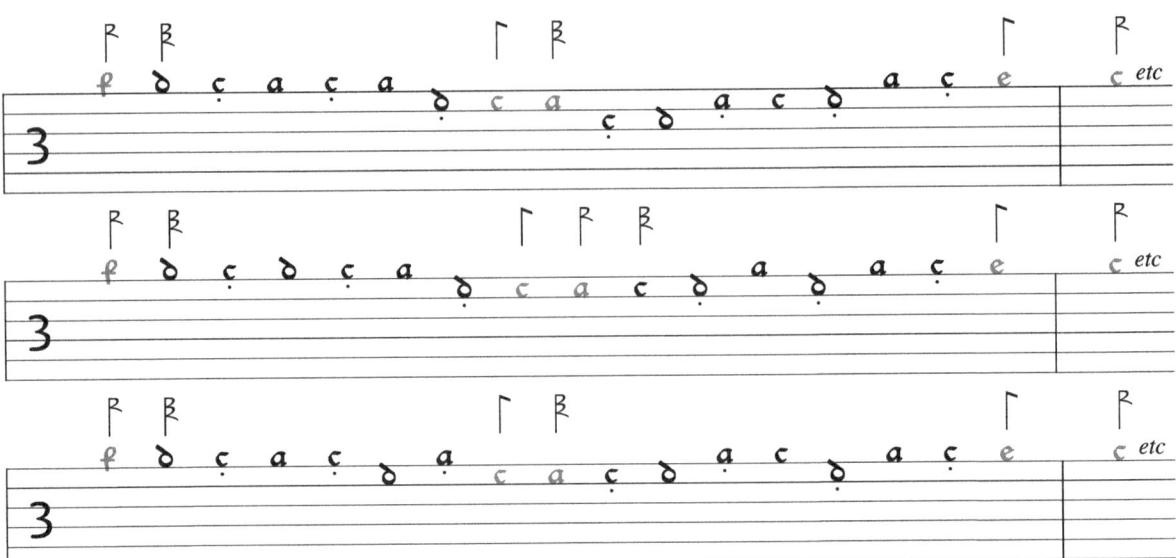

CHAPTER 21

GUIDED LESSONS IN BUILDING PATTERNS

21.1. Lesson 1 on the Ground from *The Queen's Treble* (in 10 Steps)

Patterns for practice: Interval of a fifth, ascending and descending, and simple *triad* figures.
Ground used: *The Queen's Treble* (John Johnson)
In all steps that follow, the notes of the *triad* (1, 3, or 5 of the chord) will be in grey. These are your anchor notes.

STEP 1

Here is the ground: 4 bars, chords of F, B♭, C, F. Chords I, IV, V, I in F major:

Make a recording loop, or (better) have a friend play the ground for you, repeatedly. Here are the three *triad* scales on F, B♭, and C from which we can explore some simple patterns:

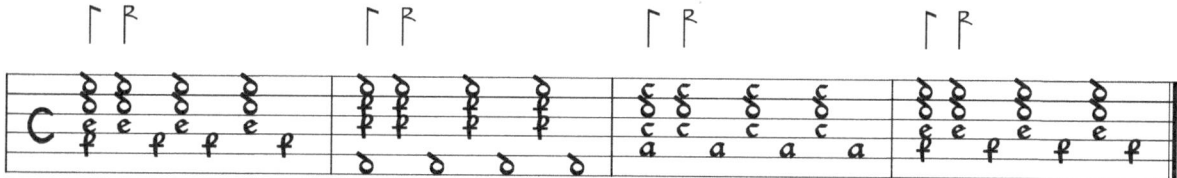

STEP 2

We will begin with an ascending scale of a fifth on each chord. Using John Johnson's treble as an excellent example, we can see that sometimes we can start on the 1 of the chord, and at other times on the 3 of the chord. This is necessary to avoid parallel octaves and fifths between the treble and ground. There are five options to consider.

Option 1

- This simplest form trains the hand in each individual ascending fifth scale.
- Each bar begins with the 1 and ends with the 5. If we only use this pattern, it will sound all right with the ground. There will be no audible parallels.
- But when we come to extend the pattern (as in Step 3 in the following), we will hear octaves when changing chords, and Johnson never allows that.

Playing with Patterns on the Lute. Nigel North, Oxford University Press. © Oxford University Press 2025.
DOI: 10.1093/9780197808764.003.0024

First option:

Option 2

- Each bar begins with the third, and only practices 3 and 5 of the *triad*, extending up to 6. This pattern is as simple as Option 1 but more naturally melodic.

Second option:

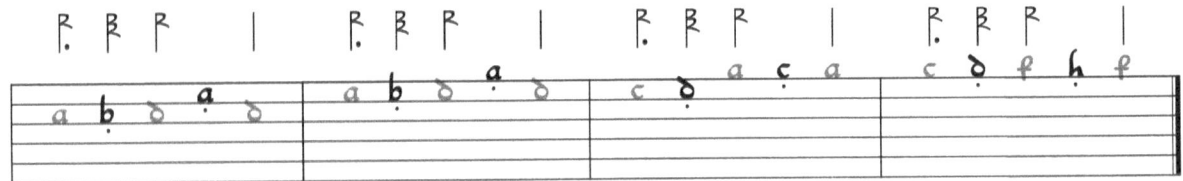

Option 3

- This option combines the previous two. Bars 1 and 4 begin with 1, bars 2 and 3 with 3 of the *triad*. This can be heard in some of Johnson's divisions and produces a very melodic line.

Third option:

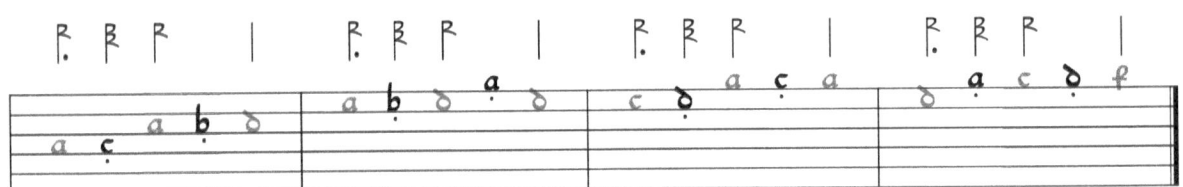

Option 4

- A rearrangement of option 3. Bars 1 and 3 begin on 3. Bars 2 and 4 begin on 1.

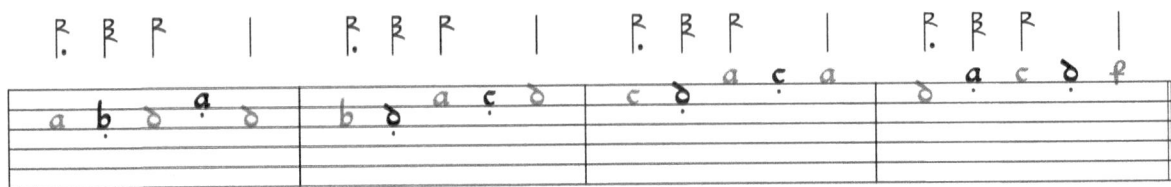

Option 5

- Each bar begins on 1 and ends on the 3 of the *triad* without parallel fifths or octaves. It is another easy pattern to repeat as each bar is the same.

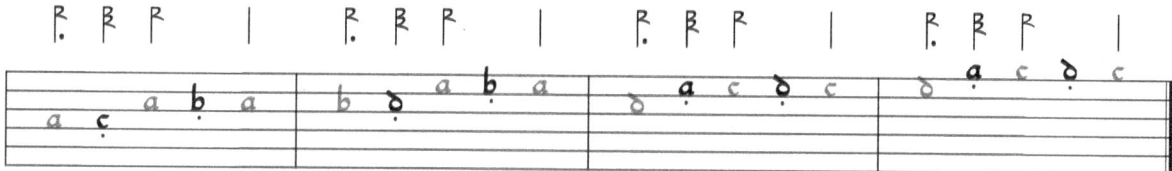

STEP 3

Extend the ascending scale with a descending arpeggio (5–3–1), just as Johnson does in his treble, using *triads* option 3 with a different bar 4:

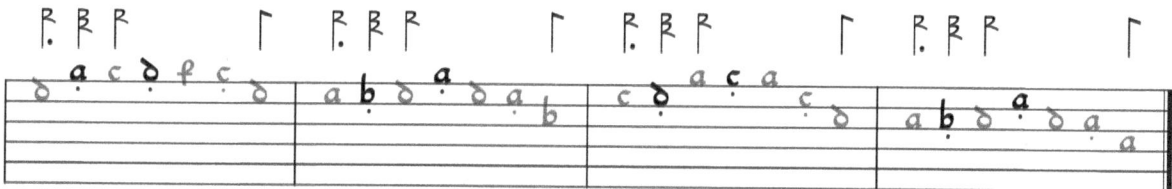

Or add a simple rhythm to connect each third of the *triad*:

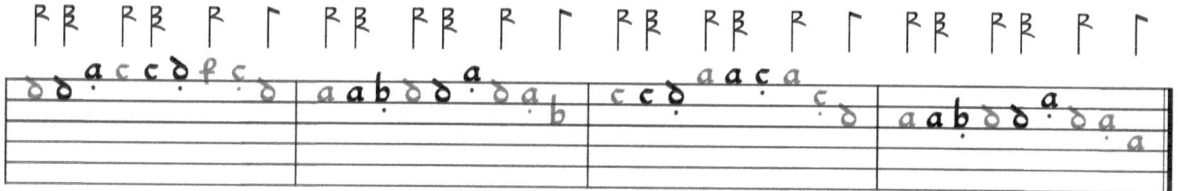

STEP 4

Using the same option as Step 3, divide the second beat with a *doubler.*

This division takes the original anchor note, descends one step, and then ascends to the next *anchor note*, at double the speed:

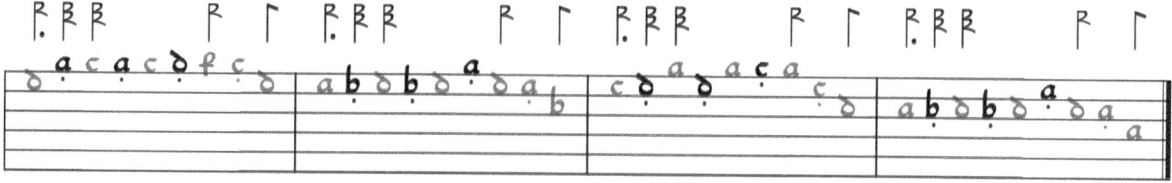

STEP 5

Add to this, dividing the first beat with a *doubler* which is constructed in the same way as Step 4:

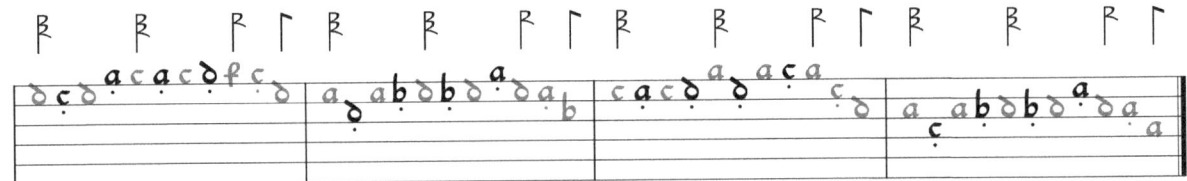

STEP 6

Add to this a simple *interval/triad* division or descending fifth, from beats 3 to 4. Now we have built a long division for each bar of the ground:

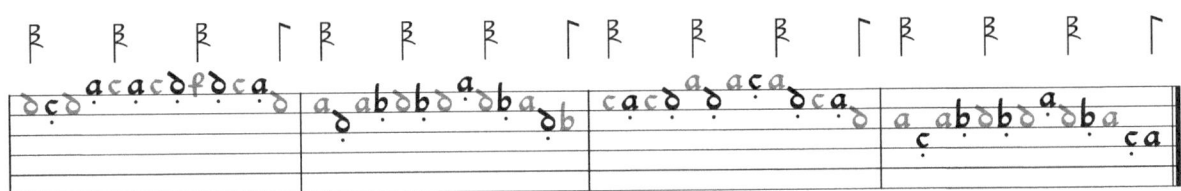

STEP 7

Now, with the confidence you have gained, try some alternatives.

Use a different division from beat 1 to beat 3. This example is constructed by descending a fourth or a sixth from the first note and then ascending by step an octave to the highest note of each *triad*, on beat 3. Don't change anything more yet. Beats 1–3, after the initial note of each bar, count as an ascending octave *simple* division.

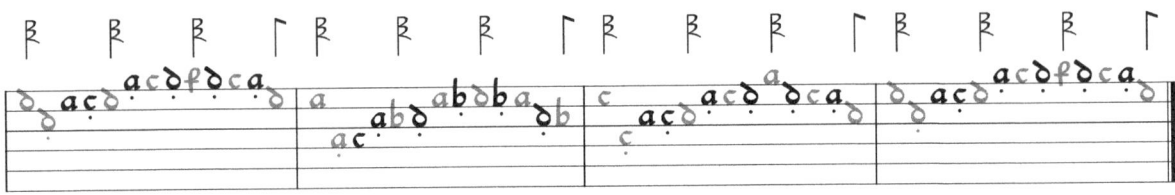

STEP 8

On the established patterns of Steps 6 and 7, you can try out different rhythms.

Here is an example in which each bar has different choices of rhythm and melody:

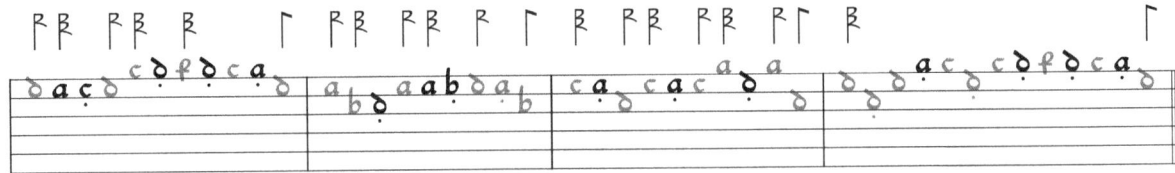

STEP 9

Using division 8 of Johnson's original as anchor notes, play and repeat using all the options we have explored in Steps 2–8:

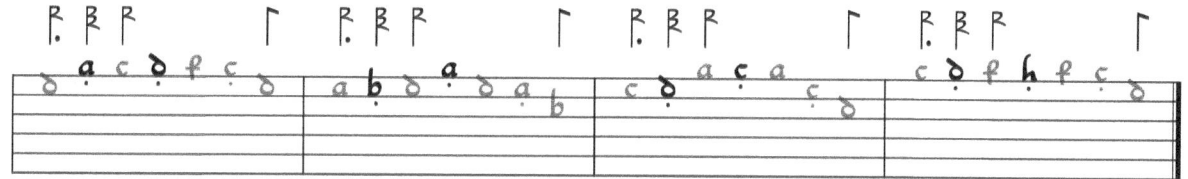

STEP 10

You can now repeat everything, in other 'keys'. Here are the grounds for G and C with an empty tablature stave for divisions!

21.2. Lesson 2 on the *Passamezzo antico* (in 17 Steps)

Figures for practice: Interval of a fifth, ascending and descending. Simple *triad* figures and *cadential* patterns. Harmonic and melodic *fillers*.

Ground used: *Passamezzo antico* in G (8 bars).

In all the following steps, the notes of the *triad* (1, 3, or 5 of the chord) will be in grey. These are your anchor notes.

STEP 1

Here is the ground. Make a recording loop, or (better) have a friend play the ground for you, repeatedly.

STEP 2

Our first aim is to play an ascending scale of a fifth on each chord, always starting with the 1 of the chord and ascending by step to the fifth. The only exception will be the cadence, which is basically I, IV, V, I. In this step we will learn some anchor notes, before learning a popular *cadential* figure.

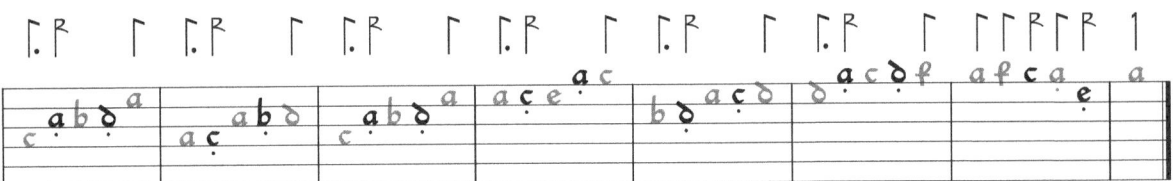

STEP 3

Let us learn some details for the ending.

In bar 7, the anchor notes 1 and 2 give us an ascending fourth followed by a descending 4th.

See the following; anchor notes, followed by simple interval divisions leading to beats 3 and 4 which can be a simple *groppo* figure:

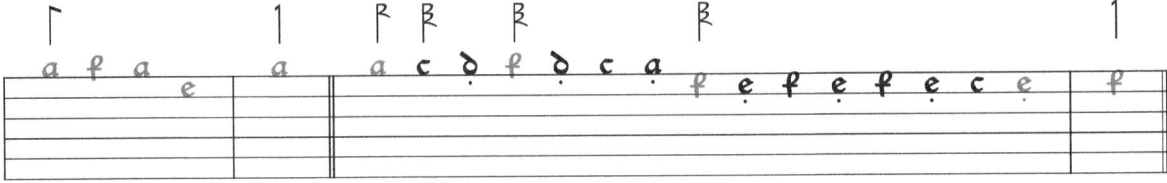

STEP 4

Bar 8 gives us the opportunity to practice different *filler* figures. Four possibilities are shown in the following. The first melodic choice would be a descending octave in its normal rhythm. To this scale we can add some chordal notes on beats 3 and 4. For an ascending octave pattern, the rhythm is a little different. To this we can, again, add some chordal notes.

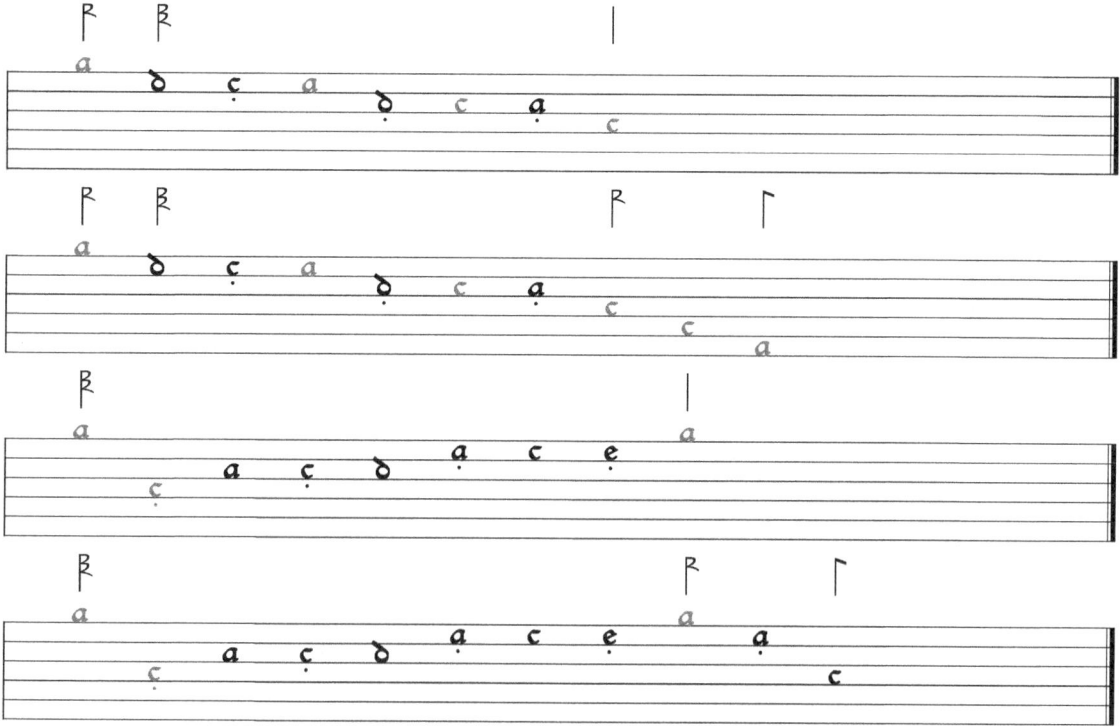

STEP 5

To all these patterns we can add *doublers*:

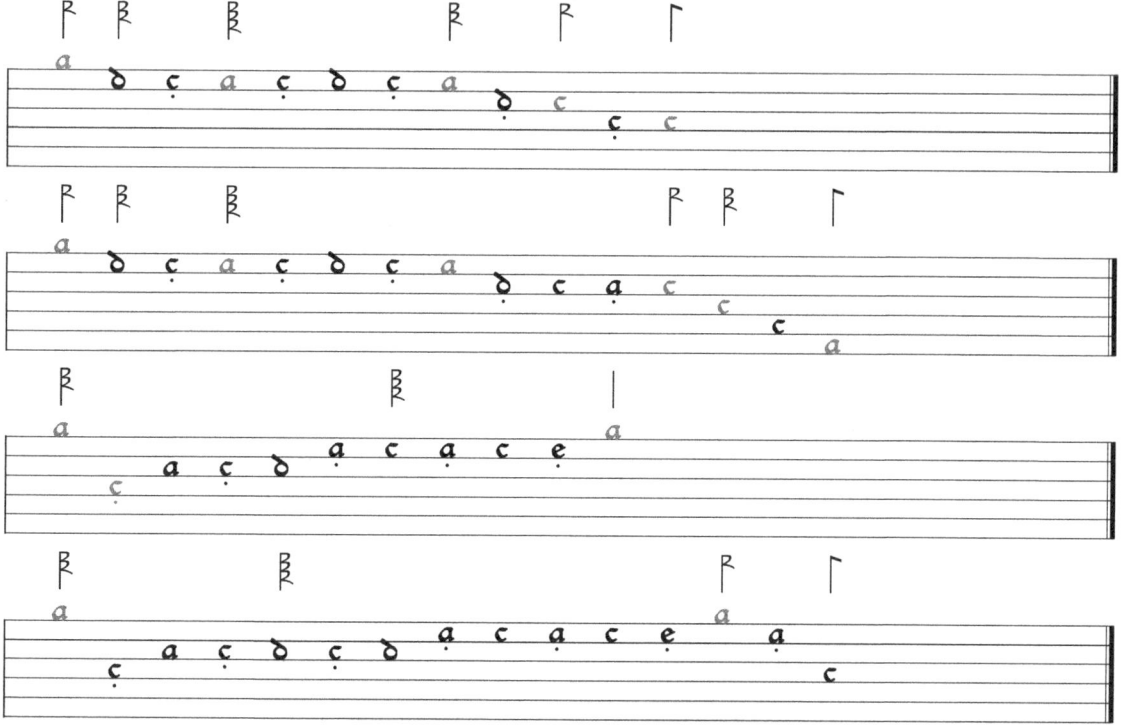

STEP 6

Our first fully divided version of the ground would include a *cadential* division as follows:

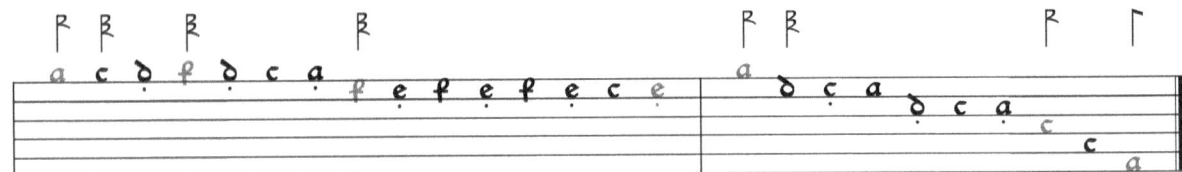

The complete first division:

STEP 7

Let us now begin to divide further. On the first two beats of each bar (bars 1–6) we can add a simple *doubler* in which the first note becomes three.

STEP 8

Add a doubler to the second beat of bars 1–6, and a *doubler* at the end of the *groppo* in bar 7:

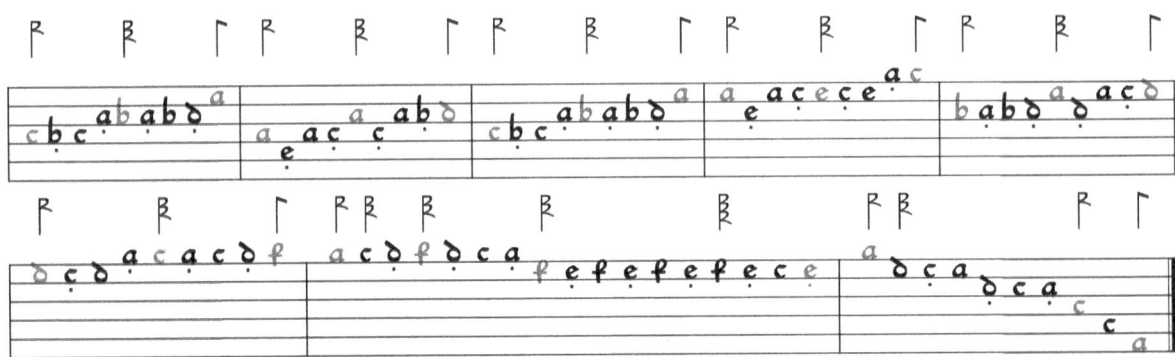

STEP 9

A *doubler* for beats 1–3 of bars 1–6, and the ascending *filler* for the final bar, and the whole ground would be:

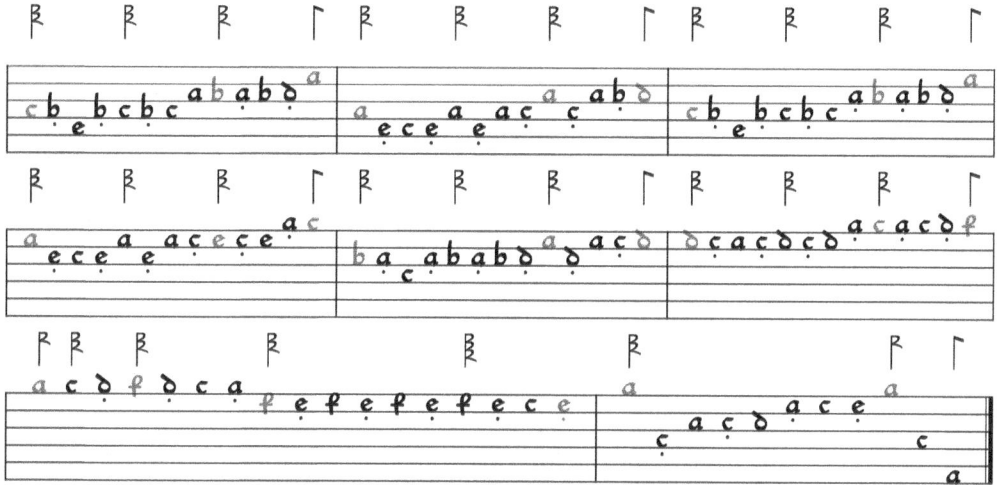

STEP 10

Now we can make a slight change of direction. Descend a fourth from the first note, and then ascend an octave to the fifth of the *triad*:

STEP 11

Descend a fourth again and then continue ascending with the figure from Step 9:

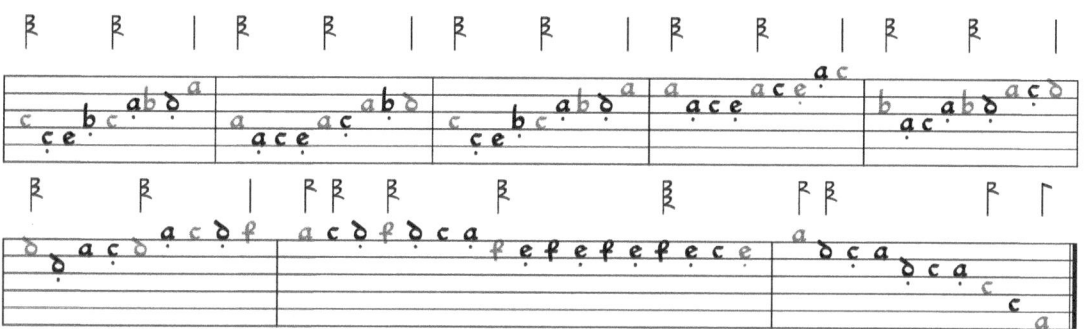

STEP 12

We can now do similar exercises with a descending fifth *triad*. Always beginning on the fifth of the *triad*, ending with the first (tonic). The first of these, using higher positions and a simple rhythm:

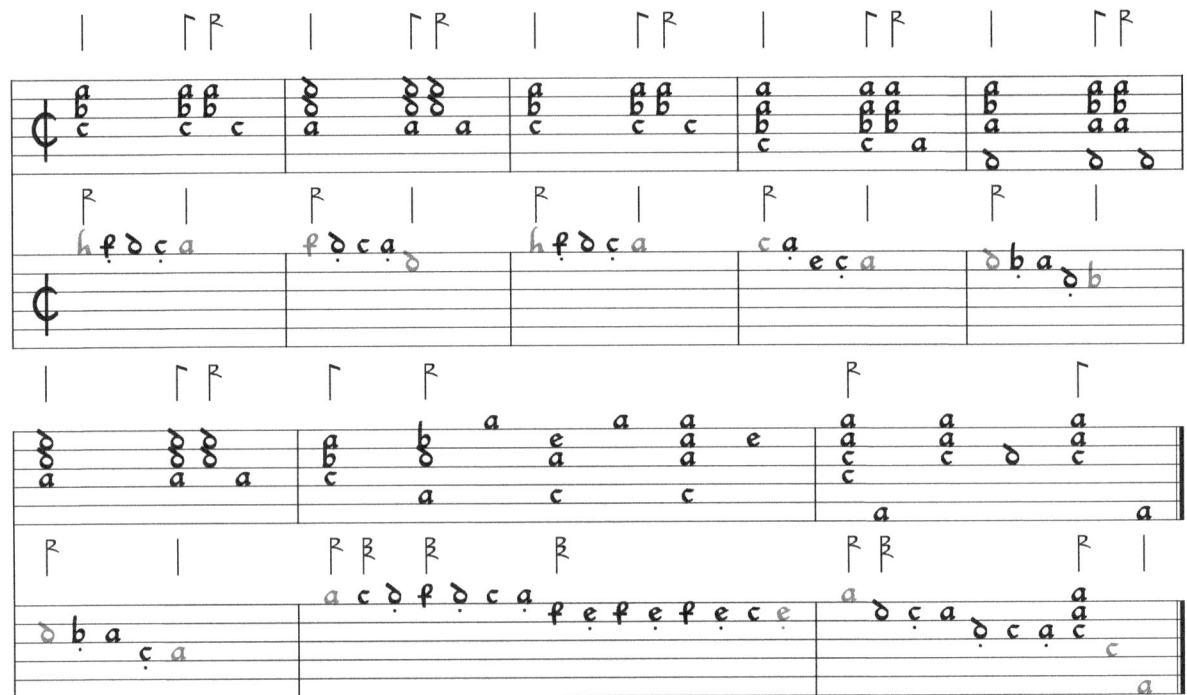

STEP 13

Similar but with another rhythm and an inverted *cadential* pattern in bar 7:

STEP 14

Adding a simple *doubler* to the first beat and a new *cadential* bar 7:

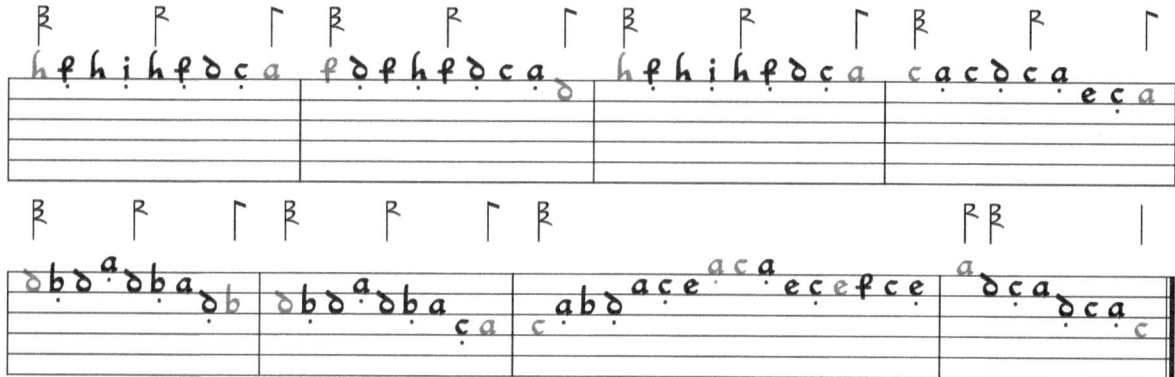

STEP 15

Add *doublers* on the third beat:

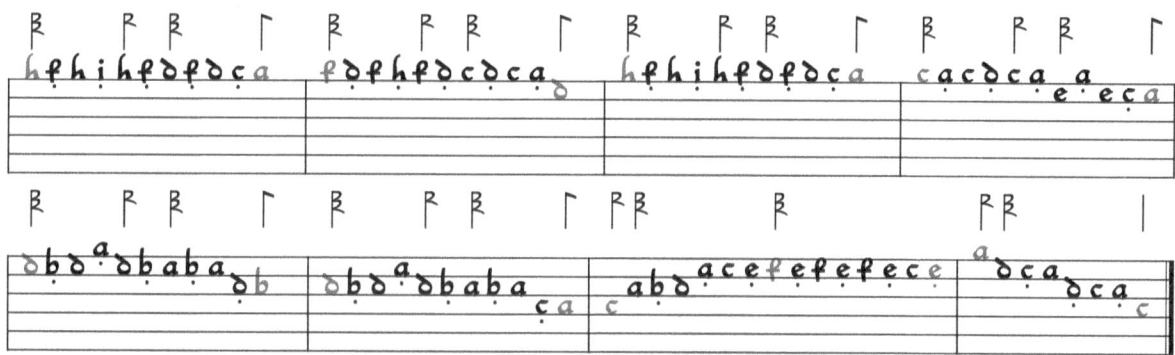

STEP 16

And finally, beats 1–3 all divided, simply, by step, and filling the interval of a descending fifth:

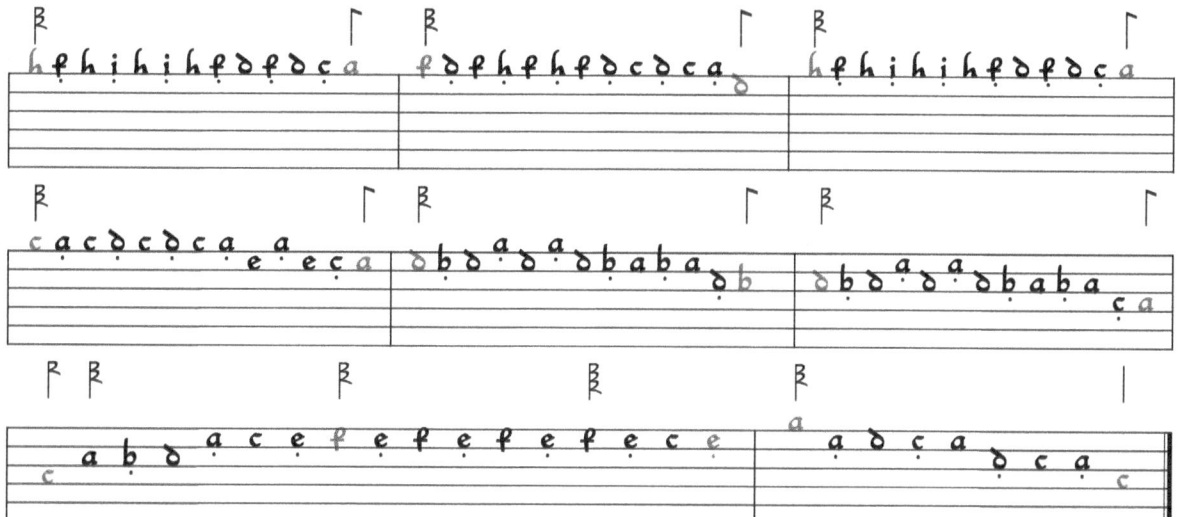

STEP 17

Now try similar training steps in two other 'keys'. Here are the grounds in C minor and D minor with an empty tablature stave for divisions!

EXAMPLE *Passamezzo antico* in C for practicing your own divisions.

EXAMPLE *Passamezzo antico* in D for practicing your own divisions.

21.3. Lesson 3: Adding Divisions to a Solo Piece (in 8 Steps)

Hans Newsidler intabulated *Ach Elslein, Liebes Elslein*, by Ludwig Senfl (first published in 1534). Newsidler's simple three-voice intabulation *Elslein liebstes, Elslein mein* was printed in two of his eight publications:

- *Ein newgeordent künstlich Lautenbuch in zwen Theyl getheylt: der erst für die anfahenden Schuler* (1536-6)
- *Das erst Buch: ein newes Lautenbüchlein mit vil feiner lieblichen Liedern für die jungen Schuler* (1544-1)

Both settings are almost identical, with more left-hand fingering indicated in 1536. We will use the 1544 version. Here is a facsimile and transcription into French tablature:

Elslein liebstes, Elsein mein, Hans Newsidler (1544):

EXAMPLE *Elslein liebstes, Elsein mein*, Hans Newsidler (1544). From: *Das erst Buch: ein newes Lautenbüchlein mit vil feiner lieblichen Liedern für die jungen Schuler* (1544-1).

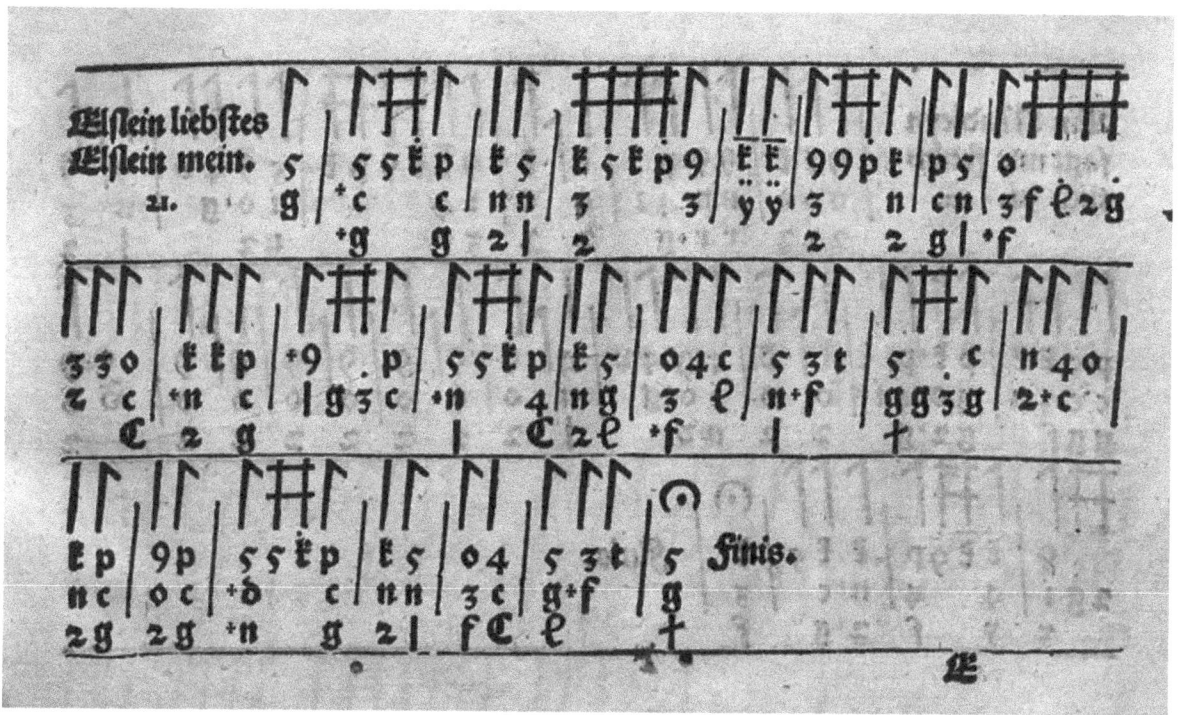

EXAMPLE *Elslein liebstes, Elsein mein*, Hans Newsidler (1544). Transcribed into French tablature.

STEP 1

Like many pieces of its kind, it gives us opportunities to practice divisions on intervals, cadences, and *static* notes. Proceeding through the piece, here are some ideas for each bar or figure with descriptions of what we can do to embellish the song.

Bar 1 is already embellished by Newsidler, we have an interval of an ascending third:

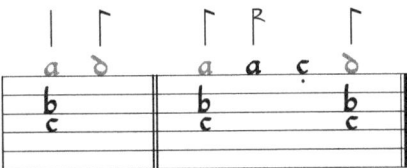

Any one of these six patterns could be applied to the *cantus* voice to ornament this bar:

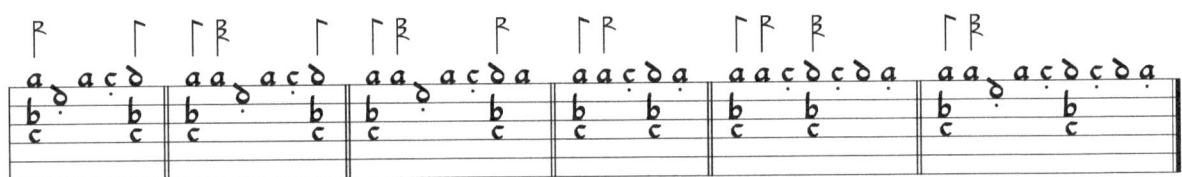

STEP 2

Bars 1 and 2:

When we consider bars 1 and 2 together and become more adventurous, we can make a *connecting* division from the *bassus* of bar 1, first chord (tablature *c*, 4th course), to the *cantus* of bar 2, first chord (tablature *c* on the 1st course). Anchor notes in grey:

From those *anchor* notes, the following three division patterns are possible.

In the first, we have a simple stepwise *connector* division covering an octave and one note. From one chord to the next:

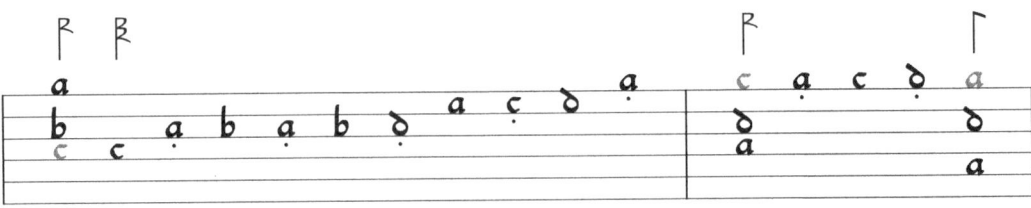

In the second division, the same journey has two more notes as the division circles back on the third course:

A similar plan is used in the third example, and the extra circling back happens at the start of the division, on the fourth course:

In each one, the *cantus* of bar 2 is treated with a simple figure of a descending second (tablature *c–a*) on the first course. This *cantus* could then be extended with another *connecting* division. Here is the evolution of bar 2:

STEP 3

Bars 3–4:

Imitating the rhythm of the division in bar 2, we can connect the *cantus* line:

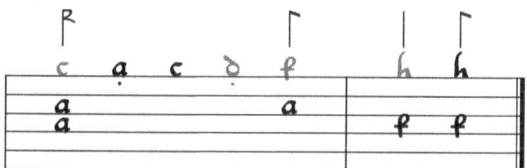

This *simple* pattern can then become one of the following three. The first division goes up to fifth fret on the first course; a simple *connector* division from the open second course. The second version does the same and then continues dividing. Version 3 is almost the same but has a *doubler* at the end of bar 3 to propel us into the following bar.

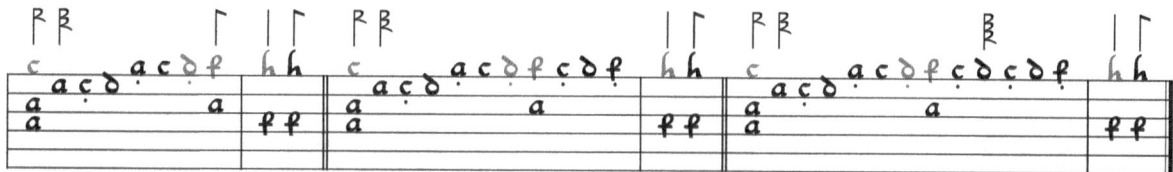

Once there, bar 4 gives an excellent chance for some simple *static* divisions.
The original, shown in the first bar here, can become any of the following examples:

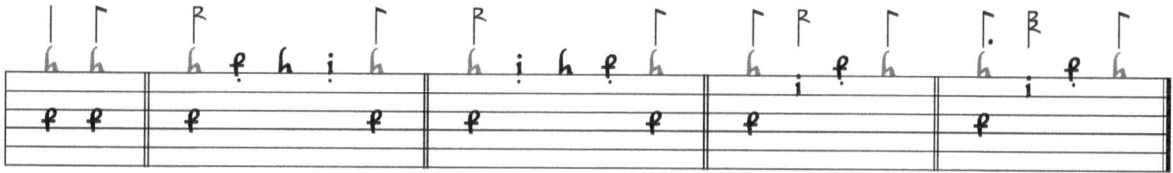

STEP 4

Bars 5–7:

Melodically we have two descending thirds, with an ascending second between the two bars and a descending second into the cadence:

These give possible embellishments, including a *connector* in the third example:

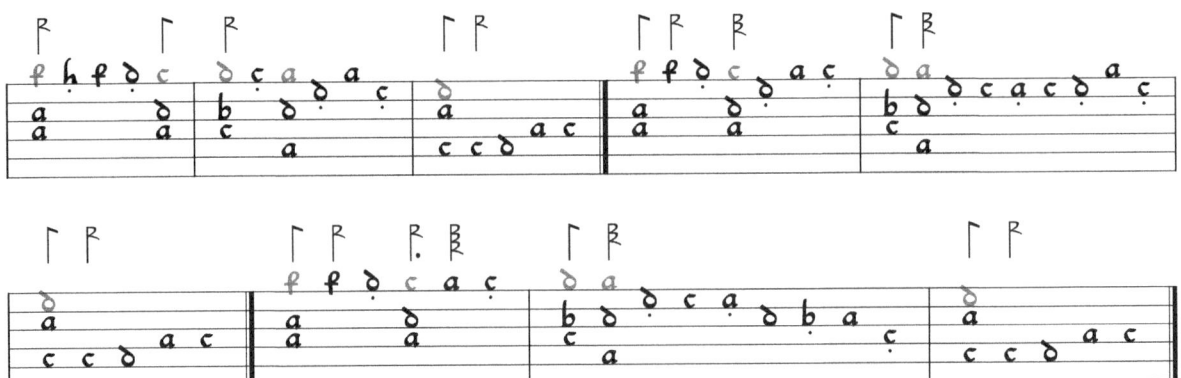

STEP 5

Bars 8–12:

Bar 8 can remain unembellished.

Bars 9–12:

Bar 9 can have a simple ascending second to join the two *cantus* notes, and an ascending third division in bar 11, giving these increasingly more complex possibilities:

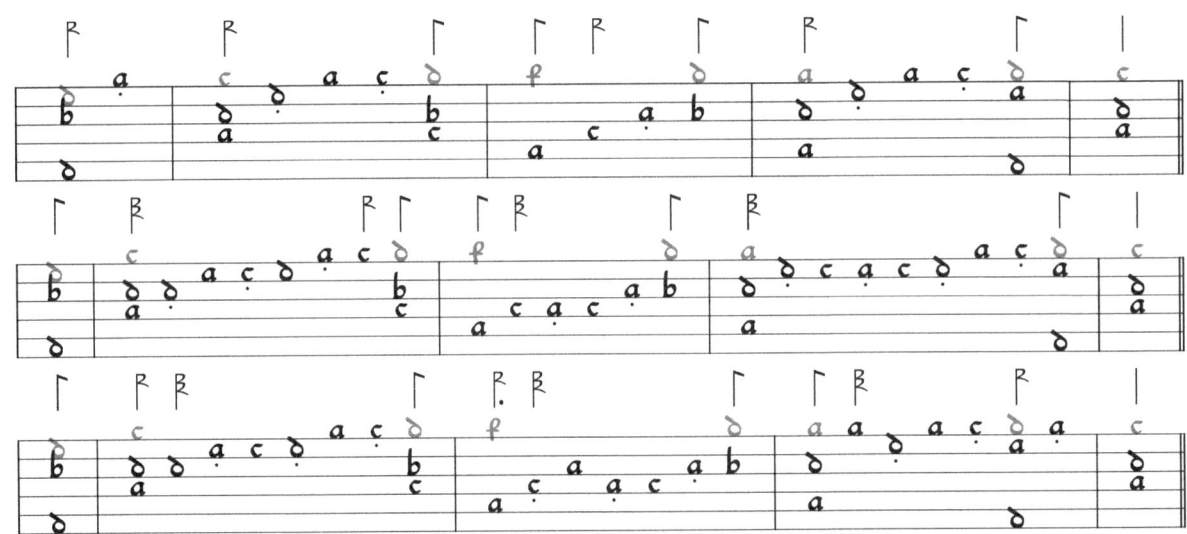

STEP 6

Bars 13–15:

Bar 14 brings us to the first of two cadences. A lutenist-composer or intabulator often shows us their favourite division patterns by using them at each cadence. Observing Newsidler's cadences, we can observe that he has a consistent repertoire of *cadential* figures. The following three examples are the most common found in Newsidler's writing:

Using the second of these examples, we could make bar 14 into this:
Bars 12–15

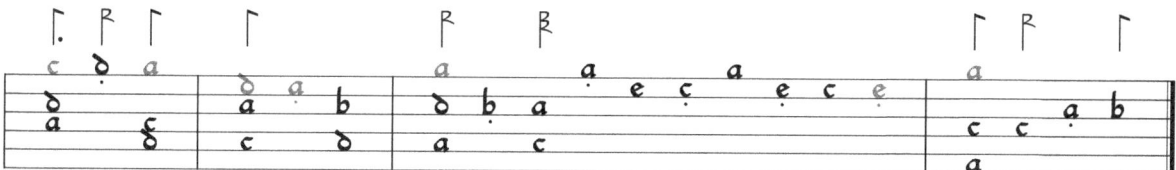

STEP 7

Bars 17–23:

Melodically these bars repeat bars 9–15, so we can embellish the same intervals but in different ways and choose a more elaborate *cadential* figure to end. In addition, bars 19–20 could include an ascending third division as shown:

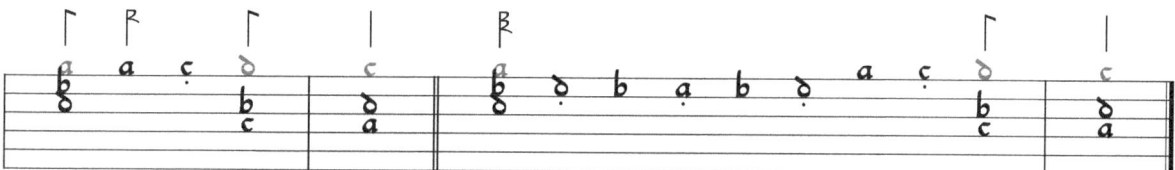

Followed by bars 20–24:

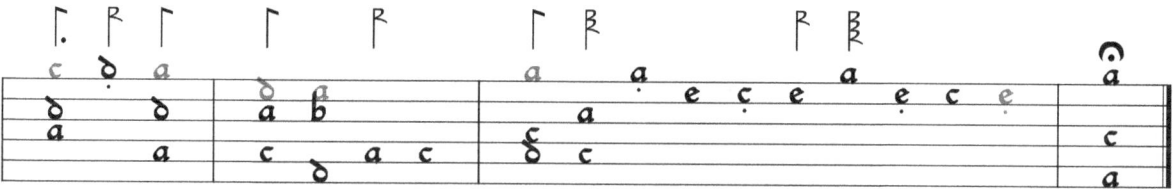

We can also embellish the bass line in bar 21, connecting the ascending fourth interval, tablature *d* on the sixth course in bar 21, to the tablature *d* on the fifth course at the start of bar 22. Here are bars 19–23:

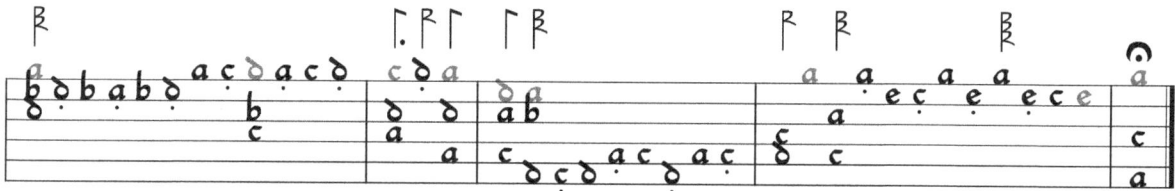

These suggestions are not exhaustive, although within the style and nature of the piece there will be a finite number of possible division figures. To end the lesson, here are three versions of the complete piece: the simple version from Newsidler and then two further ones made with some of the divisions presented earlier and, here and there, one or two new ideas.

STEP 8

Elslein liebstes, Elslein mein, Hans Newsidler (1544):

EXAMPLE *Elslein liebstes, Elsein mein*, Hans Newsidler (1544). Three versions for comparison: the original intabulation and two versions with divisions.

CHAPTER 22

PRACTICE PIECE #1: *TWINKLE, TWINKLE*

22.1. Example

With this well-known tune, familiar from its use in Suzuki violin methods, it will be easy to keep hold of the original *anchor* notes as you explore various ways of dividing. The tune is mostly composed of a *triad*, with notes 1–3–5, and 2 and 4 between. Extended only to 6, it can be seen as a fine example of a hexachord without any mutation. Before playing, observe there can be many *triad* and *static* divisions, and the principal intervals for dividing are ascending fifths and descending seconds.

Here follow three examples. In the first:

Upper stave: Anchor notes
Lower stave: The original melody:

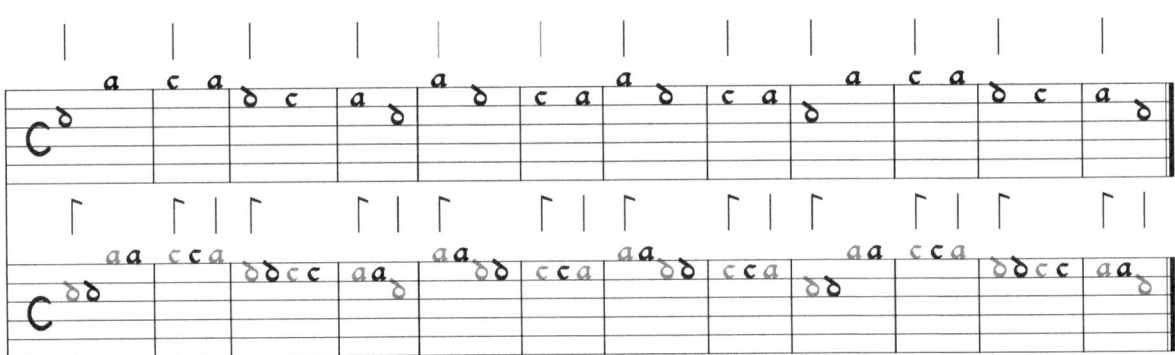

In the next two examples, you will find various division types: *static, interval, cadential, connectors,* and *doublers.* In every moment, we will find the anchor notes of the tune as the first note of all divisions, and these are marked in grey. As often found in these simple tunes, there is not much of a *cadential* suspension to divide.

First, we have two different divisions with mostly *simple interval* divisions and some *static* patterns:

EXAMPLE *Twinkle, Twinkle* with two simple division examples.

The final example has a third and fourth set of divisions which are more adventurous. Again, all anchor notes can be seen in grey and form the structure of the divided melodic line in the same way as before.

Notice in the upper stave:
   Doublers in bars 1, 5, and 9.
   Syncopations in bars 3 and 11.
   Simple *static* divisions in bar 7.
   In the lower stave:
   Harmonic *triad* divisions, bar 1.
   Syncopations in bars 5 and 7.

Divisions which do not move by step but jump a larger interval; see bars 6, 7, and 11.
   A *cadential groppo* with a *doubler* in bar 8:

EXAMPLE *Twinkle, Twinkle* with two more division examples.

22.2. Exercise

Here is the melody in six different keys, for further exploration and improvisation.

If you need harmony, it is quite simple, and almost like a *Bergamasca*, using only I, II, IV, and V. As a guide, there follows a second lute part to the C major version:

EXAMPLE *Twinkle, Twinkle* unornamented melody in many keys, for practice.

C major tune with a second lute part for accompaniment:

CHAPTER 23

PRACTICE PIECE #2: ARBEAU
PAVANE: *BELLE QUI TIENS MA VIE*

In 1589, Thoinot Arbeau (real name: Jehan Tabourot) published a dance manual, *Orchésographie*, which included the Pavane *Belle qui tiens ma vie*. The dance was printed in four voices, with text to be sung, and a drum rhythm. The form is simple, AABB, with plenty of scope for all manner of divisions. For most of the examples and exercises, we will take the *cantus* as the voice to divide. This simple melodic line rises and falls by step—so we can develop our skills for ornamenting ascending and descending seconds!

Cadences are also present, with the suspension in the *cantus* part. In fact, the cadence figures in bars 12 and 15 are like one of our previous cadence exercises. Ascending thirds and the possibility to use *doublers* and *connectors* make this a valuable learning piece. The melody will be familiar to most of us from settings by Delibes, Saint-Saens, and Warlock, so this may help our process; it is easier to improvise on a melody that we already have in our ears.

Belle qui tiens ma vie
Captive dans tes yeux,
Qui m'as l'âme ravie
D'un souris gracieux,
Viens tôt me secourir
Ou me faudra mourir.

Beautiful one, who holds my life
Captivated within your eyes,
Who has ravished my soul
With a gracious smile,
Come quickly to save me,
Otherwise I must die.

23.1. Four Versions

VERSION 1: THIS CAN BE PLAYED AS A LUTE DUET

Stave 1: The *cantus* part in notation.
Stave 2: Lute 1 (the *cantus* part intabulated).
Stave 3: Lute 2 (alto, tenor, and bass voices intabulated).

Playing with Patterns on the Lute. Nigel North, Oxford University Press. © Oxford University Press 2025.
DOI: 10.1093/9780197808764.003.0026

EXAMPLE Arbeau Pavane: *Belle qui tiens ma vie.* Version 1.

VERSION 2: THIS CAN BE PLAYED AS A LUTE DUET

Stave 1: The *cantus*, intabulated.

Stave 2: The *cantus* with first division example.

Stave 3: Lute 2 (alto, tenor, and bass voices intabulated).

EXAMPLE **Arbeau Pavane:** *Belle qui tiens ma vie.* Version 2.

VERSION 3: THIS CAN BE PLAYED AS A LUTE DUET

Stave 1: The *cantus*, intabulated.

Stave 2: The *cantus* with second division example.

Stave 3: Lute 2 (alto, tenor, and bass voices intabulated).

EXAMPLE Arbeau Pavane: *Belle qui tiens ma vie*. Version 3.

VERSION 4: THIS CAN BE PLAYED AS A LUTE DUET

Stave 1: The *cantus*, intabulated.

Stave 2: The *cantus* with third division example.

Stave 3: Lute 2 (alto, tenor, and bass voices intabulated).

EXAMPLE Arbeau Pavane: *Belle qui tiens ma vie.* Version 4.

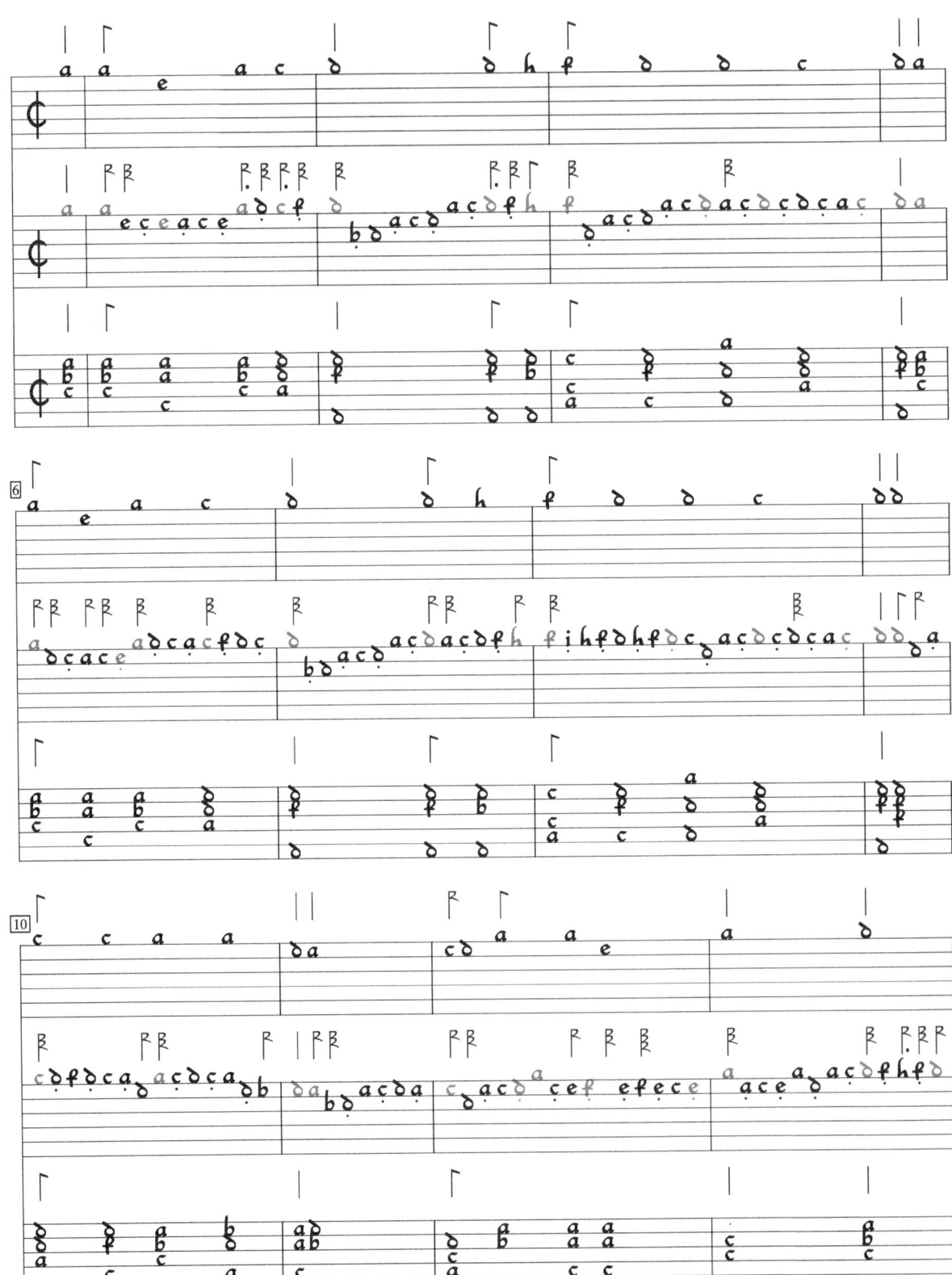

Divisions to notice and copy from these three examples:

Example 1:

> Bars 1 and 5: Alternative patterns for ascending by step.
> Bars 3 and 8, and 12 and 16: Different, simple *cadential* figures.
> Bar 10: Two ways of using the *accento*. This simple division pattern is used to embellish a descending second by ascending first.

Example 2:

> Bar 2: A simple *static* pattern.
> Bars 3 and 8, and 12 and 16: Different, simple *cadential* figures.
> Bars 9–10: An ascending seventh division.
> From bar 10 to 11: There is a very normal descending second division pattern.
> Bar 12, beats 1–2: A simple *doubler* of the original tune.
> Bars 12 and 13: Beginning to use syncopation.

Example 3:

> Bar 2 and 7: There is a *static* division which ascends an octave with a normal pattern.
> Bar 3: This imitates the previous figure but only ascends a seventh.
> Bars 3 and 8, and 12 and 16: Different, simple cadential figures.
> Bars 8 and 16: Use of a *doubler* at the end of the *groppo* both times.

EXAMPLE

The last example is for solo lute. The upper stave is a straight intabulation of the original four voices. Lower stave is, as Adrian Le Roy would call it, *more finely handled*.

Notice the various divisions used in the ornamented solo version and how some patterns can be seen in two or three different ways.

Bar 1: *Static* in the tenor.

Bar 2: *Cantus*, beats 3 and 4, ascending seconds.

Bar 3: *Static* in the tenor. *Cantus*, beats 3 and 4, simple ascending third.

Bar 4: *Cantus*, beats 3 and 4, simple *groppo*.

Bar 5: *Connector*, beats 1 and 2. Tenor, beats 3 and 4, *static* with *doubler*.

Bar 6: Beat 3, *connector*, tenor to *cantus*. Beat 4, *cantus triad*.

Bar 7: Beats 1 to 2, *triad filler*, tenor to alto. Beats 3 and 4, *connector*, alto to *cantus*.

Bar 8: Beat 1, *cantus*, anticipating descending second. Beats 3 and 4, simple *groppo* figure
from bar 4 with added *doubler*.

Bar 9: *Static* in the tenor.

Bar 10: Beats 3 and 4, tenor, simple interval patterns.

Bar 11: Bass, descending third.

Bar 12: *Cantus*, ascending third. Beats 3 and 4, *groppo cadential* figure with *doubler*.

Bar 13: Beats 1 and 2, *connector*, tenor to *cantus*. Beats 3 and 4, *cantus triad*, and/or descending second to beginning of bar 14.

Bar 14: Beats 1 and 2, *cantus triad*, and/or descending second, imitating end of bar 13. Beats 3 and 4, descending second (to 1st beat, bar 15); standard figure goes up a fourth and down a fifth, with a *doubler*.

Bar 15: Bass, descending third, as in bar 11. Beats 3 and 4, *cantus, static*.

Bar 16: Beats 1 and 2, *cantus*, ascending third. Beats 3 and 4, *groppo* with *doubler*.

Bar 17: *Filler/connector/*descending octave.

EXAMPLE Arbeau Pavane: *Belle qui tiens ma vie.* Version 5, for solo lute.

23.2. Exercises

You can now practice divisions in two ways.

Return to Version 1 and play the *cantus* (perhaps with a 2nd lute playing the A/T/B intabulation with you). After this, use the preceding simple solo intabulation and begin to add some *simple* divisions.

CHAPTER 24

GROUND #1: *LA GAMBA* (CARA COSA)

This is an excellent ground for beginners to practice many basic patterns. Apart from the two cadences, all chords are *triads* (5/3 or root position chords), and the associated treble part (*cantus*) moves simply by step and gives scope for many different figures. Here is the ground with a final of G. The simple *cantus* part presented here will serve as the *anchor notes* for all division examples which follow. You can also use this first version to try your own divisions before you read any of the following suggestions.

Playing with Patterns on the Lute. Nigel North, Oxford University Press. © Oxford University Press 2025.
DOI: 10.1093/9780197808764.003.0027

24.1. Examples and Exercises

La Gamba, ground, and *anchor notes* for making divisions:

EXAMPLE *La Gamba*, ground and *anchor notes* for making divisions.

There is a variety of divisions which can be played over this ground:

- *Static*: Bars 1–2, 8–10.
- Ascending seconds: Bars 2–5, 10–13, 17–18, 21–22.

- Descending seconds: Bars 5–8, 13–16, 18–20, 22–24, 18–20.
- *Cadential groppo*: Bars 27–28, 31–32.
- *Triad* figures on almost any note as the *cantus* moves slowly and is part of a *triad*.
- All the above can have varied rhythm, dotted pairs of notes, and syncopations.

EXAMPLES

Before finding and improvising your own versions, here are some examples to practice. First, *static* figures for bars 1, 2, 9 and 10.

  (1) Four examples with an even rhythm.
  (2) Four examples with the same varied rhythm.
  (3) Four examples with syncopations.
  (4) An example showing the use of a *static groppo* figure.

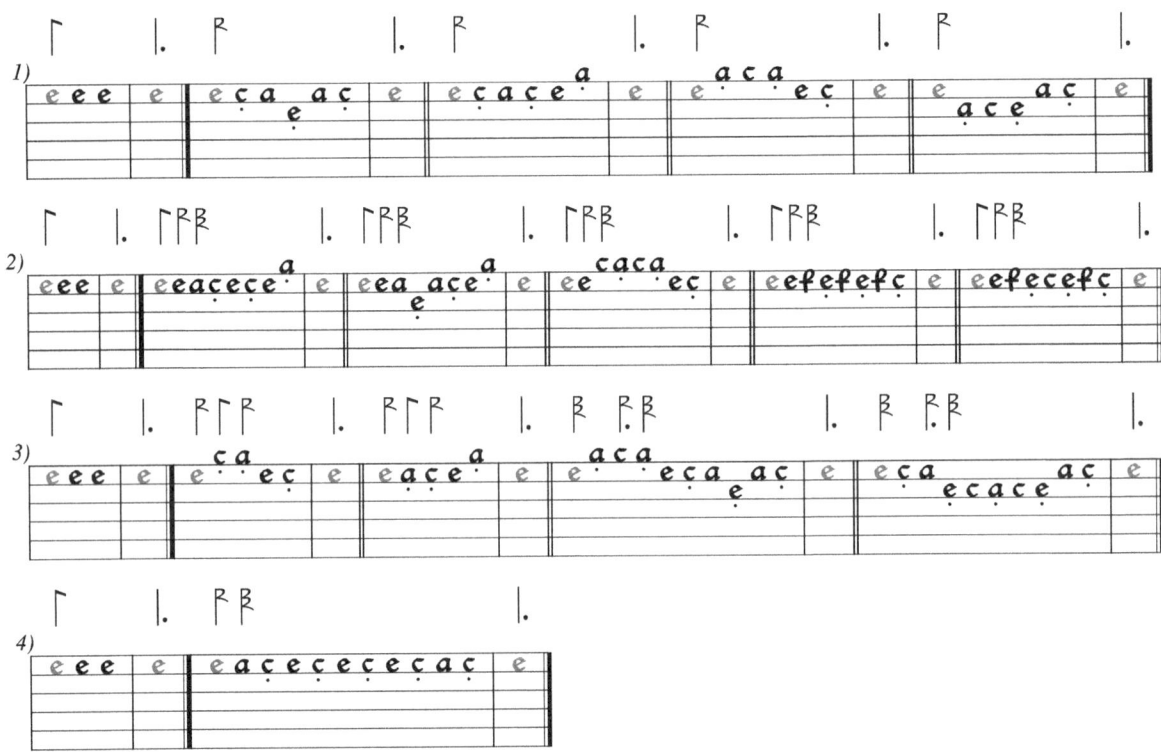

EXAMPLES

Figures for ascending and descending seconds in bars 3–8, and 11–15.

  The examples move by step except for one move of a third in each division.

  Examples 1–3 have the same rhythm. (1) and (2) are combined to make (3), ascending and descending differently.

  (4) is just a flowing, equal rhythm version of the previous three.

  (5) is a *doubler* of 4.

EXAMPLE *La Gamba*, figures for ascending and descending seconds in bars 3–8, and 11–15.

EXAMPLES

In the third set of examples, we look at bars 18–20 and 22–24, where the melody has a descending tetrachord.

(1) From the anchor note, we go an octave beneath and then play an ascending scale of a seventh to reach the next *anchor note*. This common pattern is very easy on the fingers!

(2–4) These are all connected.

In (2) we go a third above the first two anchor notes, consonant with the harmony,

The third *anchor note* has a *static* figure on G.

(3) A dotted rhythm is added to the figures of (2).

(4) Begins the same as the previous, but each step gets faster. The second and third figures are both *static*.

(5) Synopation is introduced.

EXAMPLE *La Gamba*, bars 18–20 and 22–24, where the melody has a descending tetrachord.

EXAMPLES

In the final example of division ideas for La Gamba, here are three varied sets of divisions. In all three examples I have kept the *anchor notes* mostly on the beat and then divided from there. Occasionally a division goes further afield, as an encouragement to your creativity! Look on these versions, not so much as compositions, but more as samples of possibilities.

Example 1

Bars 18–19: When descending by step, it is so natural to use the figure which goes down an octave from the first anchor note and then ascending a seventh with a scale to the second anchor note. Once your fingers and ears digest this pattern for descending by step, future use will be easy.

Example 1:

EXAMPLE *La Gamba*, first set of division examples.

Example 2

Bar 2: This shows the use of the *groppo* to ascend a second, without it being a cadence.

Bars 5 and 6: both have comparable descending patterns.

Bars 10–16: These are simple *triad* figures with some syncopation, similar to examples found in Ortiz and the *Contrapunto* from *Fronimo* (see Part 2: Tablature Case Studies).

Bar 17: A standard figure for ascending by step.

Bars 18–19: A simple version of an *accento* figure. An *accento* is when you ascend by step from the first anchor note before going down to the second anchor note.

Bars 22–23: A more extended version of the *accento* figure, by going up a fourth before descending, all by step.

Bars 27 and 31: Two different *cadential groppo* solutions, including a typical *doubler* at the end of bar 31.

Example 2:

EXAMPLE *La Gamba*, second set of division examples.

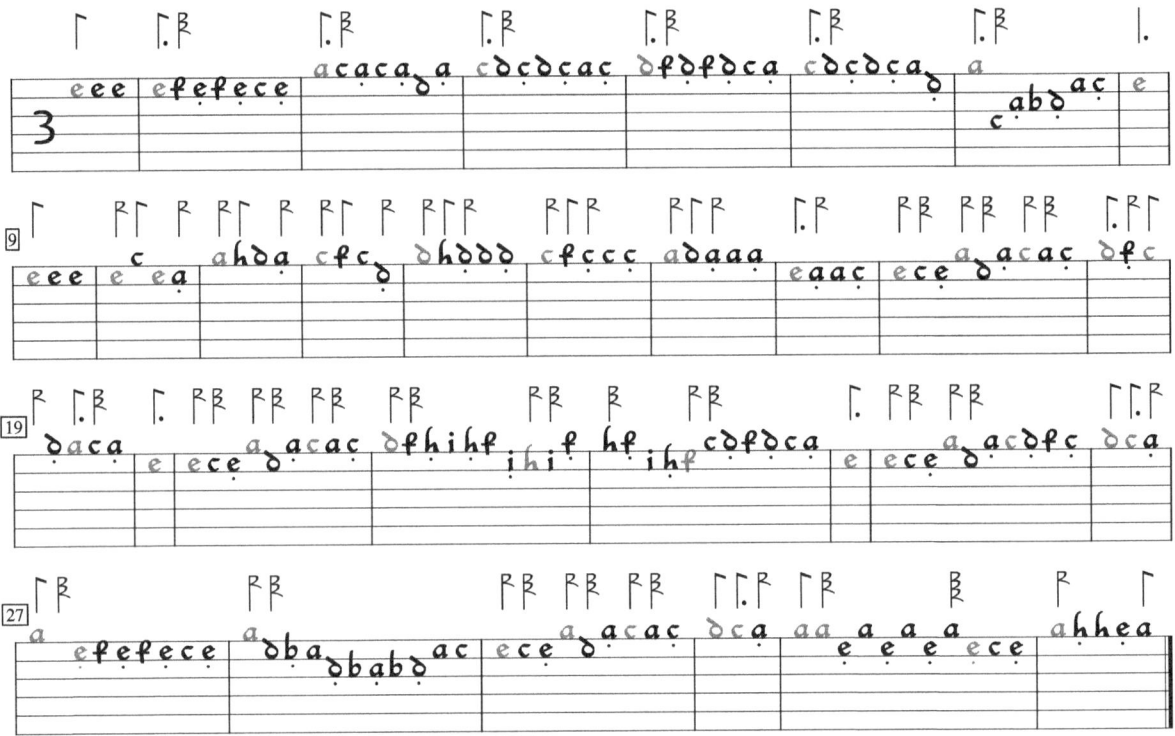

Example 3

Bar 6: A similar figure as in bars 18–19 of Example 1, but this is for ascending a third by going down a fifth and then ascending with a scale.

Bars 13 and 14: A three-note figure which has two notes twice as fast as the other note became known as a *corta*. (Bach's Third Brandenburg Concerto, in G major, 1st movement, has a typical *corta* theme.) I used some of these, in a *triad* division, in bars 13 and 14.

Each of these three examples has a final bar *filler*, all different.
Example 3:

EXAMPLE *La Gamba*, third set of division examples.

EXERCISE

Here is the ground, in G, F, and C with *anchor notes* from which you can practice divisions.

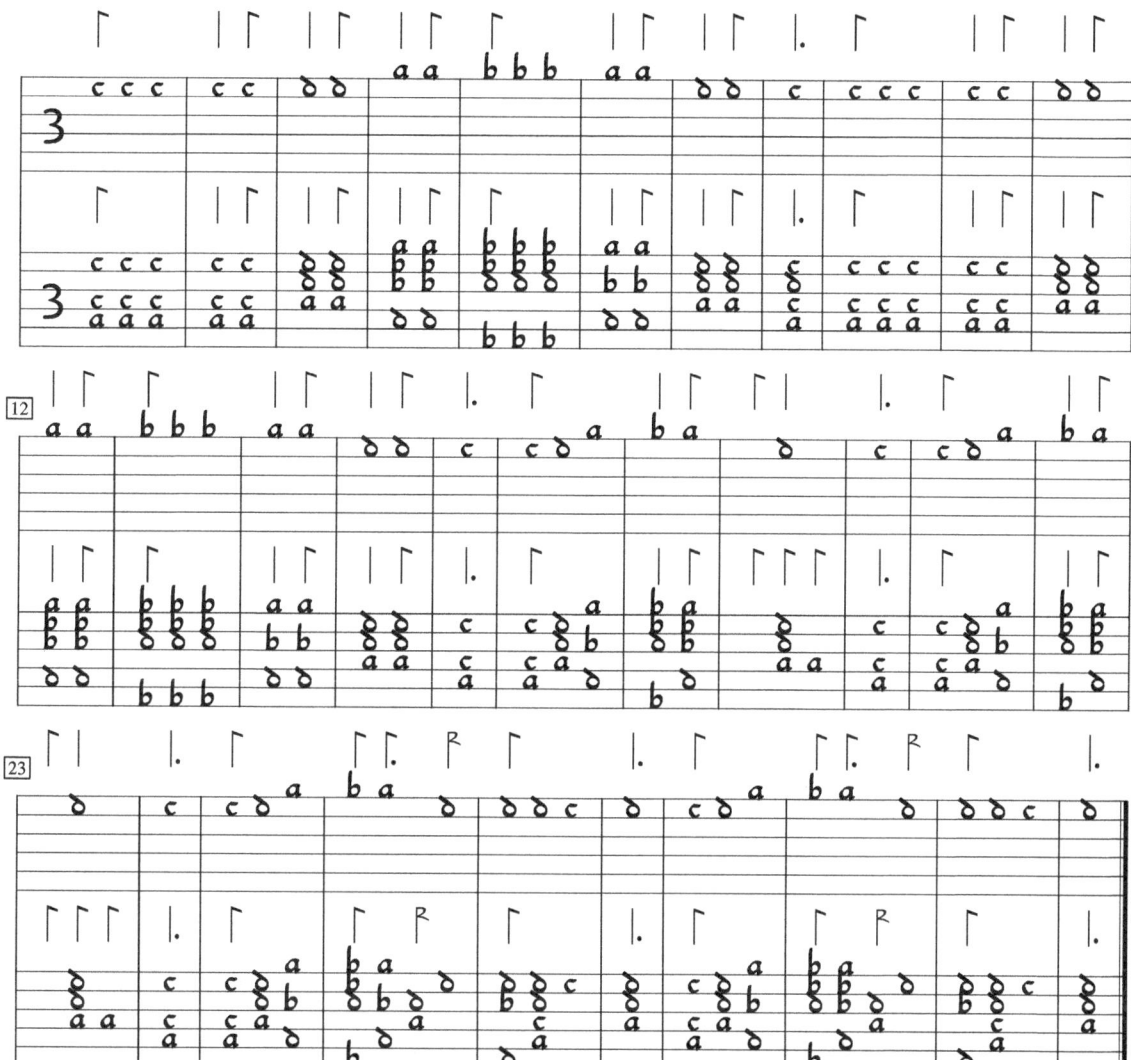

EXAMPLE Ground, in G, F, and C with *anchor notes* from which you can practice divisions.

CHAPTER 25

GROUND #2: *PASSAMEZZO ANTICO*

25.1. As a Treble and Ground Duet

La Gamba was in triple time and the *Passamezzo antico* is in duple time. This will give us opportunities for a different variety of rhythmical figurations; an alternative puzzle to solve! Before venturing into greater freedom, let us first practice using *static* figures. Here is an example: a ground (in C) with a simple line of *anchor* notes in grey as part of a division using *static* figures only, except for the final cadence, bar 14, where we need a *cadential groppo*.

Playing with Patterns on the Lute. Nigel North, Oxford University Press. © Oxford University Press 2025.
DOI: 10.1093/9780197808764.003.0028

EXERCISES

Here are three exercises to practice, in the same key. Each example has a different set of *anchor notes* to which you can find *static* patterns and *cadential* figures. Upper stave, second lute and harmonic context; lower stave, *anchor notes* which will form the basis of your improvised *static* divisions:

EXAMPLE *Passamezzo antico*, as a treble and ground duet, with examples of *static* patterns.

DIVISIONS OVER A HARMONIC GROUND

When we have a vocal line to ornament, such as the *cantus* part in *La Gamba* or the *anchor notes* in the preceding exercises, we have notes from which our divisions start and end. When dividing on the *Passamezzo antico*, or any other ground, we can do so over the harmony of the ground, not just one voice.

EXERCISE

When working from harmony alone, our choices of division figures will be more like *connectors* (divisions which connect two chords). These can be in many forms: *triad*, *interval*, *static*, and *cadential*. The first and last notes of these divisions are chosen from the notes in the harmony. As in *La Gamba*, apart from the final cadence, all harmonies are root position *triads*; these give us excellent opportunities to search out *triad* figures. The *Passamezzo* has a slow harmonic rhythm which allows us to divide in a variety of ways over the same harmony. In the following exercise, there is a suggested part of *anchor* notes. These notes do not move by step but are notes from the harmony. From these anchor notes you can find your divisions.

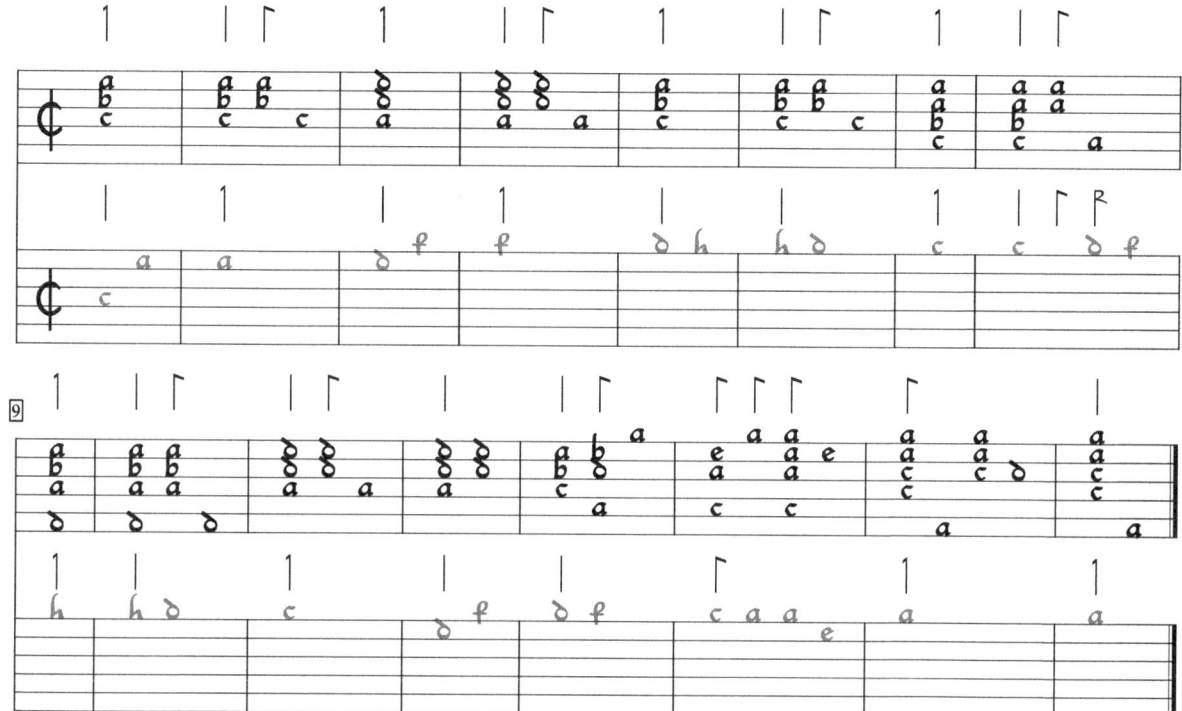

EXAMPLE

Using the same outline of *anchor* notes, here as a possible set of divisions to study; going from bar to bar, let us first identify what types of divisions are being used.

> Bars 1–2: *Triad* followed by an ascending seventh.
>
> Bars 3–4: Imitates bars 1 and 2, *triad* divisions ending with an ascending scale (a 5th this time).
>
> Bars 5–6: *Triad*, and then bar 6 is a descending scale ornamented with simple *accenti* (one step up before going one step down).
>
> Bars 7–8: *Triad* again, with bar 8 ending with an ascending *connector* octave scale.
>
> Bars 9–11: All *triad*.
>
> Bar 12: An ascending octave up to tab *f* on the first course.
>
> Bar 13: *Anchor* notes ascend a second with a *simple* division, then descend a third to the next bar using two *accenti*.
>
> Bar 14: A very common type of double *groppo* over the whole bar.
>
> Bar 15: Begins with a *static*, down a fourth and then up again to tablature *a* on the first course, followed with a final *triad* figure, leading to the closing chord at bar 16.

The first example of divisions on a ground, with anchor notes in grey:

EXAMPLE The first example of divisions on a ground, with anchor notes in grey.

The second example, with added *doublers* to practice, uses all three rhythmic levels of divisions. Compare this with the previous, simpler example and notice the differences. Mark the score with the types of divisions you notice.

EXAMPLE The second example of divisions on a ground, with anchor notes in grey.

EXERCISES

You can now explore your own creativity. Practice divisions over the *Passamezzo antico* ground, using similar methods and patterns demonstrated in the preceding two examples. Here is the ground in three tonalities. The upper staves are for Lute 2, the lower staves for you to invent a Lute 1, treble part:

Passamezzo antico: Version 1 in C:

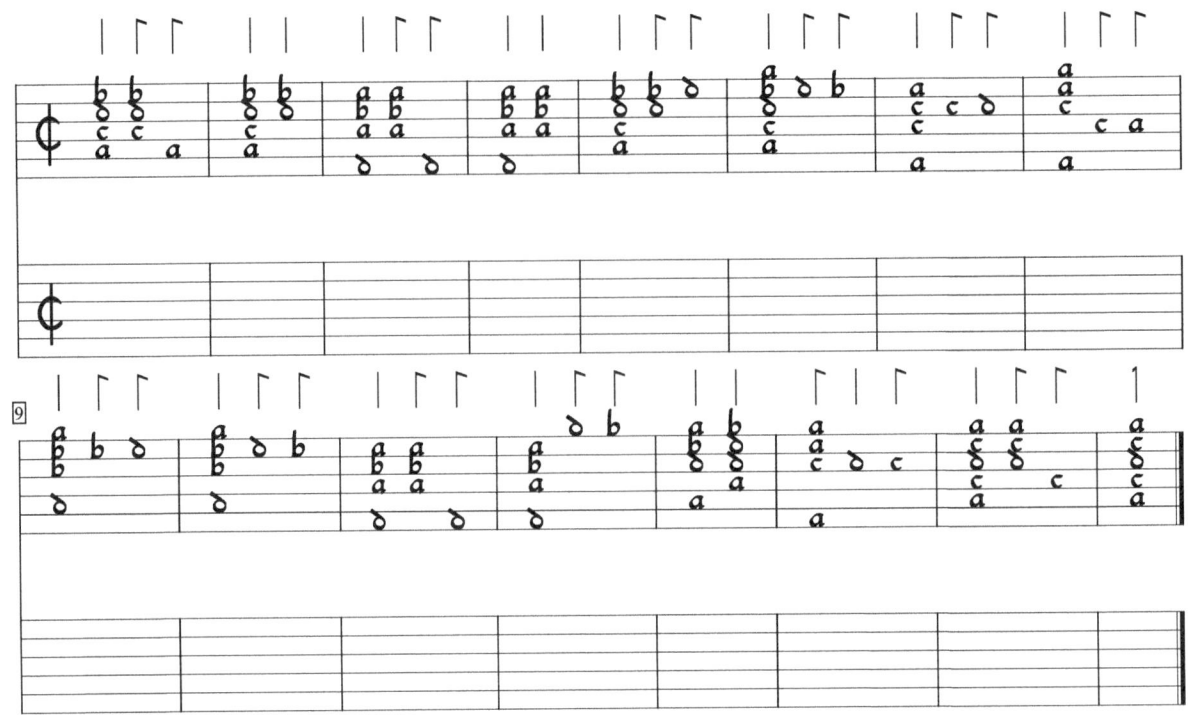

Passamezzo antico: Version 2 in D:

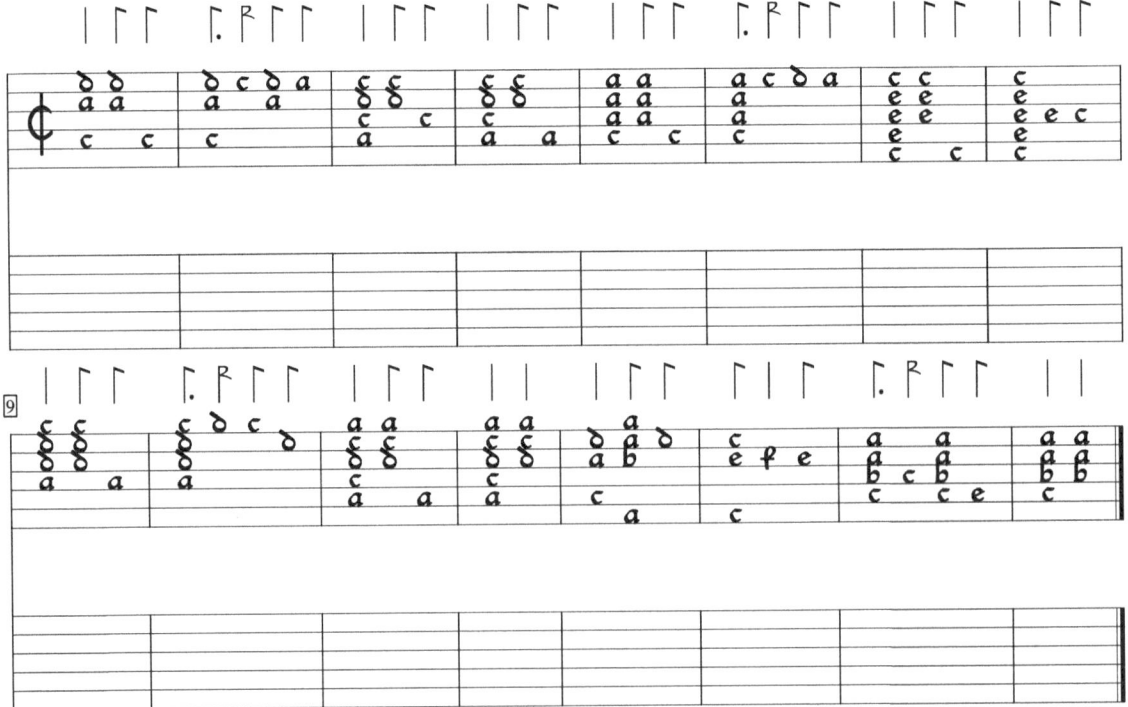

Passamezzo antico: Version 3 in G:

25.2. Solo Lute

FROM TREBLE AND GROUND LUTE DUET TO SOLO LUTE

Until now, we have been practicing divisions as a single line, in the form of a treble and ground duet. With the *Passamezzo antico*, the ground is so simple that it is now time to create some easy solo versions. (For an excellent example, see Part 2: Tablature Case Studies, Chapter 10, the *Passamezze* from Adrian Le Roy.) Giacomo Gorzanis made a whole book of 24 *Passamezzi* and *Saltarelli* (*Libro de intabulatura di liuto*, 1567, Mus.ms. 1511a, D:Mbs). It exists in manuscript form and has *Passamezzi* (*antico* and *moderno*) with their accompanying *Saltarelli* in all major and minor 'keys'—similar in concept to Bach's 'Well Tempered Clavier'. It is strong proof of the use of equal fretting on the lute—at least the one used by Gorzanis.

EXAMPLE

Here is one example. Upper stave with divisions, lower stave unornamented. As before, let us first take time to notice the division patterns used:

- Descending second: Bars 2–3
- *Static*: Bars 3, 9 with a *doubler*
- *Triad*: Bars 3, 5, 6, 10
- *Connectors*: Bars 8, 12, 13
- Ascending second: Bar 13
- *Cadential groppo*: Bar 14
- *Tirata/connector/triad*: Bar 15

EXAMPLE *Passamezzo antico*, example for solo lute with divisions.

EXERCISES

Now we can complete this chapter with three grounds, in C, D, and G, with an extra stave for your divisions. You can 'compose' them by writing them down in tablature or just be courageous and improvise them differently each time you practice.

Version 1 in C:

EXAMPLE Three grounds, in C, D, and G, with an extra stave for your division practice.

Version 2 in D:

EXAMPLE Three grounds, in C, D, and G, with an extra stave for your division practice.

Version 3 in G:

EXAMPLE Three grounds, in C, D, and G, with an extra stave for your division practice.

CHAPTER 26

GROUND #3: *PASSAMEZZO MODERNO*

Like its counterpart in the preceding chapter, the *Passamezzo moderno* can be found in several different forms. We will use four in our division practice, all of which have one harmonic characteristic in common; the sixth harmony of the ground is one tone lower than the final. For example, in the first example from Ortiz, bar 5 is in C, bar 6 is in B♭. This whole step down in the second part of each ground is very attractive and also gives us more harmonic variety with which to practice divisions.

26.1. Example

Before we practice some patterns, here is an example which uses the triple-time ground type 3, as described in the Exercises (26.2). It is the *Recercada segunda* from Diego Ortiz (*Tratado de glosas*, Rome, 1553). The qualities of Ortiz's divisions are apparent to the ear and testify to his compositional skill and taste. The rhythmic variety, frequent use of syncopation, and imitations are mostly contained in very simple *triad* division patterns. Bars 1–6 are masterfully arranged *triads*, each bar having the same basic rhythm and melodic placement within the *triad*, yet it sounds so alive and interesting. Each division ends with a melodic idea which is then developed in the following division on the ground. Besides many *triad* figures, there are a few moments which might be seen as *connectors* (bars 19, 47–48), yet Ortiz skillfully avoids *cadential* suspensions in the division part and there are no examples of a *cadential groppo*.

The following version is a transcription of this *Recercada*, originally intended for bass viol in D with harpsichord accompaniment. I have rearranged it so that all the notes lie in the same positions on the lute as they would on the viol, and the whole piece is therefore transposed up a fourth.

Recercada segunda, Diego Ortiz (*Tratado de glosas*, Rome, 1553):

Playing with Patterns on the Lute. Nigel North, Oxford University Press. © Oxford University Press 2025.
DOI: 10.1093/9780197808764.003.0029

EXAMPLE *Recercada segunda*, Diego Ortiz (*Tratado de glosas*, Rome, 1553).

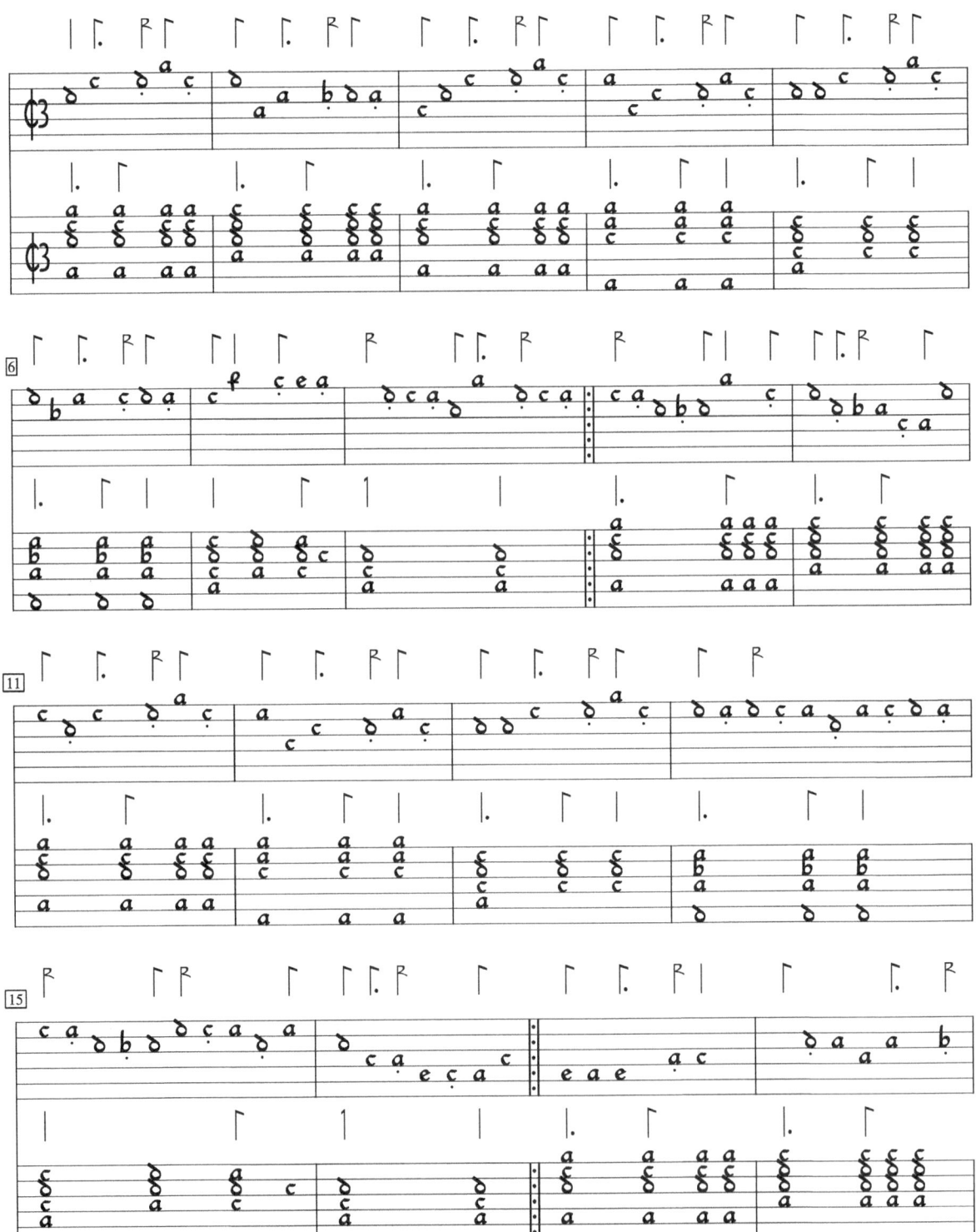

26.2. Exercises

The four versions of this ground which we will use:

Duple time ground type 1:
2 bars per harmony.
Bar 6 often has a modulating cadence.
Duple time ground type 2:
1 harmony per bar, no modulating cadence.
Triple time ground type 3:
1 harmony per bar, no modulating cadence.
Triple time ground type 4:
2 bars per harmony with a modulating cadence bars 6–7.
Hemiola, final cadence

Here are several grounds to be practiced in two forms:

- as treble and ground duets;
- as solos, using the ground lute part as a basis from which to add divisions.

In all examples, the upper stave is blank, ready for your inventions. The lower stave has a second lute part, as an accompaniment, or the basis for a solo version.

Passamezzo moderno, in duple time.

Ground 1 in C:

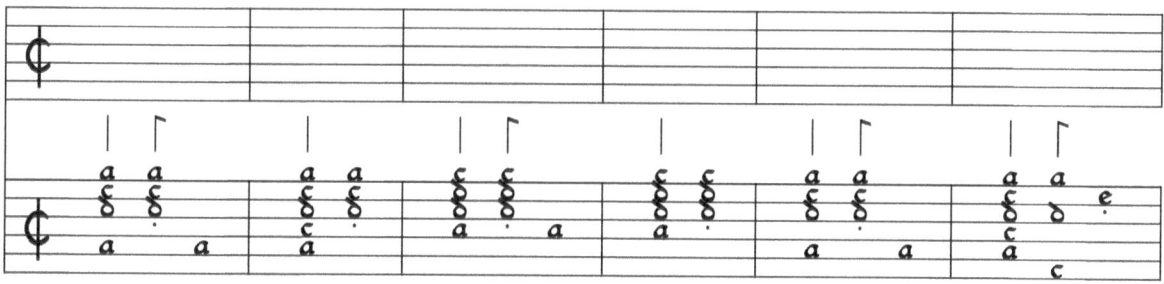

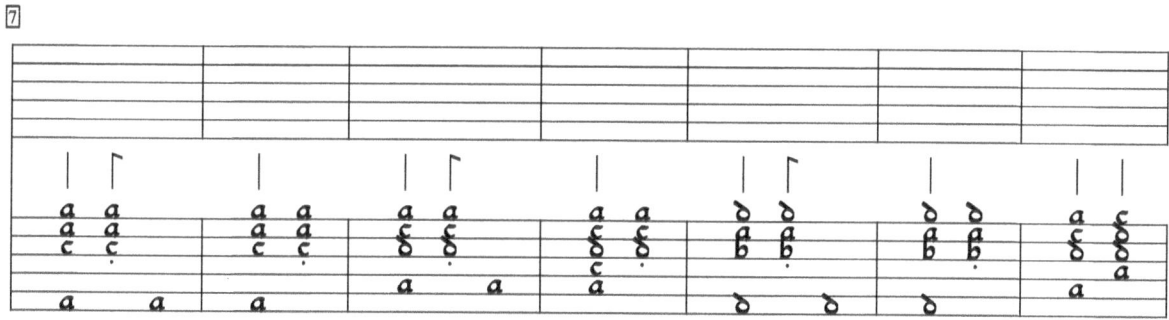

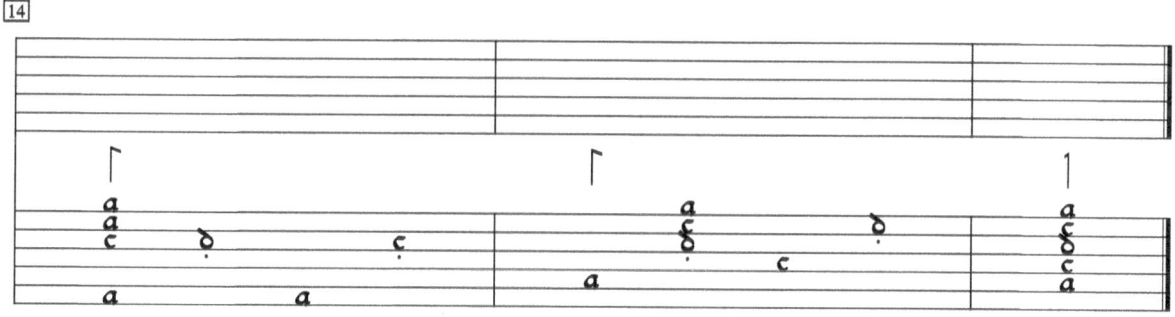

Ground 2 in F:

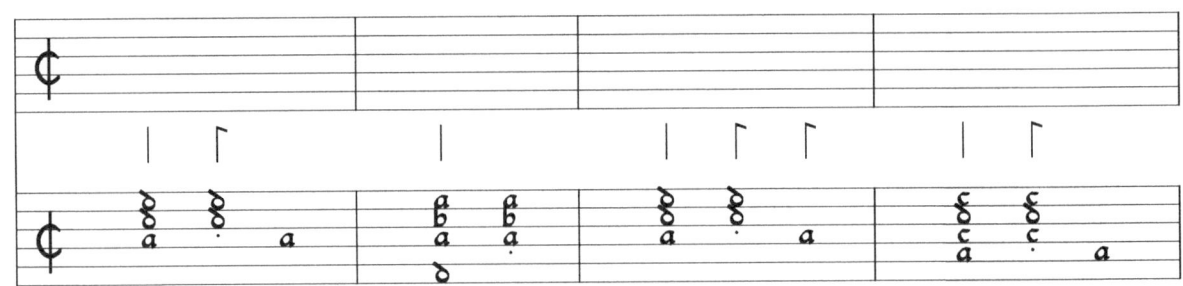

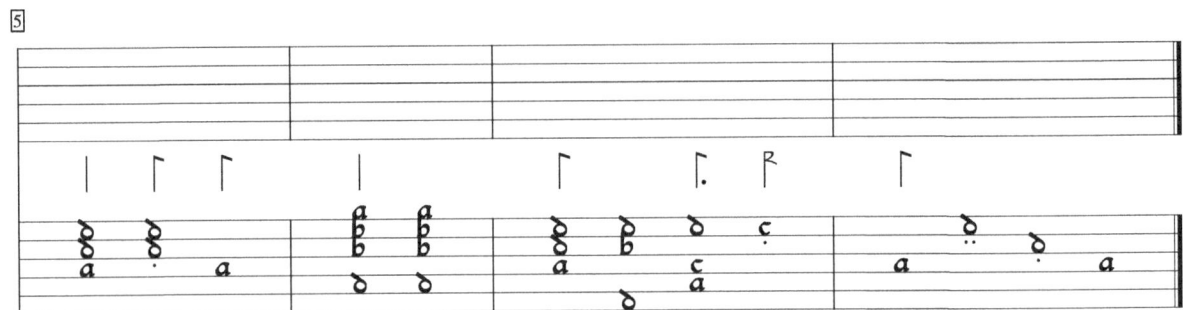

Ground 1 in G:

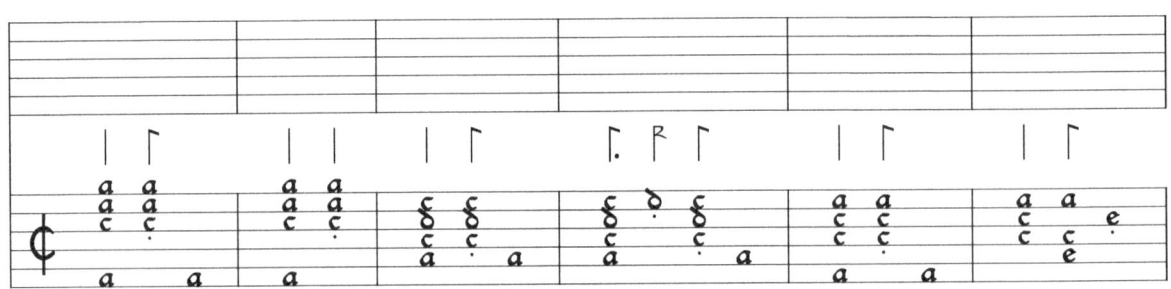

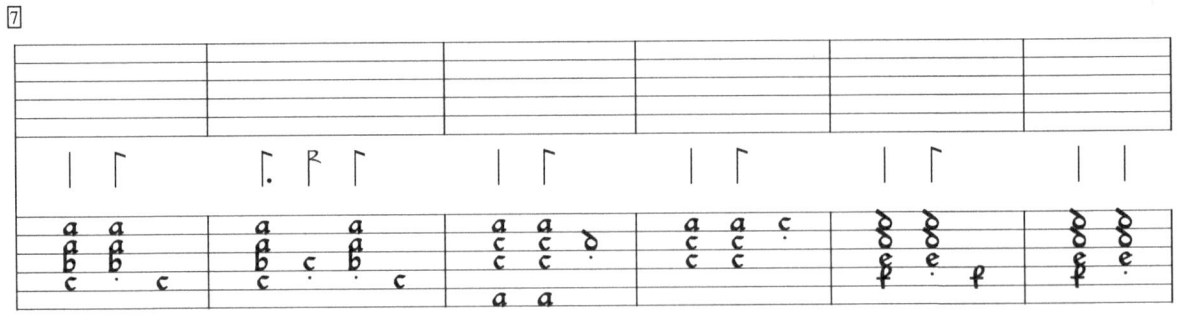

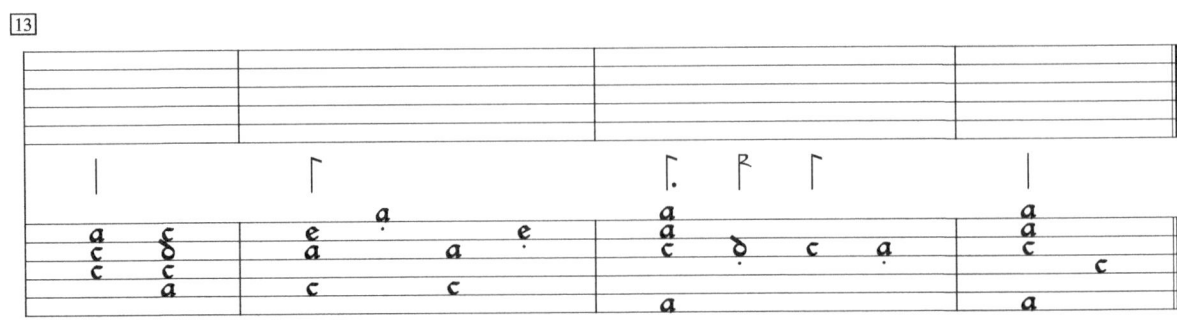

Ground 2 in B♭:

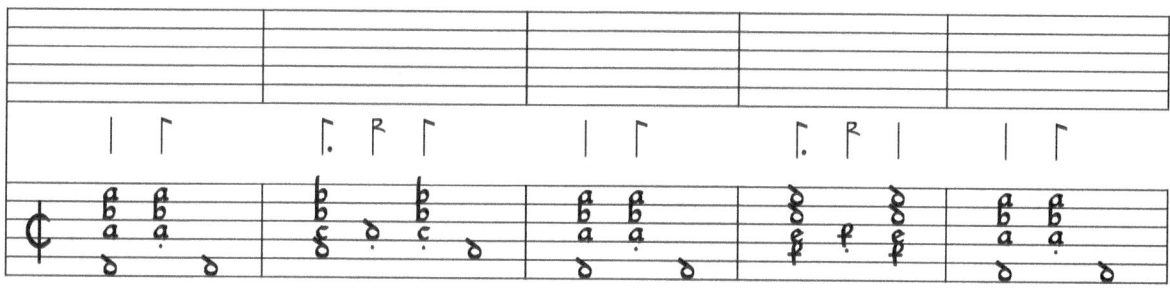

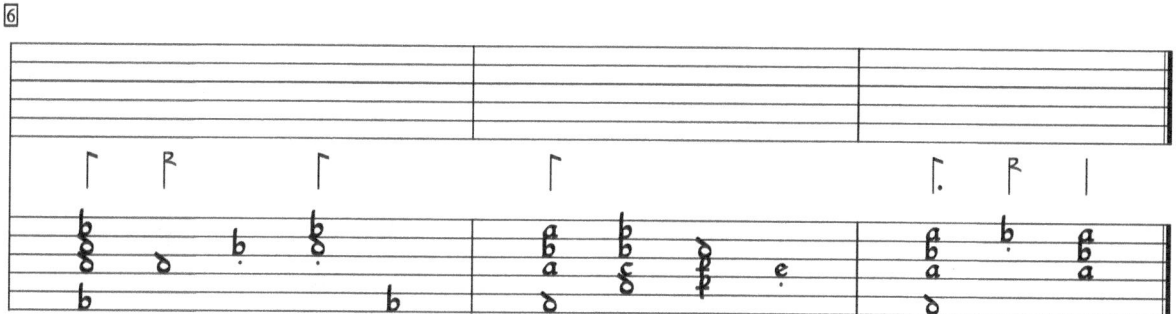

Passamezzo moderno, in triple time:
Ground 3 in C:

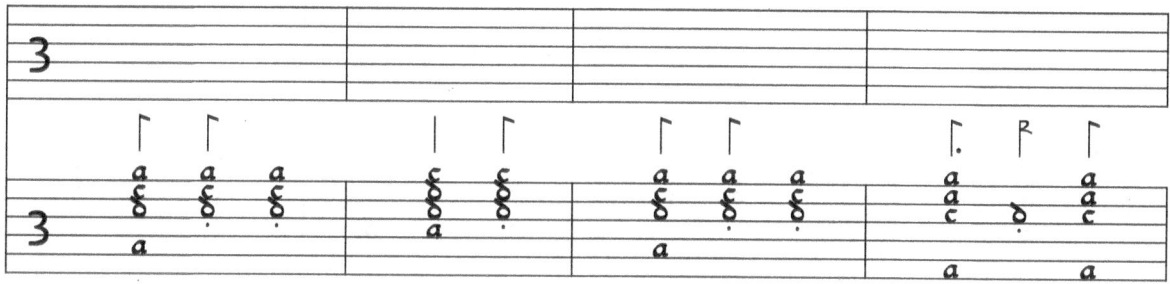

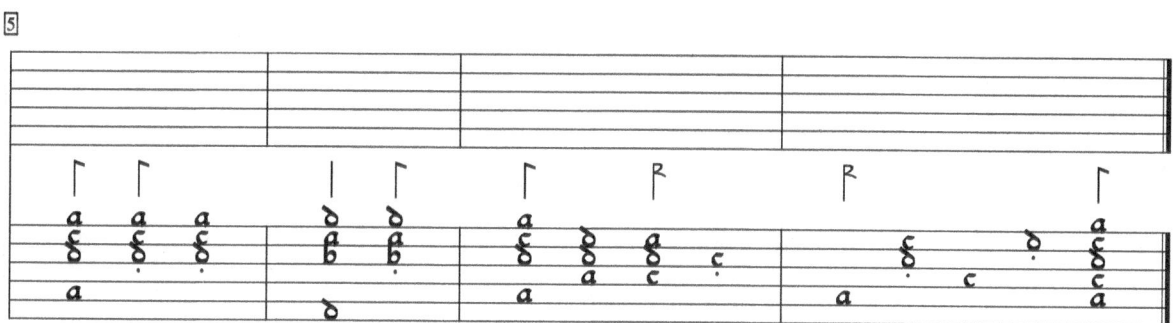

Ground 3 in F:

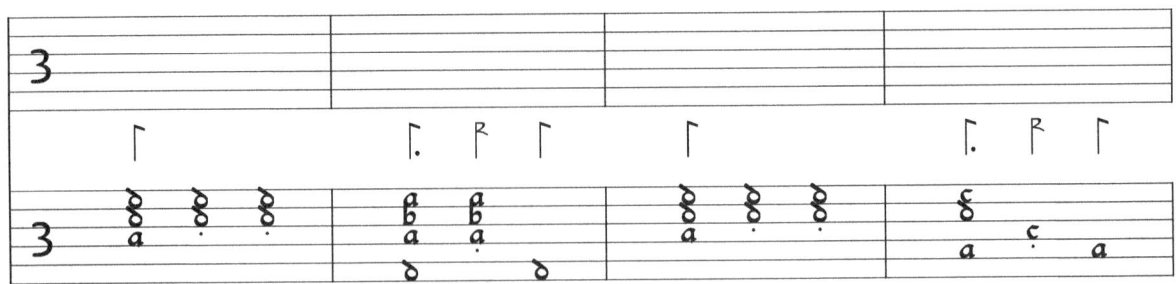

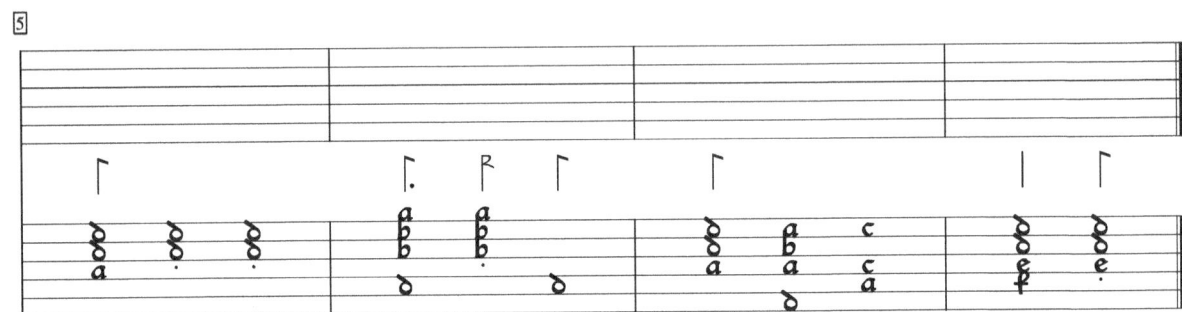

Ground 3 in B♭:

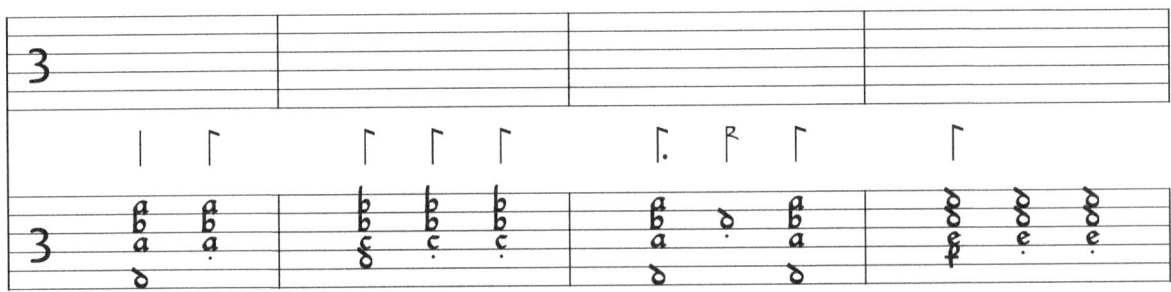

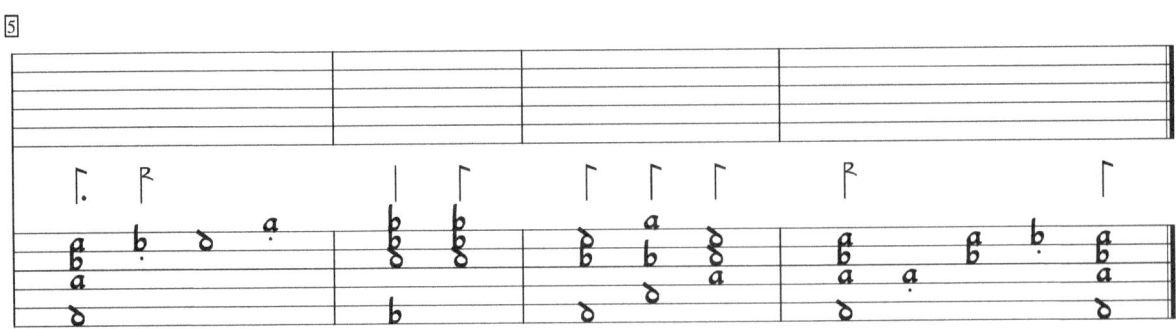

Ground 4 in G:

26.3. Example

By the late sixteenth century, the solo lute *Passamezzo* became an extended piece, with the basic harmony slowed to allow many divisions and variations. As the harmonic rhythm slowed, the bass line and harmony were ornamented, and we find passing notes and extra cadences scattered among the later dances. To inspire some solo lute *Passamezzi*, here is one from Giacomo Gorzanis (*Libro de Intabulatura di Liuto*, 1567, D:Mbs. Mus.ms.1511 a), a manuscript source which has *Passamezzi* (*antico* and *moderno*) with their accompanying *Saltarelli* in all major and minor 'keys'. This *Passamezzo moderno* is number 6 in the collection of 24 and has some moderate examples of the ornamentation of harmony and bass. Gorzanis does not use the harmony for the sixth chord, as in our earlier exercises. Here is a simple harmonic outline of the ground used by Gorzanis, followed by his set of divisions.

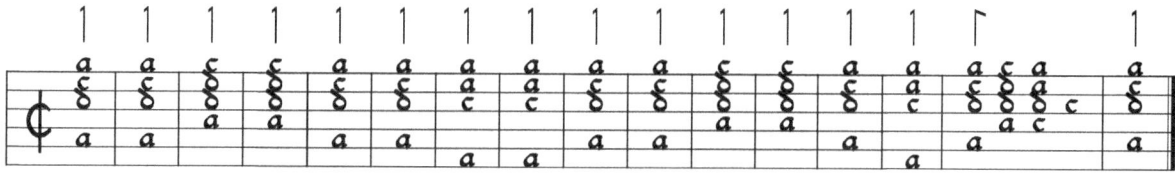

EXAMPLE *Passamezzo moderno*, Giacomo Gorzanis, 1567.

CHAPTER 27

GROUND #4: *ROMANESCA*

Like the *Passamezzo Moderno*, the *Romanesca* exists in many forms. In essence, it is a simple eight-bar ground:

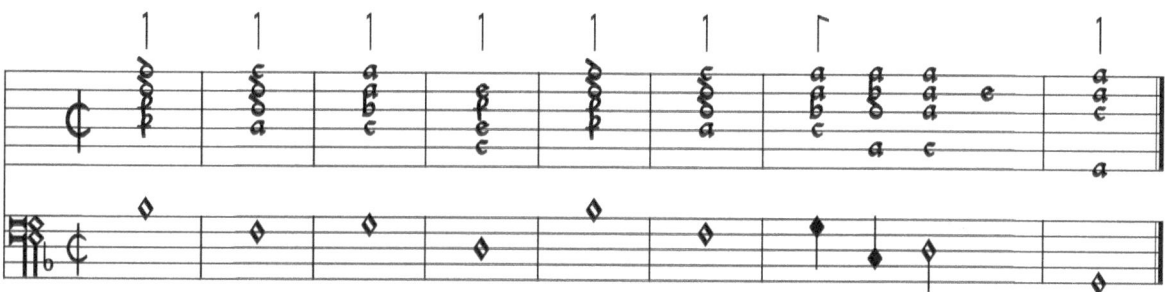

Most of the time in our sixteenth-century repertoire we can find the *Romanesca* as the foundation for triple time pieces (*Guardame las vacas* being a well-known example). The anonymous treble and ground duet, *Greensleeves* (see Part 2: Tablature Case Studies) is a *Romanesca* bass, but in duple time. For our work, we will use three different variants:

- An 8-bar, duple time version similar to the ground as shown in the preceding.
- A slow triple time (in 3/2) with a total of 8 bars.
- A fast triple (3/4) with 2 bars of each harmony. The basic ground has 16 bars, but this often came with a *supplementum* of an extra 4 bars, repeated, making a total of 24 bars.

27.1. Examples

To begin, it is helpful to work from anchor notes and later have the freedom to create a line without predetermined anchor notes. As it is the most common 'key' for this ground, we will stay with the final of G. Here is the basic ground, in duple time, with anchor notes.

Romanesca: Ground with *anchor notes*:

We follow that with an example of divisions based on these *anchor notes* in which you can observe:

Playing with Patterns on the Lute. Nigel North, Oxford University Press. © Oxford University Press 2025.
DOI: 10.1093/9780197808764.003.0030

Bars 1–4: Three different ways to descend by step.

Bar 4: We begin with part of a *triad* division, and then an ascending seventh.

Bar 5: *Static* figure on tablature *d*, first course, followed by another ascending seventh.

Bar 6: All *static* and ending with a *groppo* figure.

Bar 7: Is similar; *static* with a syncopation, followed by a normal *cadential groppo* figure with a *doubler*.

Bar 8: A *filler* made up of a descending fourth (tablature *a d b a*), followed by two *accenti*.

Romanesca: Version 1 with divisions:

Version 2 is an example of the ground in triple time, which follows the same *anchor notes* for most bars. We can observe:

Bars 1–3: All *static*, made up of a descending fourth which ascends to the *anchor note*, followed by a *static* which ascends a third and then returns.

Bar 4: Another ascending seventh which leads into the next bar.

Bar 5: Jumps down an octave and then an ascending seventh.

Bar 6: After it descends a sixth from the anchor note, the figure ascends an octave.

Bar 7: Breaks away from the anchor notes with a very common melodic line.

A new melodic line with anchor notes is shown in grey. This bar ends with a simple *groppo* figure to cadence on the next bar.

Bar 8: A triad *filler*.

Romanesca: Version 2, triple time, with divisions:

Romanesca Version 3 is the fast triple with two bars for every harmony, plus eight bars *supplementum*, as found in Ortiz. In the first example, the chords of the ground have different voicings and the anchor notes have a wider compass. They are still consonant with the harmonies but are not melodic and don't move by step:

The second example of this fast triple-time *Romanesca* is a set of divisions based on the *anchor notes* in the preceding example. In these divisions we can observe:

Bars 1–2, 3–4, 5–6, 7–8: All *triad* based, moving mostly by step.

Bar 9–10: *Static/triad*.

Bars 10–11: *Static/triad*.

Bar 12: Ascending sixth, tablature *a* on third course to tablature *d* on second course.

Bar 13: Ascending octave, one of the most common patterns.

Bar 14: Beat 2, *static* figure on tab *h* on first course.

Bars 15–16: *Triad* based.

Bar 17–19: Ascending octave, then a *groppo cadential* figure into bar 19.

Bars 19–20: Simple ascending third, followed by an ascending sixth.

Bar 21–22: *Static* on tab *i* on first course, *cadential groppo* leading to the next bar.

Bars 23–24: *Filler*, descending octave.

Romanesca: Version 3, 24 bars in triple time, with divisions:

EXAMPLE *Romanesca* ground, Version 3, with example divisions.

27.2. Exercises

Here follows the *Romanesca* ground in various versions for division creation and practice. You can make your own anchors and divide from them. In addition, you can play from the harmony without considering any anchors.

Romanesca, duple time:

EXAMPLE *Romanesca* ground, duple time for division practice.

Romanesca, triple time:

EXAMPLE *Romanesca* ground, triple time for division practice.

CHAPTER 28

ANCHOR CHE COL PARTIRE, CIPRIANO DE RORE

For the conclusion to his book *Tratado de glosas* (Rome, 1553), Diego Ortiz included two madrigals on which he wrote several sets of divisions. Taking this as our inspiration, the final piece we will be studying is a famous madrigal on which we can write or improvise two types of divisions: an ornamented *cantus* part, and a *contrapunto*.

The original: Cipriano de Rore, *Anchor che col partire,* four-part madrigal (SATB), *Primo libro di madrigali a quatro voci,* Venice (1547).

28.1. Original Madrigal a 4 (SATB)

Here is the madrigal (with text in the *cantus* part) with the text and translation:

Playing with Patterns on the Lute. Nigel North, Oxford University Press. © Oxford University Press 2025.
DOI: 10.1093/9780197808764.003.0031

EXAMPLE Madrigal: *Anchor che col partire*, Cipriano de Rore, 1547.

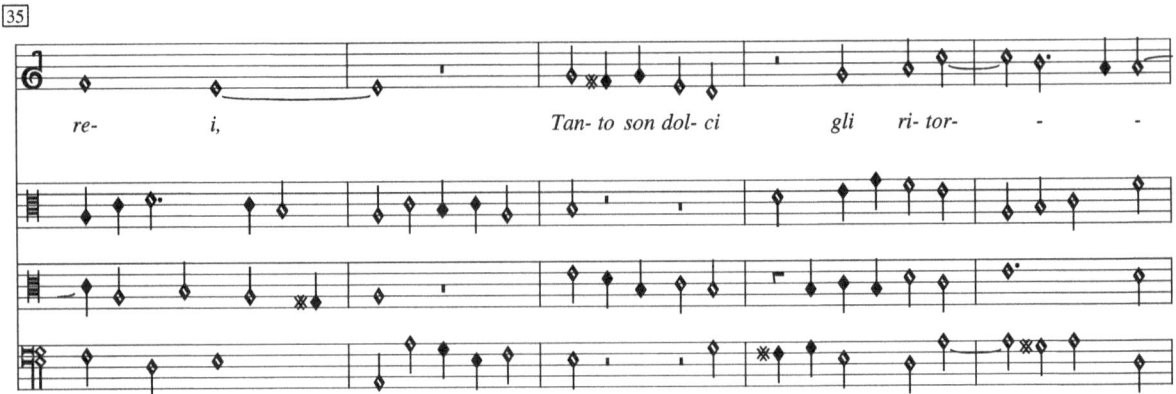

Anchor che col partire
io mi senta morire,
partir vorrei ogn' hor,
ogni momento:
tant' il piacer ch'io sento
de la vita ch'acquisto nel ritorno:
et cosi mill' e mille volt' il giorno
partir da voi vorrei:
tanto son dolci gli ritorni miei.
Alfonso d'Avalos

Although when leaving
I feel like dying,
I would be glad to part at any time, at any moment,
So great is the joy I feel
In the new life that I receive on returning.
And so a thousand and thousand times a day
I would like to part from you:
so sweet are my returns.

28.2. *Cantus* (to Practice Divisions) with an Intabulation of ATB

EXERCISE

For our lute pitches to be the same as the madrigal, we must assume an A lute. This is what we find in the intabulation from Paladino: *Premier Livre de Tablature de Luth,* Jean Paule Paladin (Giovanni Paolo Paladino) Lyon, 1560 (1560/3) f. 11v. All of the following scores will transpose the madrigal down a tone so we can continue to work with a G lute and its related pitches, just as Paladino did. Here is a lute intabulation of three voices (ATB) with the *cantus* part in staff notation transposed down a tone, and a spare tablature stave for writing or improvising divisions on the *cantus* part.

EXAMPLE Madrigal: *Anchor che col partire*, Cipriano de Rore, 1547. Lute duet: Intabulation of ATB, *cantus* with text. Spare tablature stave for division invention.

28.3. Example: A New *Contrapunto/Bastarda* Style, with an Intabulation Based on Paladino's Intabulation (1560)

The next example is a score of a lute duet I have composed to show some of the figures and devices one might employ in a *contrapunto*. Lute 1 (upper stave) is a newly composed line which weaves in and out of all the voices, and not just the *cantus*. (Similar to the Terzi *contrapunto* in Part 2). Lute 2 plays CATB, and the intabulation is based on Palatino but aligns with the *music ficta* I have chosen for the *contrapunto*.

A new *contrapunto* on *Anchor che col partire*:

EXAMPLE Madrigal: *Anchor che col partire*, Cipriano de Rore, 1547. A new *contrapunto*.

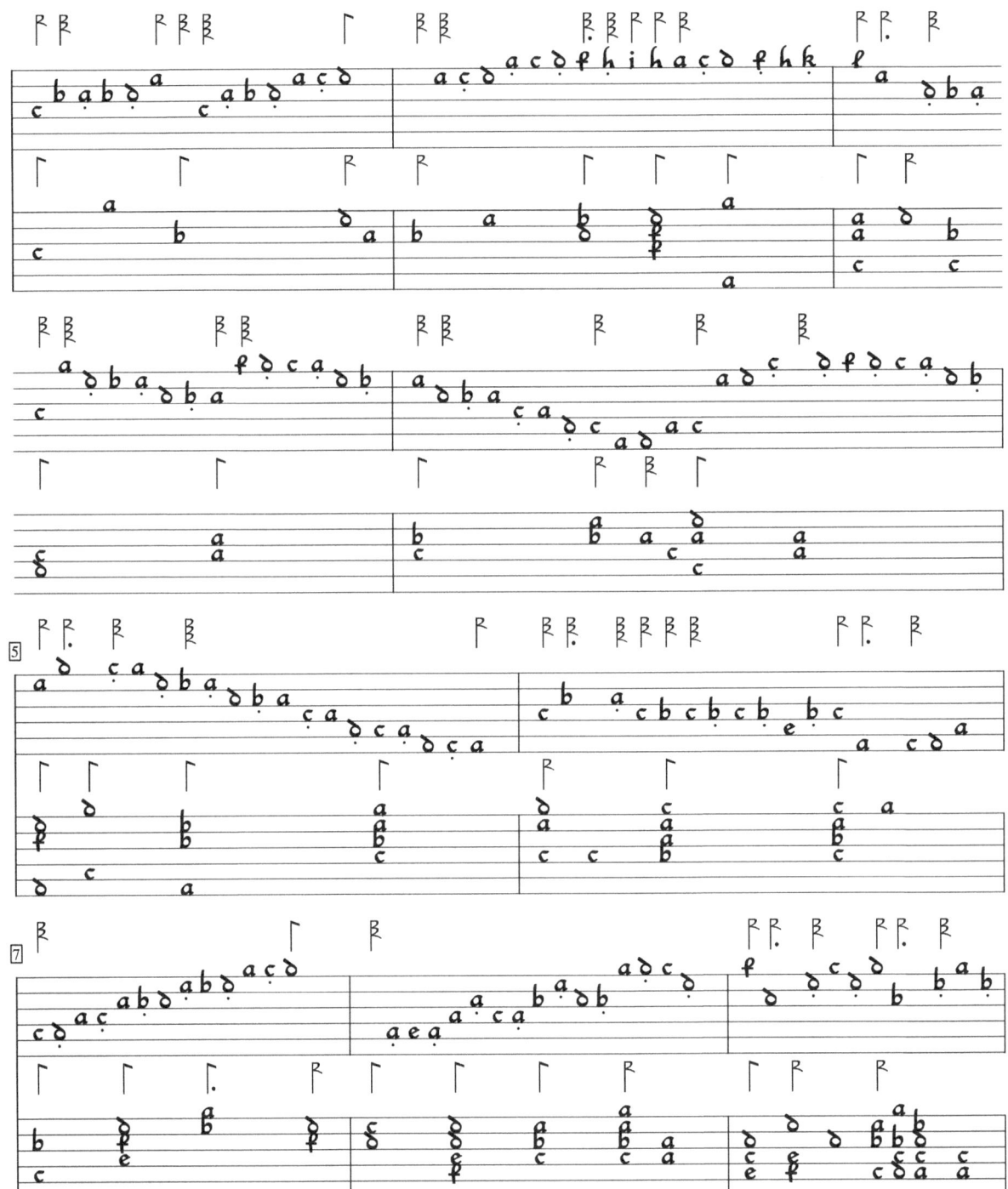

28.4. Intabulation with a Spare Stave for Improvising or Composing Your Own *Contrapunto*

EXERCISE

Finally, a score to use for your own *contrapunto*. Lute 2 (upper stave) is the same SATB intabulation as in the preceding example; the lower stave is now spare for your *contrapunto*, whether improvised or composed.

EXAMPLE Madrigal: *Anchor che col partire*, Cipriano de Rore, 1547. A new *contrapunto* waiting to be invented, on the lower stave.

ORNAMENTATION TREATISES, 1535–1620 (FOR VOICE, WIND, AND STRING INSTRUMENTS)

Eleven instruction manuals for voice and/or melodic instruments are listed; most are concerned with how to ornament a pre-existing vocal work with divisions. None of these are for the lute.

A Short Chronological Summary

Sylvestro Ganassi, 1535

Divisions and cadences for *flauto* (also suitable for bowed strings and voice).

Diego Ortiz, 1553

For *viola da gamba*. Divisions and cadences, solo ricercari, ricercari on vocal originals. Ricercari on *cantus firmus* 'La Spagna', and grounds.

Girolamo Dalla Casa, 1584

For winds, strings, and voice. Divisions on intervals and cadences with many examples from madrigals and motets. Some divisions specifically for *viola bastarda*.

Giovanni Bassano, 1585

For all instruments, and the voice. Solo ricercari, divisions on intervals, short phrases, and cadences.

Richardo Rogniono, 1592

In two parts, *Passaggi per potersi* and *Il vero modo di diminuire*.

    For all wind and string instruments, and voice. Divisions on intervals and cadences. Divisions on three complete pieces, with a variety of *viola bastarda* diminutions.

Giovanni Luca Conforto, 1593

Division manual for singers and all instruments (Conforto was a singer).

    Divisions on intervals. Examples of *trillo* and *groppo*. Scales and cadences with divisions.

Lodovico Zacconi, 1596

An extensive book on music theory with a short section with instructions for making divisions on intervals and cadences.

Giovanni Battista Bovicelli, 1594

Instrument and voice non-specific. Rules, intervals, and ornamented **superius** parts to motets and madrigals, with texts.

Antonio Brunelli, 1614

A simple set of divisions on intervals, most of which are presented as vocal duos, with text, in a style clearly apart from the virtuosic diminutions of the earlier books. It is a very accessible beginner's manual.

Francesco Rognoni Taegio, 1620

A comprehensive method by the son of Richardo Rogniono. *Parte prima* is for voice, with many examples of vocal *affetti* ornamentation. *Parte seconda* is for string and wind instruments with many instructions for articulation as well as *passaggi*.

Virgiliano, Aurelio c. 1600–1620

A manuscript with three books. *Libro primo*: copy of rules and tables of ornamented intervals, cadences, and short scales. *Libro secondo*: solo ricercari for wind and string instruments, including *liuto* and *viola bastarda*. *Libro terzo*: a list of tunings and fingering charts for several instruments used for *Libro secondo* (but there is no mention of the lute).

A List of All Sources with a Description of Their Contents

Sylvestro Ganassi, *Opera Intitulata Fontegara*, Venice, 1535

A treatise, principally for *flauto* (recorder), although Ganassi says that the ornamentation and divisions are suitable for wind and (bowed) string instruments, and for singers. The book has a few simple rules for division making and then includes many examples of Ganassi's divisions, using intervals and cadences. All examples are notated for a soprano range instrument. Ganassi's divisions are well known for their virtuosic and rhythmical complexity and are in a clearly different style from any later division manuals.

Diego Ortiz, *Tratado de glosas*, Rome, 1553

A treatise for learning divisions, principally for viol (viola da gamba); an excellent first method, and one whose musical style is tuneful and appealing.

Libro primo: Ortiz begins with a comprehensive set of divisions on cadences (*clausulas*). Most examples are for a treble instrument, but he later includes examples for making a cadence in the tenor and bass. Ortiz's style is so much more approachable than Ganassi's, and less complicated. After the section on cadences, Ortiz covers intervals.

Libro secondo has complete pieces:

• Solo ricercari in which the player can practice divisions.
• Ricercari with divisions on the *cantus firmus* 'La Spagna'.
• Four-part madrigal: *O felici occhi miei* (Jacques Arcadelt). Four ricercari with divisions for different size viols. In all ricercari the harpsichord plays the complete madrigal and the viol plays divisions on a particular voice. In the fourth ricercare, Ortiz has composed one which has a *fifth voice*. This is probably the earliest example of a *bastarda* part.
• Four-part chanson: *Douce memoire* (Pierre Sandrin) with ricercari as for the Arcadelt.
• Ricercari on various grounds for one viol with harpsichord accompaniment: *Passamezzo antico, Passamezzo moderno, La Gamba/Cara Cosa, Bergamasca, Romanesca, Ruggiero*.

Girolamo Dalla Casa, *Il vero modo di diminur*, Venice, 1584

Like Ganassi, this book is said to be for wind, strings, and voice (*Di fiato, & corda, & di voce humana*).

Libro primo has examples of articulations for wind players, followed by divisions (*passi & cadenze*) based on intervals and *cadential* formulas, and extracts of the *superius* parts to some madrigals and motets, with added divisions.

Libro secondo contains ornamented vocal parts from complete madrigals and motets. There is a set of pieces with divisions for *la viola bastarda*. Another group of pieces, *Madrigali da cantar in compagnia, & anco con il liuto solo*, in which all *superius* parts include divisions, implying that it can be sung by four voices (*cantar in compagnia*) with the *superius* singing the divisions, or as a lute song, with the lute playing the lower three voices and the *superius* singing the divisions.

The final group of pieces is a madrigal for four voices in which all voices have division (*Canzon di Cipriano A 4. Tutti le quattro parte diminuite*).

Giovanni Bassano, *Ricercate, passaggi et cadentie*, Venice, 1585

For all instruments and the voice (*Per ogni sorte d'Istrumento: & anco diversi passaggi per la semplice voce*):

Eight solo ricerari (soprano range).

Passaggi on intervals and some short phrases and scales.

Cadential formulas with examples.

One ornamented *superius* part to a Cipriano de Rore madrigal.

Bassano published another related book, *Motetti, madrigali & canzoni francese*, Venice, 1591. The original is lost, but we have a handwritten copy made by Friedrich Chrysander. The book contains ornamented versions of mostly *superius* parts from vocal originals.

Richardo **Rogniono**, *Passaggi per potersi/Il vero modo di diminuire*, Venice, 1592

Parte prima: Passaggi per potersi:

For all instruments and singers (*ogni sorte d'Instromenti et anco diversi passaggi per la semplice voce humana*).

Passaggi on scales and intervals only.

Parte seconda: Il vero modo di diminuire:

Cadential formulas and scales.

Divisions on *triads* and then other large intervals.

One motet, one madrigal with various levels of diminution for *viola bastarda*, one French chanson with various levels of diminution for *viola bastarda*.

Giovanni Luca Conforto, *Breve et facile maniera d'essercitarsi*, Rome, 1593

An engraved book, a division manual for singers and all instruments (Conforto was a singer). Divisions on intervals. One of the first to include examples of *affetti, trillo*, and *groppo*. Scales and cadences with divisions.

Giovanni Battista Bovicelli, *Regole passaggi di Musica*, Venice, 1594

This opens with some rules and examples, followed by *Diversi modi di diminuire*, division examples for intervals and cadences (simple and thorough). Primarily for singers.

10 motets and madrigals which are excellently presented with original superius parts in score, together with Bovicelli's ornamented versions.

Lodovico Zacconi, *Practicca di musica, Libro Primo*, Venice, 1596

This is an extensive book on music theory which has a very approachable short section on making divisions. These can be found in chapters LXIII–LXVI on pages 55v–76; Zacconi includes divisions on intervals and cadences and how to sing *gorgia* (vocal *passaggi*).

Antonio **Brunelli,** *Varii esercitii,* Florence, 1614

Clearly written in a later style than the previous books, and the divisions are simple and easily assimilated. The book starts with one page of examples of how to change the rhythms of the music notated, similar to comments found in the Preface to Giulio Caccini's *Le nuove musiche* (Florence, 1602). Exercises with examples for *passaggi* on simple ascending and descending figures, with basso continuo. Two sets of diminutions on the Ruggiero, for two soprano (instruments) and basso continuo.

Francesco Rognoni Taegio, *Selva de varii passaggi*, Milan, 1620

Parte prima (per cantare) selva de varii passaggi:

Rules and examples of graces and *affetti* for singers.

Division examples (*passaggi*) on intervals and cadences, including examples for a bass. Palestrina motet, *Pulchra es, amica mea*, and Palestrina madrigal, *Io son ferito ahi lasso* with *passaggi*, including a bass voice *alla bastarda.*

Parte seconda (Per gl'instromenti del dar l'archata, portar della lingua):

Observations on performance practice for wind and stringed instruments, particularly the *lira da gamba* and the *viola bastarda*. Examples of articulations and slurred bowing for string instruments. Examples of tonguing for wind instruments.

Division examples (*passaggi*) for scales, intervals, and cadences.

A few examples of ornamented vocal lines of madrigals and motets, including some for *la viola bastarda.*

Aurelio Virgiliano, *Il dolcimelo*

The only manuscript in this collection of division manuals. It is undated but thought to be ca. 1600–1620, and while it contains much, seems to remain incomplete.

Libro primo: General rules for division making (which have been often quoted), followed by *passaggi* on intervals, cadences, and scales, with three different rhythmic levels for each exercise.

Libro secondo: various ricercari for various instruments, including *flauto, viola bastarda, leuto, violino, cornetto.*

Libro terzo: fingering, tuning charts for various *viole, tromboni, cornetti, & flauti.*

THE ORIGINAL PARTS FOR LUTE 1 AND LUTE 2, G. A. TERZI (1593)

Contrapunto sopra Susanne un jour di Orlando a 5, per suonar a doi liutti in quarta
DI GIO.ANTONIO TERZI DA BERGAMO INTAVOLATURA DI LIUTO, Libro primo,
Venice, 1593, pp. 38–42
The original parts for Lute 1 and Lute 2.
Lute 1 (intabulation of the chanson). Lute in G:

EXAMPLE *Susanne un jour di Orlando a 5:* The original parts for Lute 1 and Lute 2. G. A. Terzi (1593). Lute 1 (intabulation of the chanson). Lute in G.

Lute 2 (*contrapunto* diminutions). Lute in D, a fourth lower than Lute 1:

EXAMPLE *Susanne un jour di Orlando a 5:* The original parts for Lute 1 and Lute 2. G. A. Terzi (1593). Lute 2 (*contrapunto* diminutions). Lute in D, a fourth lower than Lute 1.

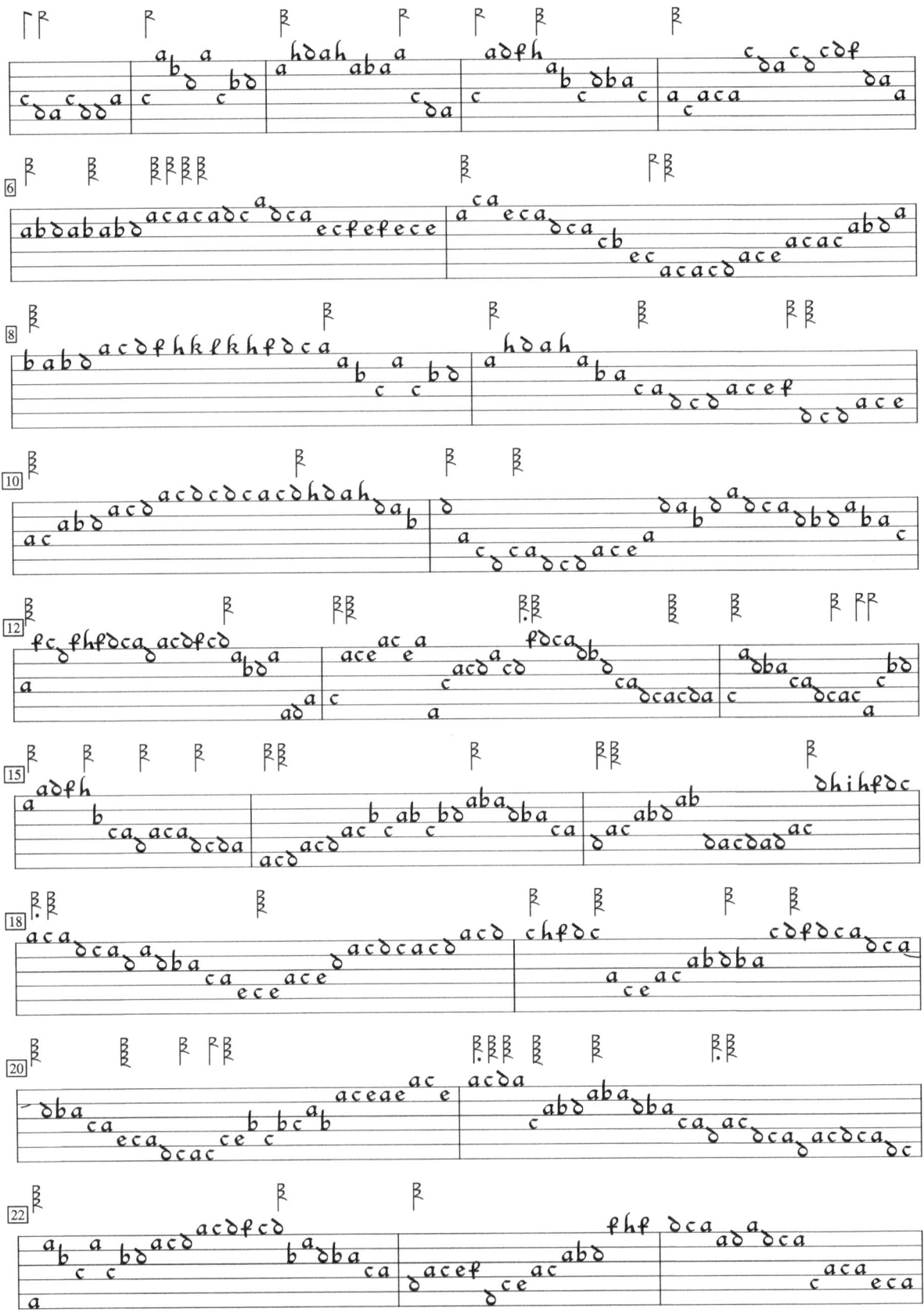

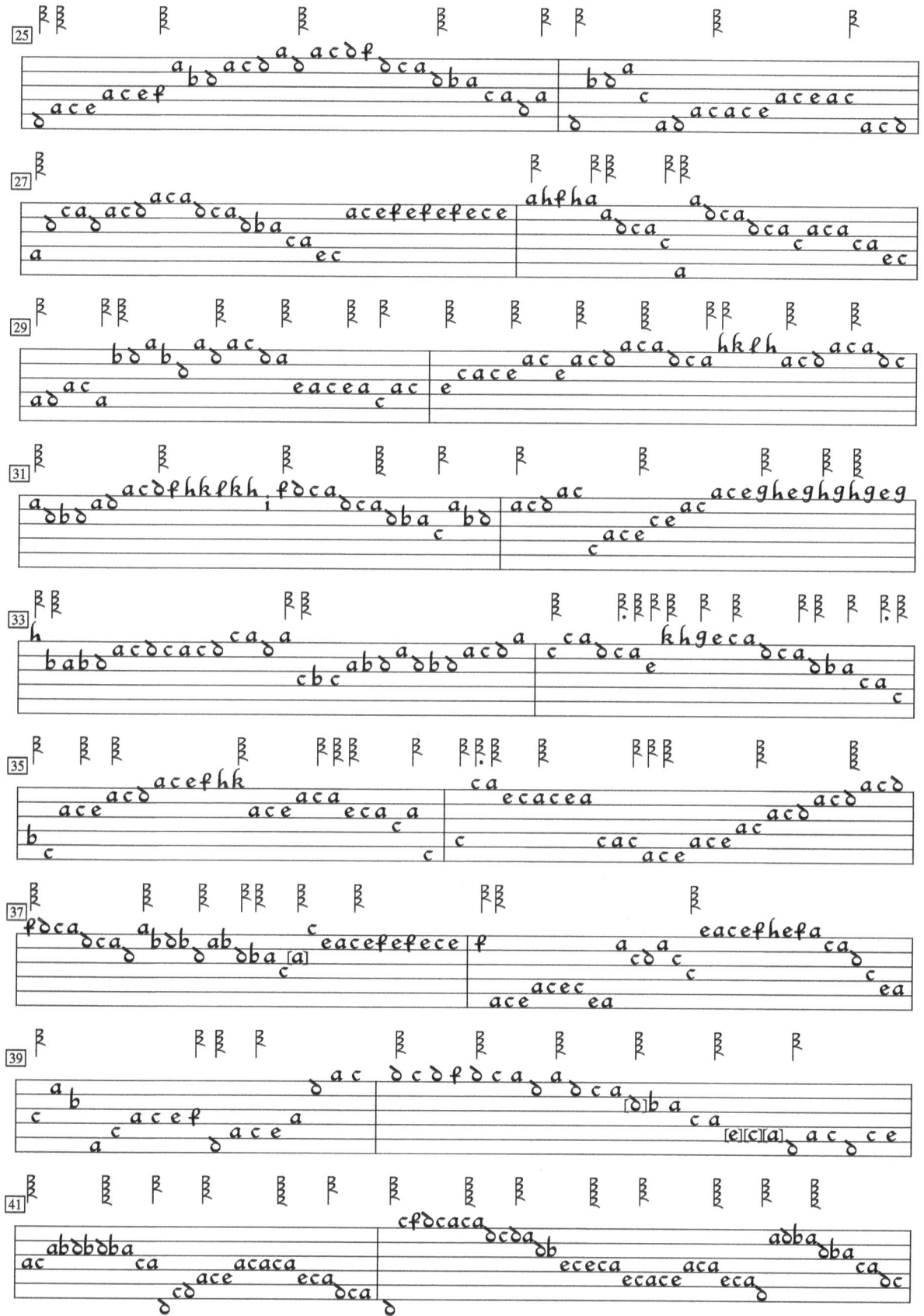

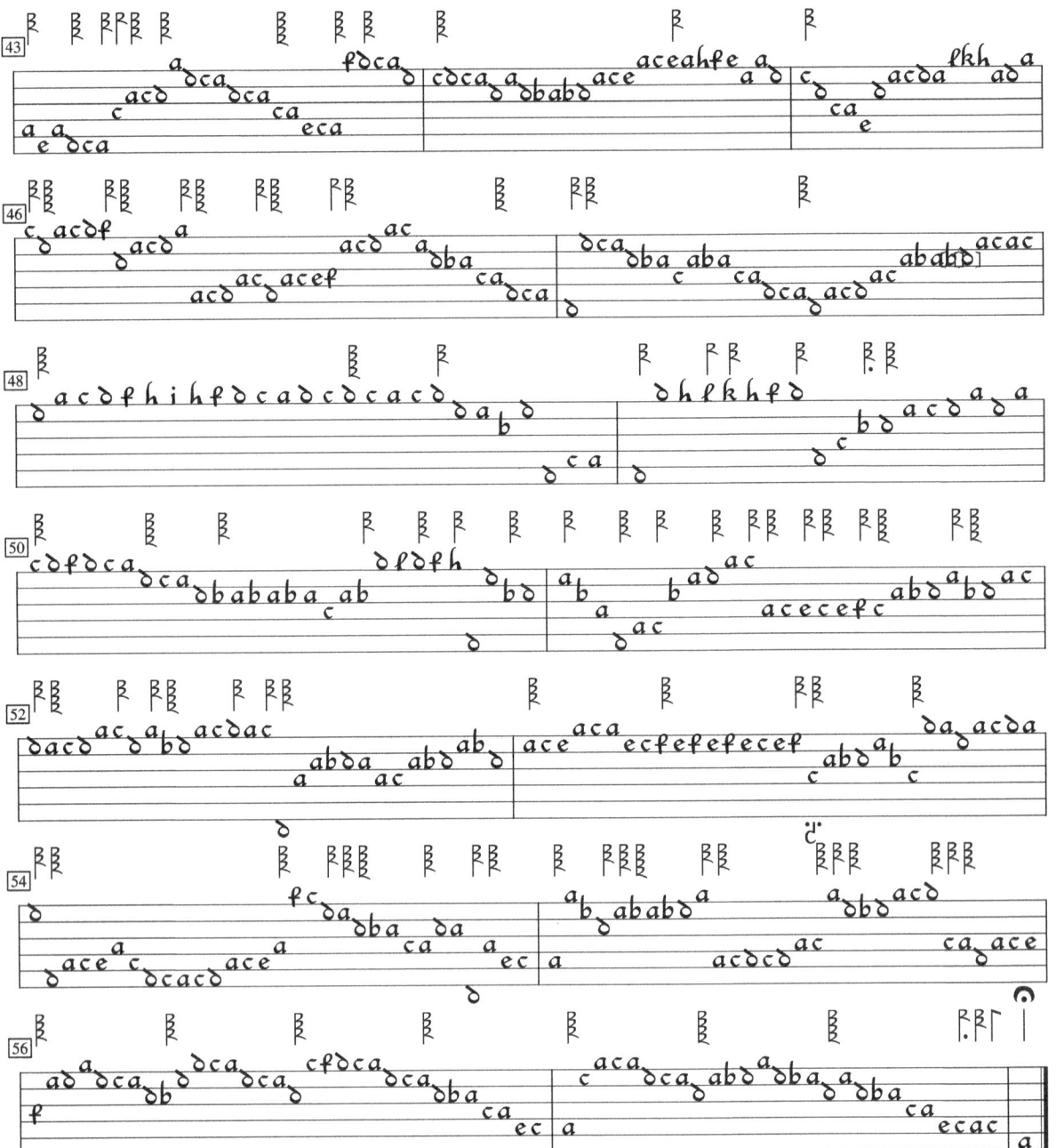

INDEX

For the benefit of digital users, indexed terms that span two pages (e.g., 52–53) may, on occasion, appear on only one of those pages.

Figures are indicated by an italic f following the page number.